MINIK

THE
NEW YORK
ESKIMO

KENN HARPER

foreword by
KEVIN SPACEY

D0974221

STEERFORTH PRESS
HANOVER, NEW HAMPSHIRE

This is a greatly revised and updated version of an earlier work published as *Give Me My Father's Body: The Life of Minik, the New York Eskimo*

For information about permission to reproduce selections from this book, write to:
Steerforth Press, L.L.C., 45 Lyme Road, Suite 208
Hanover, NH 03755

Cataloging-in-Publication Data is available from the Library of Congress

ISBN 978-1-58642-241-7

First Edition

1 3 5 7 9 10 8 6 4 2

To my daughters, Aviaq and Mikisoq
And in memory of their brother, my son,
Mamarut
May 25, 1975–August 6, 1995

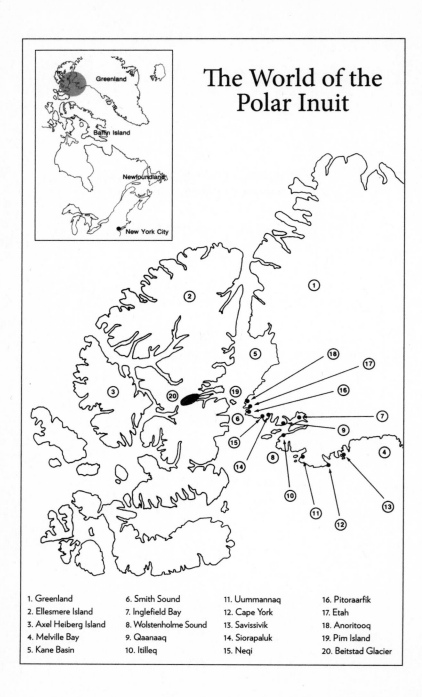

The World of the Polar Inuit

1. Greenland
2. Ellesmere Island
3. Axel Heiberg Island
4. Melville Bay
5. Kane Basin
6. Smith Sound
7. Inglefield Bay
8. Wolstenholme Sound
9. Qaanaaq
10. Itilleq
11. Uummannaq
12. Cape York
13. Savissivik
14. Siorapaluk
15. Neqi
16. Pitoraarfik
17. Etah
18. Anoritooq
19. Pim Island
20. Beitstad Glacier

To many a good person the thought at once arises: "Poor things [the Polar Eskimos] . . . why wouldn't it be a good plan to take them away from their awful home to a pleasanter region?" . . . I answer at once, "God willing, never."

—ROBERT PEARY, Arctic explorer

Our tales are narratives of human experience, and therefore they do not always tell of beautiful things. But one cannot both embellish a tale to please the hearer and at the same time keep to the truth. The tongue should be the echo of that which must be told, and it cannot be adapted according to the moods and the tastes of man.

—OSARQAQ, a Polar Inuk

This Minik seems gradually to have become a legendary figure to the Polar Eskimos who have many anecdotes to tell of him and his doings.

—ERIK HOLTVED, ethnologist

CONTENTS

FOREWORD

Anybody who makes his living in the acting business is always on the prowl for a good story, and a few years ago, in Canada, I stumbled across a great one. An article in a Toronto paper outlined the life of Minik Wallace, the youngest of a group of Polar Inuit brought to New York City in 1897 by the famed Arctic explorer Robert Peary. Four of the group, including Minik's father, soon died, and in time Minik himself was gradually set adrift by officials of the American Museum of Natural History, whose Department of Anthropology apparently had encouraged Peary to bring them an Inuk "specimen" to study; by Peary, who was preoccupied with his efforts to reach the North Pole; and by William Wallace, who took in Minik and gave him a name but whose life was eventually swallowed up by financial troubles and personal tragedy. Within a few years of his arrival in New York, Minik had forgotten his native language, his education had come to a halt, his health was shaken by recurrent bouts of pneumonia, and he was left, without family, to fend for himself.

When I managed to find a copy of the book originally published by the author, Kenn Harper, and sold mainly from a general store on Baffin Island in what is now the new Arctic territory of Nunavut—I found a story that grabbed hold of me and wouldn't let go. In *Give Me My Father's Body* [now revised and republished as *Minik: The New York Eskimo*] the saga of Arctic exploration is told for the first time through the eyes of Inuit, whose rugged endurance and knowledge of the Arctic were largely what made Peary's epic journeys possible in the first place. The wealth and power of New York City on the cusp of the twentieth century of course dazzled the child newly arrived from the world's northernmost human community. But America's excited curiosity over the Inuit quickly faded, and Minik soon encountered another side of America—one of pride and arrogance, and of a cold indifference that seemed to be explained by the boy's dark skin.

The reader watches this tale unfold much as Minik did—slowly, through small events and casual remarks. The world-famous Peary, a kind of demigod when he's first introduced, is gradually revealed to be a careless, self-absorbed man, who for years refused to return Minik to his home in Greenland. The scientists who "studied" Minik and put the skeleton of the boy's father on display were subject to crack-pot theories of racial difference. Their refusal to return the body or even give a reason why it was kept at the museum helps to explain the recent passage of laws compelling museums and other cultural insti-tutions to return to native communities sacred objects and human remains long treated as museum property.

But shining at the heart of this often dark tale, told with such care and restraint, is the spirit of Minik himself—cut off from his people, his language, and his sense of belonging in the world, he never surren-dered his hope of going "home," his demand for the return of his father's body for a proper burial, or his belief that people would under-stand and come to his aid if only he succeeded in explaining himself. Eventually as a young man in his teens, Minik finally shamed a group of Peary's backers into providing him with passage back to Greenland.

Once there he relearned his native language, became a skilled hunter, and hired himself out as a guide and interpreter to later explorers, but Minik found himself caught between two worlds. He longed to speak English, could communicate some of what he felt only to white men, and found that a part of him preferred the bright lights of Broadway to the northern lights. Inevitably, Minik began to dream of another trip "home"—this time back to New York City.

And there you have it—Minik had no home. Plucked from his own world, never wholly welcomed by another, he was condemned to look forever for what he had lost. The entire story is captured in the gaze of the child Minik in one of the photographs in this book—a small boy in spiffy cap and coat, holding a bicycle too big for him, looking directly into the heart and soul of whoever's behind the camera for something warmer than curiosity.

This too short, too sad life, unfolding at the end of the great age of Arctic exploration, was pieced together in an amazing effort of research and writing by Kenn Harper, who lived for fifty years among Inuit (as the descendants of history's Eskimos prefer to be called today). Unlike most white men in today's Arctic, he speaks Inuktitut, the language of the Inuit, and heard of Minik firsthand from Greenland Inuit in the mid-1970s. The tale had a mythic quality—the boy swept off to a magical land where fantastic adventures awaited him and a benefactor promised great wealth; his sudden return years later. But after Minik left Greenland the second time the Polar Inuit heard no more; none could tell Harper what happened to him, where he died or when. There was no end to his tale. Over a period of eight years Harper searched out the answers for himself in Greenland, in New York City, and in Denmark.

The story of Minik has the simplicity and resonance of myth. But Harper's telling of it sketches in a whole age and world, bringing to life the bustling city of New York, the infant science of anthropology, America's astonished discovery of the Polar Inuit, the American racism that treated people of color as "specimens," the huckstering public entertainers who added Inuit and other exotic peoples to their menagerie—there is not a page in this book without its horrors and its wonders.

When you get to the end of a great story there comes a moment of silence. The lights in the theater come up, or you turn the last page in a book as good as this one, and you sit stunned. There is nothing to say. And then in the next heartbeat you think of a million things to say.

But I'll stop here.

—Kevin Spacey

INTRODUCTION

No Inuit have been more studied than the small group once known as Polar Eskimos in northwestern Greenland, the most northern native inhabitants of the world. They have been described by explorers, examined by anthropologists, idealized by novelists, and, since their displacement from their favored fjord in 1953 by the American military, lionized by journalists. Their stories have been told, analyzed, and retold by numerous adventurers and academics whose international reputations received initial boosts from their work among the Polar Inuit.

This book tells the story that they all missed—Freuchen, Rasmussen, Malaurie, and all the others who have written about them in so much detail. Freuchen devoted a few pages to it, Malaurie a few lines, Rasmussen almost nothing at all.

This is the story of Minik Wallace, "the New York Eskimo," a young man whose sad and adventurous life became legend to his fellow Inuit. The legend stretches one's credulity, but the truth behind that legend is stranger still.

I first heard of Minik in the 1970s in Qaanaaq, northern Greenland, from the Inuit themselves. I already spoke Inuktitut, the language of Canadian Inuit, before I ever went to Greenland. But once there I made rapid progress in Inuktun, the very different dialect of the Polar Inuit. Ulrik Lennert, a native Greenlander who was the administrator of the community, shared my interest in Arctic history. Over coffee and cake in his comfortable home overlooking a bay filled with icebergs, he asked me if I had ever heard of Minik, a boy from the district who had grown up in America. I hadn't. Ulrik pulled a book from his shelf, the diary of a missionary, and read me a brief passage in Greenlandic about Minik, the first words I had heard about him. There's a story here, said Ulrik, a story that has never been told. I was hooked.

Because I spoke their language, I was always welcome in the humble homes of the community's Inuit hunters. I had always listened to their stories—what better way to learn their language—shared over never-ending cups of tea. Now I found myself asking them for specific stories, reminiscences of Minik, anecdotes from the memories of the eldest Inuit in the community. And they shared. It was not often, they said, that anyone took an interest in these episodes from the past. They're all gone now—Inuutersuaq, Imiina, Qisuk, Qaaqqutsiaq, Amaunnalik, Avoortungiaq, and others. But their memories, and that first kernel of information from Ulrik Lennert, were the genesis of this book.

Uncovering the life of Minik led me far from Qaanaaq—to the Royal Library in Copenhagen; the US National Archives in Washington; the American Museum of Natural History, the New-York Historical Society, the New York Public Library, and the Explorers Club, all in New York City; and the library of the American Philosophical Society in Philadelphia. It took me also to the small town of Cobleskill and the hamlet of Lawyersville in upstate New York, and to Pittsburg in the mountains of northern New Hampshire.

This is not a book about Robert Peary and Frederick Cook, although both men play major parts in the story, Peary a more prominent one than Cook. It is not a book about the North Pole controversy, a vicious debate over which of the two men was the first to reach the Pole. The resulting dispute was fought in the press for months and has been fodder for numerous books since. Although the controversy is mentioned, I have avoided taking sides in it.

This is a book about Minik, an Inuit boy taken by Peary to New York, where he grew to manhood before returning to his native Greenland. It is the story of a life shattered by the greed and insensitivities of others, and of Minik's resilience in the face of obstacles.

Many of the people once known as Eskimos prefer today to be known as *Inuit*. That's the plural form; the singular is *Inuk*. The adjectival form in current usage is *Inuit*, whether the modified noun is singular or plural. Exploration and anthropology knew the people of northern

Greenland as *Polar Eskimos*; I use the term *Polar Inuit*, and use it and *Inuit* interchangeably. Today the term *Inughuit* is sometimes used to distinguish the Polar Inuit from other groups of Inuit living elsewhere in the Arctic. The Polar Inuit were quite distinct in language and culture from the people, also Inuit, living south of Melville Bay along the Greenland coast. I have referred to those people as Greenlanders and their language as Greenlandic. They were also quite distinct from Canadian Inuit and of course from Inuit farther to the west in Alaska. The language of the Polar Inuit is Inuktun.

I have used the term *Eskimo* in the title, as Minik was known to many during his life as "the New York Eskimo." I have also used it in direct quotations.

1

Arrival in America

Robert Peary's chartered ship, the *Hope*, a three-masted sealer, had made a brief stop for fuel in Sydney on the northern tip of Nova Scotia. Now, heavy in the water on the last day of September 1897, she was gliding past the Statue of Liberty and heading toward the East River, where she would soon be fast to Excursion Wharf at the foot of Dock Street in Brooklyn.

From Sydney, Peary had wired New York the news of the ship's imminent arrival, and the city's newspapers were only too pleased to print it.

Robert Peary needed no introduction to reporters or the American public. A seasoned explorer, his adventures had been reported to an eager public for a decade. He had made sure that his expeditions were well covered in the press, for he depended on favorable publicity for his funding and ultimately for his success. This last foray had been a summer excursion to Greenland.

Peary had been to Greenland before—that was hardly news anymore. But what set the city abuzz this time was news of the cargo he carried: a large meteorite and six Inuit—"Eskimos" to the curious people of New York—as well as the sealskins, furs, kayaks, and harpoons they brought with them, all tools and clothing that New Yorkers would find exotic.

As the vessel drew close to the Brooklyn Bridge, the Inuit, "curious, long-haired individuals, clad in furs and skins," were on deck, awed by the sight of the city's skyline. Suddenly they began to gesticulate wildly. The closer the ship came to the bridge, the more animated their gestures became, as if they, and they alone, knew some disaster was imminent. In fact they were vainly trying to warn the captain that the topmast would surely be knocked off if he tried to pass under the bridge. The Inuit were concerned; the crew and the few passengers aboard were amused. The Inuit had had their first taste of the wonders of the city.

The following day twenty thousand people showed up in Brooklyn to see the ship and, for the first time, real live Inuit who hailed from Smith Sound in the northwestern corner of Greenland. Of equal interest was the enormous meteorite that Peary had brought back; over the course of a few years it had been wrenched from the frozen ground and hauled a mile to the shore before being laboriously loaded onto the ship.

Authorities had expected there to be crowds upon the *Hope*'s arrival. To bring some semblance of order they granted admission by ticket only.

Three days later, on October 3, the *Hope* was moving again as tugs towed the vessel to the nearby Brooklyn Navy Yard, where the public's enthusiasm continued. The meteorite was lifted by derrick from the ship and nestled into a huge timber platform on land. As many as a thousand people a day would come to view it.

"The crowd afterward boarded the vessel to see the Eskimos, who had attired themselves in their native costumes for inspection," *The New York Times* reported. The writer mentioned two Inuit children in particular, a girl, Aviaq, and a boy, Minik, and said they "attracted considerable attention, and were plentifully supplied with candy and peanuts, which they seemed to enjoy immensely."

A ship's officer was quoted as saying, "The children are sick from the quantity of sweet things given them. We feed them with raw meat, and the candy has had a bad effect on them."

To the little group of Inuit, these throngs of New Yorkers were overwhelming. Thirty thousand visitors in two days alone! Peary had told them that many people lived in America, but so many? The Inuit had grown accustomed to seeing strange new faces when the occasional ship from afar arrived at their Greenland settlements, but no amount of prepping by Peary could have prepared them for this turnout. Their own tribe back in Smith Sound, indeed their whole world, numbered fewer than 250 people. Peary had promised they would be safe. Now they were seeing, for the first time, a city skyline and street traffic and the human masses of New York, in all colors, shapes, and styles of dress. The experience was as unsettling as it was exciting. The Inuit would quickly learn that they were completely dependent on Peary and those who did his bidding.

Why had Peary brought six Inuit—three men, a woman, and two children—to New York? Was it a selfless gesture, a way to reward those who had served him so loyally during his earlier adventures in Greenland, as he would maintain? Or was there something sinister in this? Could he not have imagined that there might be unfortunate consequences from taking Inuit from their homeland and relocating them to New York City?

In short, what kind of man would take such liberties with the lives of other people? Who, exactly, was Robert Peary?

Robert Edwin Peary was born into a poor family in Pennsylvania in 1856. When he was not yet three, his father died of pneumonia at the young age of thirty. Robert's mother promptly packed up her son and returned with her husband's body to the family's native Maine, settling near Portland. She never remarried, and young Robert would remain an only child. Though of limited means, she doted on the boy she called Bertie. A mama's boy who was pampered and indulged, he was raised for a time as if he were a girl. Indeed, his own daughter would eventually write, "Gentle, pious Mary Peary had no previous experience with small children, especially small boys. . . . She tried her best to make her son over into the gentle little girl whom she would have known so well how to handle. She tried to implant in him the idea that he was not strong, that he was too delicate to play with other boys."

The boy was also hampered by a pronounced lisp, which he worked steadfastly to overcome before he reached adulthood. Mrs. Peary sent him to a succession of boarding schools, making sure that she always moved to a community quite nearby. In high school, perhaps as a form of rebellion against his mother's dominance, he took up outdoor activities, although he never liked team sports. He also became an expert in taxidermy and ornithology.

In 1873 Peary enrolled in Bowdoin College in Brunswick, Maine, on a scholarship, and his mother again relocated to be close by. After four years he graduated as a civil engineer. In 1879 he found employment with the Coast and Geodetic Survey in Washington. He found the city stimulating but the work boring—he was merely a draftsman occupying a desk and dreaming of greater glory, for he was nothing if not ambitious.

Peary applied for a position as civil engineer with the US Navy in 1881. The job appealed to him because it came with the rank of lieutenant and the prestige that accompanied that rank. He had earlier written to his mother: "I cannot bear to associate with people, who, age and advantages being equal, are my superiors. I must be the peer or superior of those about me to be comfortable." The naval position would put him in the company of people who would notice his abilities and drive, and place him on the path of advancement. In the same letter, written when he was twenty-four, he outlined for his mother an ambitious and arrogant description of how he saw himself by age thirty:

> Tall, erect, broad-shouldered, full-chested, tough, wiry-limbed, clear-eyed, full-mustached, clear-browed complexion, a dead shot, a powerful, tireless swimmer, a first-class rider, a skillful boxer and fencer, perfectly at home in any company, yet always bearing with me an indefinable atmosphere of the wildness and freedom of woods and mountains, master of German, Spanish, and French . . .

Peary excelled at his work with the navy. In early 1882 he was sent to the US naval station at Key West, Florida, as an inspector to oversee the work of a contractor on the construction of a new pier. The contractor botched the job; Peary canceled the contract and oversaw the completion of the project himself, which he brought in under budget.

By 1884 he was in Nicaragua on the first of two trips there to survey a possible route for a transoceanic canal from the Atlantic to the Pacific. On both trips he served under the authority of a senior naval civil engineer. In 1887 and 1888 Peary served seven months there, and effectively laid out the route of the proposed canal. But back in the United States most of the accolades went to the senior engineer, whom Peary came to detest as a result. He resolved that from then onward he must always be in command.

In between the two trips to Nicaragua, Peary turned his attention northward. In 1886 he took passage on a whaler, the *Eagle*, to Disko Bay, midway up the west coast of Greenland. From the Danish colony of Ritenbenk, accompanied by one other white man and using man-hauled sleds, he traveled onto the ice cap and penetrated into the interior about a hundred miles. The expedition didn't accomplish much, but he returned alive and published an account of the adventure, which brought him attention. It resulted in his election to the American Association for the Advancement of Science, and enhanced his reputation in Washington society. These were important first steps on his road to influence.

Immediately upon his return from Nicaragua, Peary married Josephine Diebitsch, whose father was a scholar at the Smithsonian Institution. Peary's mother accompanied them on their honeymoon.

He longed for fame and recognition. At one point he wrote to his mother, "Remember, Mother, I <u>must</u> have fame." He decided that it lay in the north, in Greenland. He contemplated a return to the central west coast and a complete west-to-east crossing of the ice cap. But then news came that a Norwegian, Fridtjof Nansen, had made a successful crossing in the opposite direction. Undeterred, Peary decided that his future lay even farther north. He would determine the outline of the northern coastline of Greenland, in effect proving its insularity.

Some self-promotion would be required to pull this off and secure the requisite support. And so in 1890 he lectured before scientific institutions in Brooklyn and Philadelphia, and the prestigious American Geographical Society in New York. All three institutions voted their support for his proposed expedition, and this helped him secure his leave of absence from the navy. Thus had begun Robert Peary's eighteen-year involvement with northwestern Greenland and the Polar Inuit.

Peary prided himself on being a man of science. In his books and speeches he often described his expeditions in the far north, particularly those in search of the North Pole, as research, a learning quest. He brought back scientific specimens from his various expeditions and many made their way, often circuitously, to the American Museum of Natural History in New York, which had become one of his biggest supporters. Perhaps these Inuit whom he brought on this autumn day in 1897 could be viewed as legitimate specimens, not unlike the human skulls and skeletons he had collected earlier for the museum, but, of course, much more interesting because blood still coursed through their veins.

Certainly, Peary felt an affinity for the six Inuit, since three of them, the men, had been in his employ, hunting and carrying supplies by dogsled. But he had also felt an odd and morbid affinity for several deceased Inuit he had known by name but whose bodies he had nevertheless exhumed from fresh graves the year before. They had died from diseases brought by his ship in 1895. That was unfortunate, but it didn't stop him from shipping their skeletons south to New York to become museum specimens. He had written about it in his diary on August 22, 1896, citing the name of one specimen. "The ship's men brought off the cask containing Qujaukittoq and his wife and the little girl together with the accessories of his grave," Peary wrote dispassionately. And the American Museum of Natural History, just thirty years old but already an important institution, eagerly and unquestioningly purchased the macabre specimens from the explorer.

Peary maintained an important personal connection to the museum. He had found and cultivated a patron with the highest connections there, a wealthy man to be humored, coddled, and flattered—one who could help him immensely were the US Navy, in which Peary still served, ever to grow tired of his requests for leave for purposes of exploration. Sooner or later Peary might need to rely on private sponsorship for his northern adventures and his ultimate dream of reaching the North Pole. He would need significant financial backing.

The patron was Morris Ketchum Jesup, who had made a fortune in banking and railroad supplies. In 1884 he had retired to devote his life to philanthropic interests. A religious man, he helped found the Young Men's Christian Association. He made substantial gifts to the Union Theological Seminary in New York, to Yale, Harvard, and Princeton universities, and to the Woman's Hospital in New York. But he reserved his greatest love and his greatest gifts for the American Museum of Natural History. He had been one of its founders in 1868, and he assumed its presidency in 1881.

Like Peary, Jesup was not a scientist. Unlike Peary, though, he never pretended to be one. Still, he revered scientists and their work and strove to further scientific research. Wielding his considerable wealth, he dedicated himself to bringing science to the common man. Indeed, it was during his presidency, which lasted until his death, that the American Museum of Natural History became a respected instrument of popular education and research.

Peary undoubtedly felt that the scientific benefit to be derived from an anthropological study of "his" six living Inuit would benefit the museum and, through it, boost Jesup's stature. The museum president had already shown interest in the Arctic by endowing one major archaeological research foray, a scientific journey eponymously known as the Jesup North Pacific Expedition. Peary, of course, had in mind possible sponsorship for his expeditions to the northern reaches of Greenland and beyond.

Yet Peary decided to bring the Inuit to the United States apparently without Jesup's knowledge. There's no evidence Jesup had asked him to bring back living specimens for research, and Jesup seemed genuinely surprised when he learned that Peary had. Others at the museum were not surprised; at least one scientist had suggested to the explorer that he bring a single Inuk to New York for a year. And a later memo in Jesup's hand said, "I understand Peary brought this party here at the suggestion of the Department of Anthropology."

It was the museum's Dr. Franz Boas who gave Peary the idea. As a young geographer, Boas had spent a year among the remote Inuit of Cumberland Sound on the east coast of Baffin Island in northeastern Canada, a year that shifted his interest from geography to the young science of ethnology. With the publication of papers on his year of Arctic research, the scientific world had taken notice of his work.

A German immigrant to the United States, Boas received the recognition he sought when the Smithsonian Institution published his large monograph, *The Central Eskimos*, in 1888. It was the first detailed ethnological study of any Canadian Inuit, and Boas used his instant academic acclaim as a springboard to a distinguished career in American anthropology.

Boas never returned to the Arctic, but he maintained a deep interest in it and its people. From 1892 through 1894 he served first as chief assistant in anthropology at the World's Columbian Exposition in Chicago and then as curator of the museum established there to house its permanent collections. Inuit had been brought to Chicago from Labrador for "exhibit" at that exposition. In 1895 he joined the staff of the American Museum of Natural History and became assistant curator there the following year. It was in that year that he asked Peary to bring back from his summer's cruise one Inuk for a year's stay. Such a thing had previously been done, he claimed, without the individual suffering. Peary liked the idea but was unable to execute it until the following year.

As Peary was planning his 1897 voyage north, Boas again contacted him, writing, "I beg to suggest to you that if you are certain of revisiting North Greenland next summer, it would be of the very greatest value if you should be able to bring a middle-aged Eskimo to stay here over winter. This would enable us to obtain leisurely certain information, which will be of the greatest scientific importance."

Boas expected the arrival of one Inuk in New York, so he was probably as shocked as Jesup at the arrival of six. But he later wrote, "It was believed that much valuable information of an ethnological character could be obtained from them, and that their presence here would be very instructive to scientists interested in the study of the Northern races."

Peary may have thought that if the presence of one Inuk would enhance his reputation with the institution, then a larger group would earn him even more prestige. He would later deny that he was involved at all in the decision to bring the Inuit to New York, claiming he was acting only on the Inuit's own suggestion. This was a silly and irresponsible denial. There is no doubt that he brought them to secure the goodwill of the officials of the museum and to obtain favorable publicity for himself. One of his most ardent admirers later admitted as much when he wrote that "it was his idea that they would provide an interesting ethnological and anthropological study."

This was a golden age of exploration, when hardy American and European adventurers, acting in the name of science, set their sights on both the Arctic and Antarctic, hoping for fame by being the first to reach the Poles.

This was also the heyday of newspapers, especially in New York, which had more than a dozen big dailies that were expanding their coverage of the world, broadening their readers' knowledge and stoking their imaginations.

Among them were Joseph Pulitzer's *World*, with its huge circulation of some four hundred thousand, and William Randolph Hearst's more flamboyant *Journal*, plus others such as the *Herald*, the *Sun*, the *Tribune*, the *Post*, and the *Times*, all competing against one another with muckraking series, legitimate news items, and sensational features and scoops. Peary would have little difficulty in gaining the exposure he craved; his problem would be in avoiding negative publicity on those occasions when things went wrong.

Reporters were quickly drawn to the Inuit story and would publish many articles. Some ridiculed the Inuit for their appearance and their behavior. But as it became apparent that the small party of six—far away from their homeland and with no possibility of returning home for a year—was deeply unhappy and often poorly treated, the ridicule turned to sympathy and in some cases even outrage.

Peary intended, too, to carry on the Arctic explorers' tradition of exhibiting Inuit before audiences as a means of securing funds for the continuation of his explorations. Even while the *Hope* was at Excursion Wharf, an admission fee had been charged to allow the curious to view the attractions, human and otherwise, that he had brought from the Arctic. But one person whom these New York crowds did not see was Peary himself—he had left the *Hope* at Sydney and proceeded by train to Washington to report to his superiors at the navy.

At every stop, he was met by reporters, and he told them, "We have on board six Eskimos, namely, three men, one woman, a boy, and a girl. . . . They will remain with me here this Winter, to arrange the ethnological specimens, and will return with me next summer." He had already laid plans for the next summer's voyage, and he claimed, "When I leave again . . . it will be to remain up there until I reach the pole, or lose my life in the attempt."

Although Jesup was unaware of it, Peary expected all along that the Inuit would go to the museum. And so, on October 1, the day after their arrival at the docks, *The New York Times* reported, "A collection of the implements, tents, sleds and clothing of the 'Greenland Highlanders' . . . was brought back. These will be placed in the American Museum of Natural History. Six Eskimos were carried on the steamer . . . and will help Lieut. Peary arrange the materials he brought home." And two days later the same paper reported, "All of the Eskimos will leave the ship today and go to the Museum of Natural History, where they will arrange the exhibit of their implements."

While Peary assumed that the museum would be happy to have the Inuit, neither he nor Boas had made arrangements for their reception there. A museum memo at the time stated,

> It was felt that it would be unwise to place the Eskimos in an asylum or in a hospital because the artificial, and to them, unnatural confinement of such places would prove unfavorable. Mr. Morris K. Jesup . . . was appealed to and . . . rooms were provided for the temporary occupancy of the Eskimos, who were placed in the custody of Mr. Wallace, in whom he

had every confidence. . . . These rooms were clean, and . . . the Eskimos received kind and considerate attention.

William Wallace, middle-aged, married, and the father of a young son, was buildings superintendent and a highly trusted and valued museum official.

Years later Minik, the youngest of the party, recalled that arrival in New York: "Oh, I can remember it very well, that day when we first saw the big houses and saw so many people and heard the bells on the cars. It was like a land that we thought must be heaven."

But he added another observation, one of consternation and disapproval over part of the cargo that Peary landed:

When they took us ashore, they brought five big barrels—they held the bones of our people who had died, and I had seen them digging them up out of their graves to bring here.

When we asked them why, they told us that they were bringing them here to put in nice boxes, where they would be kept safe forever. But I don't know where they are now. Our land is cold and stony, but I guess they would have been better off there if they had been left in the stone graves my people made for them.

The Inuit were housed at first in the museum's basement, but even there they were not free from the eyes of the curious. *The New York Times* referred to "the several scores of visitors, who received permission from Superintendent Wallace of the museum to inspect the newcomers." But there were many others who were denied admission:

The unusual crowd that thronged the museum was disappointed when told that the Eskimos were not on exhibition. Some of the visitors understood that they could have access to the temporary abode of the strangers, and came there for that purpose, but they had to content themselves with a glimpse through a grating above the basement, and many lay prone, peering through the spaces in the hope of catching a glimpse of the Eskimos.

The Inuit were not sure which was more oppressive, the heat or the crowds. Nonetheless they tried to bear the former and be polite to the latter. They had looked forward to this trip to America, with all the wonders that Peary had described, and to all the treasures they would take back home. Peary was surely a great leader, and everyone in northern Greenland considered it wise and, indeed, profitable to do his bidding. If these hordes of white-faced strangers in America were Peary's people too, then it might be wise to treat them respectfully.

Visitors to the museum were treated to a round of handshaking with every member of the little party. Matthew Henson, Peary's black servant, whom the Inuit had come to know and trust during Peary's expeditions, was on hand to help with interpretation. He was the only one of all those who ever accompanied Peary north who learned to speak the language of the Inuit in anything but a halting fashion.

The New York Times commented on the appearance of the Inuit:

> For the first time since their arrival in this city, they laid aside their fur garments, and yesterday wore a combination of American and Eskimo costumes, which, while by no means picturesque, presented a striking appearance.
>
> Qisuk, the head of the party, and ranking chief, by grace of one of the attendants got hold of a light overcoat, and, though several sizes too large for him, he wrapped it around his body and seemed proud of it. His nether garments consisted of a pair of golf stockings of rather loud pattern and somewhat too comfortable a fit.

The men of the party expressed a tremendous interest in American girls and "insisted upon their rights to propose an exchange of wives." Until their stop in St. John's, Newfoundland, on the voyage to New York, they had seen only two white women in their lives. One was Peary's wife, Josephine, who had wintered twice in northern Greenland. The Inuit recalled with amusement how Equ, a hunter, had met her during Peary's visit in 1891. Equ had heard that the chief of the recently arrived white men had brought his wife along, and so the Inuk made a trip to the camp to see this spectacle. Upon arrival he presented himself outside the house and asked to see the white woman. Robert Peary and his wife both stepped outside. It was the first time Equ had seen either. After looking them up and down for a few moments, he asked, "Which one is the woman?" Upon learning the answer, he promptly proposed an exchange of wives with Peary.

Peary hadn't liked that, they remembered, though they all thought a man should be flattered by such an offer. But perhaps it was still worth a try here in this large American city. They knew that after Mrs. Peary had left Greenland, Peary had developed a fondness for Aleqasina, one of the most beautiful of the Inuit women, and that he often borrowed her from her husband, Piugaattoq, rewarding him much more liberally than the other hunters under the guise of paying him for his services as a hunter and driver.

The happy-go-lucky Qisuk, Minik's father, could do with a partner to help him with his son. Another member of the party, Uisaakassak, was also impressed by the American women, who interested him more than the flat-chested Aviaq, to whom he was betrothed. Perhaps a few could be induced to go north with him and share their polar nights.

A reporter wrote that "when . . . some ten or fifteen young women were introduced to them they at once began instituting inquiries as to the willingness of their new acquaintances to enter into matrimonial agreements. Through the interpreter they gave an account of their possessions and what consideration they were willing to allow for the acquisition of a good-looking wife. They had no special preference, but would take anyone who would present herself for acceptance. When their rather verbose offerings were declined with thanks, they showed keen disappointment."

The newspaper report is the first to mention how little Minik, seven years old, first took to America. "Qisuk's little son," it stated, "was happy in the possession of a knickerbocker suit and blue flannel waist, which he took great delight in exhibiting to the callers, his chubby, greasy, little face beaming with delight at his civilized appearance. For the first time in his life, probably, he had a real bath yesterday, and, though it took some coaxing to get him to enter the tub of water, after the performance was over, he was so pleased that he has been anxiously inquiring through Matthew Henson, the coloured interpreter, when the next bath was forthcoming."

William Wallace took Minik for a ride through Central Park and reported that "the little fellow could hardly be torn away from the menagerie, where he saw some polar bears, and the sight of a bicycle made him howl with glee. He would not let riders pass without hailing them, and was amazed at the size of the 'big dogs,' as he called the horses he saw in the driveways."

Within a few days of their arrival the Inuit were sick. They had all caught colds. It was fall in the city, and while to the New Yorker autumn can be sunny and splendid, the Inuit found the seasonal heat oppressive, and their colds quickly developed into pneumonia. They knew they were seriously ill.

The newspapermen, however, did not realize the gravity of what they saw in the museum's basement one day in early October, and one insensitively reported, "One of the most amusing forms of entertainment consisted in an illustration of the manner in which the Eskimos attempt to conjure away illness. This in their opinion can only be accomplished by rubbing the sides of the body and singing a weird sort of a lullaby that with all its peculiarities is not absolutely discordant."

It was not, however, a mere exhibition. It was an attempt, perhaps by old Atangana, the shaman, to invoke the helping spirits to ward off illness. It didn't work. The helping spirits—the *toorngat*—did not respond, and the Inuit would later claim that "in the United States . . . the *angakkoq* [a spiritual intermediary, a shaman] has no power, because there are no *toorngat*."

By November 1 the entire group was in Bellevue Hospital. All were ill with pneumonia, Atangana the most critically, and it was thought for a time she would die. She survived, and they all returned to the museum where drier and more comfortable quarters had been prepared for them in an apartment on the sixth floor, an apartment that had been meant for a custodian.

Minik and Aviaq, the children, had been the favorites of the staff at Bellevue. The attendants became deeply attached to the children, and the nurses amused themselves by teaching both children English words.

Boas, who observed the group closely, commented that Minik "had begun to pick up a few English words as soon as he reached this city" and counted him the brightest of the group.

2

Peary's People

The first white man to visit the isolated Polar Inuit of northwestern Greenland was the British explorer John Ross. At the time, in 1818, he was a commander in the British navy, charged with sailing to this corner of the frozen world in search of a Northwest Passage, a shortcut to Asia, that might prove to be a convenient trade route.

Some time before his arrival, a woman of the tribe prophesied that "a big boat with tall poles would come into view from the ocean." And sure enough, on an early-summer day Ross's ship arrived at the ice edge. The Inuit thought it a marvel of ingenuity, and described it as "a whole island of wood, which moved along the sea on wings, and in its depths had many houses and rooms full of noisy people. Little boats hung along the rail, and these, filled with men, were lowered on the water, and as they surrounded the ship, it looked as if the monster gave birth to living young."

The ship remained long enough for Ross to interact with the Inuit. Fortunately, he had along a West Greenlander—an Inuk from much farther south in Greenland—who could interpret, after a fashion, the words of the Inuit, although his dialect was very different from that of the Polar Inuit. Then, as unexpectedly as it arrived, the ship "turned towards the sea with the sun shining on its white wings and disappeared into the horizon."

Ross was surprised to find anyone living this far north. And the Arctic Highlanders, as he called them, were equally surprised to meet Ross, for in their isolation they thought they were the world's only humans.

It was, indeed, a small world that they inhabited. They lived along a narrow strip of coastline bounded by tall, nearly impassable glaciers and the sea. The broad expanse of water in what is now known as

Melville Bay and the glaciers separated the Polar Inuit from the native West Greenlanders and a few Danish settlers far to the south.

When Elisha Kent Kane, the American explorer, met the Polar Inuit thirty-six years later, he noted: "If you point to the east, inland, where the herds of caribou run over the barren hills . . . they will cry 'Sermeq,' glacier'; and, question them as you may about the range of their nation to the north and south, the answer is still the same, with a shake of the head, 'Sermeq, sermersuaq,' 'the great ice-wall': there is no more beyond."

In Ross's and Kane's time, these Inuit were a society of about two hundred people who relied on hunting and collecting for their food. They lived in small camps, usually of a few families each, and were nomadic within the confines of their ice-enclosed coastline. A long and oppressively dark winter dominated their lives. The sea ice usually did not break up until late July or early August. Then the short summer brought warmth but not freedom. For some unaccountable reason, over previous decades they had lost their knowledge of both the kayak and the larger open craft, the umiaq. Their loss confined the population to shore during the brief ice-free season. They lived in summer on caches of food put up during the long and glorious spring. They chose summer camping grounds where they could supplement their diet with the meat and eggs of the little auk, the godsend that came by the millions to nest on the fabled bird cliffs. They were such easy prey that everyone—men, women, children, and the aged—was able to take part in the catch. The birds provided not just food but skins for inner coats.

Winter presented a different set of challenges. The midwinter darkness made travel by foot or dogsled hazardous. Four months separated the autumn setting of the sun from its February reappearance, and the height of the dark season was a time of lethargy and occasional depression. When Kane wintered there for the first time, he had with him a young Inuk from the far southern reaches of Greenland, hundreds of miles away, below the Arctic Circle, where the sun still shone in midwinter. The man described his shock at that first winter in the far north:

Then it really grew winter and dreadfully cold, and the sky speedily darkened. Never had I seen the dark season like this, and, to be sure, it was awful. I thought we should have no daylight any more. I was seized with fright, and fell a-weeping. I never in my life saw such darkness at noontime. As the darkness continued for three months, I really believed we should have no daylight more.

In October the Polar Inuit would leave the bird cliffs and move to their winter settlements in stone houses. Before the dark was totally upon them, they hunted marine mammals at the floe edge—ringed seal, bearded seal, walrus, and narwhal—and sealed on the smooth ice at the heads of the fjords. Polar bears, indispensable for clothing, were also hunted in early winter. Often the Inuit food caches proved insufficient, and hunger, even starvation, was a worry by late January and February.

At times like these, hunters gathered at Neqi—the very name means "meat"—where open water was close by throughout the winter. There they hunted walrus until the more favorable conditions of spring allowed more travel and sealing on the ice.

Despite the hardships, this was home to a small tribe of people who lived for the magnificent months of sunshine that are the High Arctic spring. The sun made its reappearance in mid-February and, from then until mid-June, rose progressively higher in the sky each day. By early April the darkness had been supplanted by twenty-four hours of daylight, and families packed and traveled over the still-smooth sea ice to visit friends and kin. Sea mammals were plentiful in the waters at the floe edge, and seals basked on the ice surface. Indeed, life was splendid.

As late as the mid-nineteenth century the Polar Inuit were without knowledge not only of how to make and use seagoing vessels, but also of how to craft bird spears, fish leisters, and the bow and arrow. Incredibly, they were unable to hunt the local caribou. A fortuitous immigration of Canadian Inuit from Baffin Island in the 1860s reintroduced the kayak and weapons of the hunt. By the time Peary arrived they were, as a result, better supplied than they had been in Ross's time.

Still, they lacked one important item.

When Kane lived among them, he noted tersely: "They had no wood." Driftwood rarely found its way to their shores, so the Polar Inuit relied on bone and ivory as substitutes. Bear and walrus bones and the narwhal's pointed tusks were fitted together as weapon shafts, while the larger whale bones were used as sled runners. Driftwood, when found, was a treasure. It was the desire for wood, above all else, that made the infrequent arrival of ships such welcome events. And the greatest bonanza of all was a shipwreck—which could never happen often enough as far as the Inuit were concerned.

In the wake of John Ross's visit, two distinct types of white men began to frequent Melville Bay and Smith Sound. One group, men like Ross himself, came to learn and pursue seemingly elusive goals. It was hard for the Inuit to fathom the visitors' motivations, but intentions mattered little as long as they traded or paid for the services of the Inuit men with wood, guns, knives, needles, and other commodities.

The Inuit could make more sense of the ways of the other newcomers, for they were skillful hunters who came in the years when they could negotiate the unpredictable drift ice of Melville Bay. They arrived in sailing ships in the late spring or summer in search of the largest treasure of the northern sea—the bowhead whale. The Polar Inuit had dubbed them *upernaallit*, meaning "those who arrive in spring." These men, too, carried trade goods. They also expressed more than a passing interest in the Inuit women, and many were especially generous with gifts for the men who let their wives visit the ships.

Peary, in his first visit to the far north, had approached the Polar Inuit with some wariness, influenced by reports of earlier explorers about the natives' treachery and thieving nature. Their behavior aboard ship had amazed Kane, who called them "incorrigible scamps," and wrote:

> When they were first allowed to come aboard, they were very
> rude and difficult to manage. They spoke three or four at a time,
> to each other, and to us, laughing heartily at our ignorance in
> not understanding them. They were incessantly in motion,

> going everywhere, trying doors and squeezing through dark
> passages, round casks and into the light again, anxious to touch
> and handle everything they saw, and asking for or endeavoring
> to steal everything they touched.

Before long they were busily running back and forth from the ship to their sleds, carrying off loot.

After studying narratives of Arctic exploration, Peary began developing some practical notions about how best to travel in this region of Greenland. He concluded that the travel methods endorsed by earlier explorers had led to unnecessary hardship and death. British explorers in particular had disdained the use of dogs for hauling sleds—they claimed the dogs ate too much—and they used man-hauled sleds instead. As a result many expeditions that went north had stayed in the north, with the remains of the explorers left on the tundra and the beaches.

Peary shunned their "orthodox" methods, and instead would go among the natives, live close to them, and adopt their means of travel. What could make more sense, he thought, than to use the Inuit dogs as a means of traction, and the Inuit themselves to hunt for fresh meat for dogs and men alike? They would be paid cheaply with trade goods brought from the United States, so all sides would benefit.

And so he overwintered in 1891 as an experiment to see if his "radical" ideas about living off the fruits of Inuit hunting were practical. He was pleased to discover they were.

In 1893 Peary returned to overwinter, this time for two years. His announced goals for the expedition were to continue the mapping and surveying of northern Greenland, complete the ethnographical studies of the Polar Inuit, and, if conditions allowed, reach the North Pole. After the favorable experiences of his previous expedition, he felt confident in relying more on the Inuit, and he developed close ties with some of them. Two of them, Qisuk and Nuktaq, had already worked for him and were pleased to do so again. They were impressed with his tenacity and personal toughness. Here was a man who at least had enough common sense to use the native dogs to haul the sleds, although they were perplexed and amused by the donkeys he brought to haul supplies from the beach to his house site.

Peary also brought his wife, an act that had convinced many of his critics in the south that he was indeed crazy, for Mrs. Peary was obviously pregnant with her first child when the ship left for the north. The baby was born in December and named Marie Ahnighito. She was nicknamed the Snow Baby.

A Peary biographer summarized the explorer's adaptation to his northern environment:

> He learned to drive and care for dogs in native fashion.
> . . . He learned to dress like an Eskimo. . . . He learned the technique of building a snow-igloo. . . . He learned the value of laying in a supply of fresh meat during the proper hunting seasons. . . . He learned where game was most plentiful by listening to native teaching, and what methods of search were most successful. He discovered the psychology of the native, and so was able to organize the tribe almost with the efficacy he would have used with a large band of trained white helpers.

But although Peary lived among the Inuit, he did not consider them his equals. They and Matthew Henson, his black assistant and dog driver whom he once berated for not calling him "sir" often enough, were in Peary's estimation members of inferior races. Strong, knowledgeable, and reliable providers, they were somehow not as good as white men. They, even more than his white colleagues, were the means to an end. He once wrote,

> I have often been asked: "Of what use are Eskimos to the world?" They are too far removed to be of any value for commercial enterprises; and, furthermore, they lack ambition. They have no literature; nor, properly speaking, any art.

They value life only as does a fox, or a bear, purely by instinct. But let us not forget that these people, trustworthy and hardy, will yet prove their value to mankind. With their help, the world shall discover the Pole.

Peary's attitude toward the Inuit on whom he depended, often for his life, tarnished the work he might have accomplished. He was intimately associated with the Inuit for almost two decades, yet, in the opinion of a noted anthropologist, he "did not produce a single good ethnographic or archaeological study." He was unable to speak the Inuit language well, even after years of association with them. He misunderstood many aspects of their culture.

The Inuit knew him as Piuli—the best they could do at pronouncing his name—or Piulerriaq. He was, they realized, a man of tenacity. One man, Uutaaq, who accompanied him on his final poleward dash in 1909, called him "a great leader," but to others he was an enigma.

Knud Rasmussen, a Danish explorer with a dash of Inuit ancestry, put it the most charitably when he said "their respect for the man was greater than their love." An anthropologist who heard the Inuit talk about Peary almost half a century after his Greenland adventures had ended characterized him as a man who accomplished his aims "by threats, coercion, and the power of his authority."

Peary had essentially appropriated the entire band of Polar Inuit for his own purposes. They were his, just as surely as were his sled, his Arctic gear, and anything else he needed in the fanatical pursuit of his goals. They could work only for him. Their dogs, he insisted, were to be available to him alone for barter. It was the same with their furs and the ivory tusks of walrus and narwhal, which he acquired in exchange for cheap goods from the United States and later sold in America for a handsome profit.

In his writings, the Inuit were "my faithful, trusty Eskimo allies, dusky children of the Pole" and "effective instruments for Arctic work." At the end of his Arctic career, he wrote that "these people are much like children, and should be treated as such."

His ego was enormous. He felt that "their feeling for me is one of gratitude and confidence," and he concluded that "it would be misleading to infer that almost any man who went to the Eskimos with gifts could obtain from them the kind of service they have given me; for it must be remembered that they have known me personally for nearly twenty years. . . . I have saved whole villages from starvation, and the children are taught by their parents that if they grow up and become good hunters or good seamstresses, as the case may be, 'Piulerriaq' will reward them sometime in the not too distant future."

To be sure, some Inuit genuinely liked the man. The influential Uutaaq was among them. But many others retained a quite different memory of him.

In 1967 an elderly man in tiny Siorapaluk, the region's most northerly village, reminisced about Peary, to whom he referred as "the great tormentor":

> People were afraid of him . . . really afraid. . . . His big ship . . . it made a big impression on us. He was a great leader. You always had the feeling that if you didn't do what he wanted, he would condemn you to death. . . . I was very young, but I will never forget how he treated the Inuit. . . . His big ship arrives in the bay. He is hardly visible from the shore, but he shouts: "*Kiiha Tikeqihunga!*—I'm arriving, for a fact!"
>
> The Inuit go aboard. Peary has a barrel of biscuits brought up on deck. The two or three hunters who have gone out to the ship in their kayaks bend over the barrel and begin to eat with both hands. Later, the barrel is taken ashore, and the contents thrown on the beach. Men, women and children hurl themselves on the biscuits like dogs, which amuses Peary a lot. My heart still turns cold to think of it. That scene tells very well how he considered this people—my people—who were, for all of that, devoted to him.

3

The Iron Mountain

When John Ross first encountered the Polar Inuit in 1818, he observed with surprise that they used metal tools. They alone, of all Inuit, had discovered a local source of iron—three meteorites at the northern extremity of Melville Bay, about thirty-five miles to the east of Cape York. A legend had grown up around these meteorites that they were a woman, her dog, and her tent, hurled from the sky by a supernatural power. The Inuit tried to explain to Ross how they obtained their metal tools, but he understood them imperfectly. When he reported the event, he inadvertently created another northern myth, that of the existence of an iron mountain on the shores of Melville Bay.

After Ross's visit, many expeditions went in search of the mythical mountain. Most were sent out for exploration or whaling; finding the iron was a secondary objective. Still, they searched for, but never found, the iron mountain. Yet over the years they learned that the iron was meteoric in origin. In 1883 Baron Adolf Erik Nordenskiöld, a Finnish-Swedish scientist and explorer, tried to reach Cape York with the sole purpose of discovering and bringing home the meteorites, but the ice of Melville Bay proved impassable that year. Until 1894, no white man had laid eyes on the treasure.

Robert Peary heard about the meteorites in 1892 from the Inuk Qisuk, one of his regular hunters and dog drivers. When Peary returned to Greenland the following year, it was with the announced intention of locating the so-called iron mountain, which he, too, was convinced must be meteoric in nature. The Inuit hesitated to take him there. After all, wasn't this their source of iron? What would he do with it? Would he be content merely to look at it? One could not imagine a man wanting to undergo such a lengthy journey just to gaze at three large stones. Perhaps he would carry them away, as he was carrying off so many other things from their land. It was true that they used the stones less now than had their forefathers; they traded for knives and other metal implements with the *upernaallit* who stopped by from time to time, and now with the great Peary himself, but one could never be certain that these voyages would continue. Perhaps there would come a time when they would need again the woman, her dog, and her tent.

If Peary planned to carry the stones away, the Inuit wanted no part of it. Only bad luck could ensue from any such attempt, and it would surely follow those who helped in it. Many years before, a group from the northernmost part of the region had tired of the exhausting trip to Savissivik—literally "the place where one finds metal"—and they laboriously detached the head from the woman to cart it off to their wintering area. They lashed the head to a sled and started for home, but it was late spring and the ice was rotten; when they were well out from shore, it gave way under the tremendous weight of their cargo. The sled, the dogs, and the woman's head all disappeared beneath the water. There could be no misunderstanding such an event—it was a punishment exacted by the spirit of the iron woman on the hunters for trying to remove the stones. Since that time it had been considered bad luck to take more of the iron than was needed. The iron lady had never begrudged them the small fragments they had chipped from her scarred body over the centuries, but one must not be greedy.

At last Peary found a guide to take him to the place. After a long and difficult sled journey from his headquarters in Inglefield Bay, they reached the site on a day in May 1894, dug away the snow, and found a large brown mass. His guide, Aleqatsiaq, identified it as the headless woman. It would take some stretch of imagination, Peary thought, to see this as a woman. He spent the following afternoon measuring, sketching, and photographing the treasure, then claimed it as his own: "I scratched a rough 'P' on the surface of the metal, as an indisputable proof of my having found the meteorite." Aleqatsiaq also showed him the site of the largest of the meteorites, the tent, on Bushnan Island, a few miles offshore.

When Peary returned to his headquarters, a place he had named Anniversary Lodge, he told his wife, "This means that if the ship comes I can put one or two of the meteorites aboard her. By their sale or exhibition your brother . . . can raise enough to send a ship next year." The ship, the *Falcon*, did come, but she was unable to reach the site, for the ice of Melville Bay once again protected the meteorites from intruders. Peary remained in the Arctic for a second winter. The following summer, with the relief steamer *Kite*, he was more fortunate. He reached the site in August, and, with the help of a crew of Inuit, he struggled to winch the three-ton woman and her thousand-pound dog aboard and then departed for America.

Peary was accustomed to being in total charge when he was in the north. Back in America, it pained him to realize once again that he was a mere lieutenant in the navy. He was beginning to feel heat from powerful critics, jealous people in the navy who resented the time off he had already been given to pursue what they thought were personal and frivolous pastimes. It rankled them that leave was accompanied by half pay. They thought that Peary ought to devote himself to naval duties, some going so far as to say that, as a civil engineer, he was merely a civilian lucky enough to have a rank.

He was fortunate to have secured the meteorites, for at least he had something tangible to show for his two-year absence. However, he had failed to accomplish most of his other professed aims, and the scientific results of the expedition were meager. He had not even made an attempt on the North Pole. Before departing from Greenland in August 1895, he penned a simple entry in his diary: "I have failed." By the time he arrived in the United States, he was despondent. "I shall never see the North Pole," he told a reporter, "unless someone brings it here. I am done with it. In my judgment such work requires a far, far younger man than I."

But with Peary, whom a biographer characterized as "the man who refused to fail," such despair never lasted long. The navy assigned him to a post in Brooklyn, and while there he began planning to return north the following summer to bring the largest meteorite, the tent, to the United States. He requested leave for a summer voyage in 1896. There was strong opposition to it, but through the influence of powerful friends his request was granted.

Peary took the *Hope* north that summer. Again using an Inuit workforce, he and his crew excavated the largest meteorite and got it to the shore, but bad weather prevented him from maneuvering it aboard the ship. His empty-handed return to the United States again made him an easy target for critics, and he was derided in the navy and the press for his fruitless obsession with Greenland. This was the time in his career when his future as an Arctic explorer seemed most in jeopardy.

Yet even before leaving Cape York to return to America, he had instructed Qisuk and Nuktaq, his two most trusted aides, to be at the cape awaiting his arrival the following summer. He would return, he promised. "The summer's voyage and the Arctic atmosphere," he wrote, "had brushed away the last vestige of the previous year's exhaustion and morbidness. I felt once more my old-time elan and sanguineness."

He also began planning for a major expedition to reach that one geographic prize that remained in northern exploration—the North Pole. On January 12, 1897, the American Geographical Society presented him with its first Cullom Gold Medal for establishing the insularity of Greenland and for his explorations about Inglefield Bay. It was at the society's awards ceremony that Peary announced his strategy for reaching the top of the world. He described what would come to be known as the American Route to the Pole. He would acquire a strong ship and force her through the passages separating northern Greenland from Ellesmere Island, the ice-choked waters of Smith Sound, Kane Basin, and Kennedy and Robeson channels, right to the Arctic Ocean. There he would establish the northernmost land base possible, on either the northern shore of Ellesmere Island or Greenland, and from this base he would "assault" the Pole.

As with the Inuit whom he had appropriated for his own ends, so with the American Route to the Pole. Peary came to look on all of northwestern Greenland and Ellesmere Island as his private domain. Any other explorer who ventured there was a trespasser, an interloper, a poacher. He claimed that "the knowledge an explorer has acquired of the particular route which he is . . . developing and by which he hopes, by repeated efforts, to reach the Pole, is as much a part of his capital as the gold and silver in the vault of a bank, and until he abandons that route, no one else, without his consent, has any more right to take and use it, than a stranger has to enter the vaults of the bank and take its treasure."

But his critics were busy again, and this time they included the secretary of the navy himself. On April 12, 1897, while he was still planning his expedition, Peary received orders to transfer to the West Coast for a new, rather inconsequential position with the navy. He realized what was afoot. On the west coast he would be far removed from the influence of his friends in New York and Washington. If he transferred west, he was finished.

Peary had deliberately cultivated friendships with people of influence. It had started a decade earlier with his election to the American Association for the Advancement of Science. His lectures before scientific institutions were designed solely to bring his name to the fore in scientific circles. The year after the American Geographical Society had awarded him its prestigious medal, the influential Royal Geographical Society gave him its Patron's Gold Medal. But while this ensured that he was known to the scientific establishment and those wealthy individuals who might financially support his endeavors, it was like salt in a wound for his critics in the navy department. They were determined that he would secure no more leave.

He countered the announcement of his transfer west with a most audacious proposal—a request for five years' leave. Even the intervention of his wealthy and influential patron Morris Jesup, simultaneously president of the American Geographical Society and the American Museum of Natural History, was unsuccessful, and the navy denied his request. But Peary was both lucky and determined. A chance encounter with a prominent New York Republican, Charles A. Moore, who had been active in the election of President McKinley, resulted in Moore going directly to the president and calling in a favor. The president granted Peary five years' leave.

"Never was a man more fortunate in his friends than I," wrote Peary a year later. It was true, but more than sheer luck was involved. The friends had been carefully cultivated over the years for the influence they could bring to bear in his favor. Peary would call on them again and again in the future.

Although the five-year leave was granted, there was insufficient time to prepare for an expedition of the scope he envisioned in the few short months remaining before summer. But there was still the matter of the remaining meteorite. Securing it would increase his prestige in America even more. So in 1897 Peary left again on the *Hope* for a summer voyage to Melville Bay. He reached Cape York on August 12. Ice conditions were favorable, and Peary decided to try for the meteorite immediately. He embarked Qisuk and Nuktaq and all the other able-bodied men at Cape York, and headed for Bushnan Island.

Nuktaq was the older of the two Inuit, a swarthy fellow with a straight black mustache and a small beard. He was in his forties. A stocky man, he measured one inch over five feet and was incredibly strong. He had had three daughters with his first wife, who had died. His present wife, Atangana, said to be a powerful shaman, was perhaps five years older. She was four feet ten inches tall and rather plump. Peary held a special interest in the couple, for in 1894, when his wife, Josephine, had returned to America, she had taken with her Nuktaq's young daughter Eqariusaq. The girl had passed the winter with Mrs. Peary and the Peary's own baby girl and returned to her northern home the following summer.

Nuktaq was somewhat used to the strange ways of white men in the north. He had heard stories of their erratic behavior from his father, the famous Qulutana, who in 1854 had befriended a desperate party of eight white men, led by Dr. Isaac Hayes, who were deserting from the expedition under Elisha Kent Kane. Qulutana and his fellow hunters had generously supplied Hayes and his deserters with food, but the Americans came to distrust their benefactors and thought the Inuit were about to murder them. While the Inuit were asleep, the Americans stole their clothing, sleds, and dogs, leaving them naked in their tent. When the Inuit woke they quickly fashioned makeshift clothing from blankets, and boots from strips of cloth, and set out in pursuit of Hayes and his party. The Inuit overtook the Americans, who turned their guns threateningly on them. Hayes made the Inuit understand that if they would drive his group back to Kane's ship at Rensselaer Bay—for he had reconsidered his desertion—he would not harm them. Otherwise he would shoot them on the spot.

Qulutana realized that these white men were like children out of their element and must be humored. He agreed—what choice did he have?—but he first fashioned a snowhouse and took Hayes and his perplexed party in for a feast and a much-needed rest. After Qulutana had delivered the recalcitrant deserters to the ship, Kane and he became fast friends; Kane described him as "a man of fine instincts, and, I think, of heart."

Nuktaq had heard his father tell this story, and he grew up wary of the unpredictable white man. But Peary tried to recruit the best hunters of the tribe, and Nuktaq was certainly one of them. The items with which the explorer paid were the items a man with a family needed, and so Nuktaq worked and hunted for Peary. Moreover, he liked Peary, for they had many qualities in common; Nuktaq respected him for his independence and toughness.

In the winter of 1894, Nuktaq and his family had lived in a small house attached to Anniversary Lodge in Inglefield Bay. When Peary left the following summer, he told Nuktaq that he and his family could have the entire lodge as soon as his ship had disappeared from view. The impatient family entered the house almost immediately after the ship left and began to inspect every nook and cranny. Atangana, in her curiosity, dropped a torch, and the lodge burned to the ground before the ship was even out of sight.

The other man was Qisuk, a younger man in his late thirties with shoulder-length hair. A good three inches taller than Nuktaq, he, too, was strong and said to be one of the best hunters. He was known for his good nature, and Peary had nicknamed him the Smiler. Eivind Astrup, who participated in two of Peary's expeditions, described him this way: "His face was broad and round, and looked as if it had been cut in wood in a great hurry by a carpenter. When very happy he would laugh so that the corners of his mouth stretched upwards to the back of his head, at the same time closing both his eyes; when in danger of his life, however, never more than one was shut." He was, Astrup added, "a thoroughly splendid man. A bolder and more energetic companion for one's travels it would be difficult to find, or one with greater powers of physical endurance." He inherited his easygoing manner from his father, Arrutarsuaq, of whom Peary once wrote that "the old man is aging . . . though still sturdy. . . . He is just as affable and unassuming as ever."

Unassuming he may have been, but Qisuk's father was also a powerful shaman. Once, at the floe edge where he was hunting, a rope had broken and a bear he harpooned had escaped, causing his harpoon to sink into the water. Calling upon his helping spirits, Arrutarsuaq entered into a trance-like state and dove to the sea bottom to retrieve it. His hunting partner would long recall the sound of his chanting deep under water. Arrutarsuaq retrieved the harpoon.

Qisuk had been working off and on for Peary since 1891. When Peary first met him, he was living on the southern coast of Inglefield Bay with his wife, Mannik, and their year-old son, Minik. Mannik had worked for Peary, too, as a seamstress, preparing the skin clothing that Peary insisted members of his expeditions wear. In 1892 she gave birth to a daughter, a sister for Minik.

Mannik was Atangana's daughter. The older woman was therefore Minik's grandmother and Qisuk's mother-in-law. Nuktaq, who was Atangana's second husband and not Mannik's father, was Qisuk's stepfather-in-law.

But the family dynamic changed in late 1894 when they were living at another of the small camps in the bay. Peary noted in his journal, "Panippak . . . tells me that . . . he saw Majaq on his way from Natsilivik up the gulf to Quinisut, to exchange wives with Qisuk. This shows that the sound is frozen over as far out as Natsilivik, and that Majaq has a soul above monotony."

Wife exchange was common among the Polar Inuit. It often occurred for a night, but was more often for longer periods of time.

Rarely it became permanent. But this was one of those rare instances when it did. So Majaq took Mannik as his wife, and Qisuk took Majaq's young wife, Arnakittoq—she was only seventeen—as his. Minik remained with his father and teenage stepmother. Of course, both men and their extended families remained on cordial terms.

Arnakittoq soon became pregnant and gave birth to a daughter, a half sister for Minik. She was named Akitteq.

Then in the winter of 1895–96 tragedy struck the families and indeed the entire region. Mannik died in an epidemic that had come with the ship in the summer; it killed thirty-seven members of the tribe.

Minik was devastated by the epidemic, for not only did his mother die but his stepmother as well. Both his sisters died, too—the three-year-old daughter of Mannik and the newborn daughter of Arnakittoq. His great-grandmother, Atangana's mother, perished and so did his maternal aunt, Amaunnalik, her husband, Qujaukittoq, and their daughter, Minik's cousin Ilaittoq. The epidemic wiped out most of the significant women in Minik's young life.

Qisuk was wifeless again, but a hunter could not remain so for long, especially a hunter with a young son to raise. A partner was needed to prepare skin clothing and tend to the home. So in 1896 Qisuk took a new wife, fourteen-year-old Serminnguaq. She became Minik's third mother, but in fact she was only eight years older than he and was more like an older sister.

This was the situation in 1897 when Peary returned.

Peary arrived well equipped for the task of finally securing the meteorite. He brought along powerful hydraulic jacks, timbers of fourteen-inch by sixteen-inch white oak sixty feet long, and heavy steel railroad track as well as a rail timber car. Despite the *Hope*'s arrival at Bushnan Island in a blinding snowstorm, work began almost immediately. The crews used the oak beams to construct a bridge from the shore to the ship. They laid the steel rails on the timbers, and the timber car on them. Laboriously, the meteorite was set on top of the railcar, and the entire mass slid slowly across the tracks.

As the meteorite neared the edge of the vessel, the Inuit left the ship, superstitious perhaps, or simply fearing that the weight of the object might crush the ship. The meteorite continued its slow journey until finally it rested above the ship's hatch. The bridge was removed, and the hydraulic jacks lowered the meteorite into the hold. It had been a monumental task, for the tent weighed 37.5 tons (a far cry, though, from Peary's estimate of 90 to 100 tons). But by August 20, it was safely on board.

Peary was never one to miss a photo opportunity—as the meteorite started its inch-by-inch ride across the improvised bridge, his daughter who, with her mother, was along for the summer cruise, smashed a bottle of wine against it and christened it Ahnighito, her own middle name.

While the task of getting the meteorite aboard was underway, the scientists and others who had come north aboard the ship were busy. One had promised a jackknife to the first child who could deliver him an Arctic owl.

Peary wrote in a children's book he published some years later:

Little Minik . . . had heard of the promised knife, and started up the cliff to see if he could capture a real *uppissuaq* [snowy owl]. He had climbed some distance when he saw far above him a gerfalcon [gyrfalcon], which he knew was waiting for his prey. Minik had with him his little bow and arrows, which he could use with much skill. Climbing still nearer, and moving cautiously so as not to frighten the bird, he drew his bow and sent the arrow flying to the mark and killed the falcon, which tumbled almost at his feet. . . . He then found the owl's nest, and hiding himself, awaited the coming of the owl. After a long wait he saw her flying towards him with a bird in her claws, and it was not long before she reached the nest and received the arrow that was sent from Minik's bow. Minik came down the cliff with the two birds. He received a knife and a piece of board as his reward.

Qisuk was proud of his young son, a hunter already!

The *Hope*, with its load of iron, left the island and steamed six hours to Cape York. There, Peary wrote, "I sent my faithful Eskimos ashore, accompanied by several barrels of biscuit, and loaded with guns, knives, ammunition, and numerous other articles, which I had brought to reward them for their faithful service."

All the Inuit did not leave the ship at Cape York, though. Qisuk and Nuktaq and their families remained aboard. They were Peary's people, and like the meteorite in the hold, they were bound for America, a reward from Peary, they thought, for their services. Nuktaq would be accompanied by his wife and his daughter, Aviaq, a pleasant girl of about twelve with straight blue-black hair falling to her shoulders. Qisuk would leave his young wife behind but take Minik.

Many years later Minik recalled the beginning of his southern odyssey. In his brief account he telescoped several years of Peary's activities in the north:

> I can remember very well when the big ship came far up there where I lived with my father and my people. I was a little boy then, and I had never seen a ship before. I had never seen anything bigger than my father's kayak. The big ship brought to our little village more white men than we had ever seen.
>
> I lived in a little igloo with my father. My mother was dead, and I had no brothers or sisters. And so I loved my dear father very much, and he loved me. He promised me that just as soon as I was big enough he would make a little kayak for myself, and when the traders came again he would buy me a knife.
>
> He and the rest of the men saw the big ship when it was far out in the water, and they went out in kayaks to meet it. I stayed on shore and watched. Soon Lieut. Peary and the white men came ashore and tried to make us understand. We knew what white men do, so our men hid all the furs and ivory to keep them from being stolen. Soon we understood that they were going to stay there and build a house. We helped them, and the men got knives and pieces of board as pay. A piece of board is one of the most valuable things we can get.

> . . . Lieut. Peary (eventually) asked if some of us wouldn't like
> to go back with him where there were great buildings and rail-
> way trains and lights and many people, and where the sun shone
> every day in winter and where people didn't have to wear heavy
> furs to keep warm.
>
> He coaxed my father and the brave man, Nuktaq, who were
> the strongest and the wisest heads of our tribe, to go with him
> to America.
>
> They promised us nice warm homes in the sunshine land, and
> guns and knives and needles and many other things. So one day
> we all sailed away for New York.

This was a convincing invitation, coming from the man of whom
the Inuit would later tell the explorer Rasmussen, "He asked with so
strong a will to gain his wish, that it was impossible to say 'no.'" Of
course, the Inuit were eager to please this man who now, it was apparent, controlled the supply of trade goods in their region. And anyway,
hadn't Nuktaq's daughter, Eqariusaq, returned well fed and unharmed
from America a few years earlier? How could they refuse?

Minik continued:

> Our people were afraid to let them go, but Peary promised
> them that they should have Nuktaq and my father back within a
> year, and that with them would come a great stock of guns and
> ammunition, and wood and metal and presents for the women
> and children. So . . . my father believed that for so much good
> and comfort for his people they should let him and Nuktaq
> make the trip. Nuktaq could not part from Atangana, his wife,
> and his little girl, Aviaq, so he took them with him. My mother
> was dead, and my father would not go without me, so the five of
> us said a last farewell to home and went on Peary's ship.

From Cape York the *Hope* steamed north as far as Cape Sabine,
stopping at various Inuit camps along the way. Peary wanted to meet
certain Inuit whom he had come to know and give them instructions

for the winter for laying in supplies of meat that he could utilize when he returned the following year to begin his attempt on the Pole.

At one of these camps he met a young man, Uisaakassak, who petitioned him for permission to go to America as well. His reason was simple—it had been decided that twelve-year-old Aviaq should someday become his wife, and he did not want to part from her. A brief entry in Peary's journal for August 26, 1897, reports, "Uisaakassak wants to go to America & I take him."

4

An Inuit Orphan in New York

octors at Bellevue Hospital who had treated the Inuit for influenza and pneumonia had a suggestion: Move the six Greenlanders from their makeshift quarters at the museum to a private house, where they might be more comfortable and less exposed to germs from the public. Morris Jesup, the museum president, following up on the recommendation, once again turned to William Wallace, his buildings superintendent. Wallace had a home on Featherbed Lane in the Highbridge area of the Bronx, a pleasant place with a six-room cottage and barn on the property, and Jesup thought it might be ideal. The Inuit were moved to the cottage in the first week of December, and a housekeeper was hired to look after them.

She was Esther Enutsiak, age twenty-one, an Inuk from Labrador. She had been in America for five years, having come as part of a group of Inuit who were exhibited at the 1893 Chicago World's Fair. When her family returned to Labrador, Esther remained in New York. She was known to staff at the museum, and Wallace was fortunate to hire her as a maid. Esther moved into the Wallace cottage with the Polar Inuit so that she could help them day and night.

Esther could talk with the Inuit, though with considerable difficulty, for the dialect of Labrador differs markedly from that of the Polar Inuit. Nonetheless she brought to three the number of New Yorkers who were able to speak with the Inuit in their native tongue, though all used different dialects. Matthew Henson was the one they could understand the best, for he spoke their language with ease. The other was Franz Boas, who spoke a Baffin Island dialect and saw them occasionally.

Typically, the Inuit rose for breakfast about eight o'clock. Esther prepared boiled meat for all three meals, and the men had ravenous appetites. They had come to love coffee and tea. She also took them on excursions to see the sights of the city. She recalled for a reporter their astonishment at seeing their first train, with whistle sounding and bell clanging. The men had scurried up a hill and back to the safety of home. It probably reminded Esther of her and her family's reactions to similar sights five years earlier.

Reporters continued to take an interest in the Inuit. They took a particular shine to young Minik, one having described him as "the life of the party" and "as lively as a cricket." Among his favorite toys were a policemen's nightstick and brass buttons that an officer had given him at Bellevue. The boy strutted about the cottage imitating the policeman, twirling the nightstick and puffing out his chest. He and Wallace's son, Willie, were inseparable. Esther took a kindly interest in Minik. Perhaps he reminded her of her daughter, only two years younger, who had returned to Labrador a year earlier.

The Inuit passed some of their time making model kayaks and sleds. Esther's husband taught them how to play cards, which they enjoyed. It was, nonetheless, a boring life they led in the Wallace cottage. A reporter asked Boas, "What do the Eskimos do all day?"

"Oh, we try to give them little things to keep them busy," he answered. "Their work doesn't amount to much, but they have made some carvings, and occupied themselves either indoors or around the place with any employment that suggested itself to them. They do not seem discontented."

William Wallace's wife, Rhetta, had a different opinion. "They just sit there and look heartbroken," she explained in an article that appeared in the *The New York Sun*. "When they first moved up here they had to spend most of their time indoors; they were so delicate; but now they stay outdoors when the weather is fine, and seem to enjoy it." She worried about their future. "I fear the poor things are doomed," she said. "It was a great mistake to bring them to this country. They have suffered fearfully and are so homesick. They can do nothing but wait, wait, wait for Peary's ship, and the time seems very long to them."

In early February things took a turn for the worse. The Inuit were sick again and back in Bellevue Hospital.

On February 17 Boas received a letter from the hospital reporting that Qisuk was dying and the other Inuit should be removed from the institution and returned to the Wallace cottage. Then, suddenly, Qisuk died that very day. Minik was now an orphan far from home.

From Minik's own hand we have an account of his father's death in those last heartrending days in Bellevue:

He was dearer to me than anything else in the world—especially when we were brought to New York, strangers in a strange land.

You can imagine how closely that brought us together; how our disease and suffering and lack of understanding of all the strange things around us . . . made us sit tremblingly waiting our turn to go—more and more lonesome and alone, hopelessly far from home, we grew to depend on one another and to love each other as no father and son under ordinary conditions could possibly love. Every morning he would come and sit beside me until I wakened, almost crazy to know how I felt, and yet too tender to arouse me from my rest. How he would smile if I was a little better, and how he would sob, with tears in his eyes, when I was suffering.

Aside from hopeless loneliness do you know what it is to be sad—to feel a terrible longing to go home, and to know that you are absolutely without hope? Ah, you cannot know. And then add to this the horror of knowing that death was waiting nearby for us, and that one must go first and leave the other all alone—awfully alone; no one who even understands your language—no one except grief! Aside from these tortures my poor father was suffering frightfully from disease. His neck was swollen from tuberculosis, and his chest ached so badly that he could not rest. And yet, in spite of all this, his whole thought was constantly of me. He watched over me night and day, denying himself sleep and even food, and when anything was brought for me to eat he insisted on giving it to me himself—coaxing me and praising the food—and if I seemed to like it, big tears would come in his eyes, and he would laugh—half laugh and half cry—and pat me on the cheeks.

He wanted to do everything for me with his own hands and watched everyone who came near me. His greatest suffering was when he grew so weak that he was obliged to remain still in bed and could not come to me. And I cried all the time, and could no longer eat for fear my father would die. Then I grew better . . . because I was so anxious to be with him, and soon I was allowed to go to him and lie near him. He did not notice any of the doctors' torture after that.

One day a doctor accidentally or carelessly burnt my arm with an iron. My father saw the sore, and when I told him that it was a burn, he got out of bed, enraged, as weak and sick as he was, and I am sure he would have killed the doctor. I was terribly frightened, and for the first time I lied to my father; I told him that I had burned my arm on a gaslight. Then he took me in his arms and kissed me and said in Eskimo, "Minik must be careful for his father's sake." The next morning my father was dead. The strain had been too great for him, and he nearly suffocated during the night, and cried out for his home, his family, his friends and me. I put my head under a pillow, crying hard. They tried to take me from the room, and my father saw them and realized what it was. He called to me and I ran into his arms. He knew that he must leave me, and his grief was terrible. "Father's spirit will stay with Minik always," he said in Eskimo, choking hard. Father was dying then I know, but I think his poor heart broke, and that is what killed him.

I thought my heart was broken, too! That sad, long, lonesome day!

On March 16, less than a month after the Inuit had moved back to the cottage at Highbridge, tragedy struck the small group again.

Atangana, the wife of Nuktaq, died. She had been the first to become seriously ill in the early winter and had never fully recovered. She had enjoyed the cottage in Highbridge. She would ask Esther to prop her up by the open window so she could enjoy the fresh air. She kept her sense of humor to the end, often patting her thin face and telling Esther that her husband had lost interest in her since she had lost her fat. But fresh air was not enough, and she succumbed to her illness a month after Qisuk's passing.

One of the scientists who studied the hapless group of Inuit in New York was an American-born ethnologist of German descent, Alfred Kroeber. In 1897, when he first met the Inuit, he was only twenty-one years old, about the age of Uisaakassak, so perhaps he empathized with the unfortunate young man. Kroeber studied the Inuit, under the direction of Boas, during the winter and through the period of the deaths of Qisuk and Atangana. He published a pioneering study of the Smith Sound Eskimos, as he called them, an amazing feat considering he never traveled to the Arctic. He did it by observing this displaced group. Of all the scientists involved with the Inuit, Kroeber was in human terms the warmest. A liberal both politically and socially, throughout his life he maintained an enormous interest in, and sympathy with, common people.

Boas was Kroeber's mentor, and Kroeber's study contains a lengthy description of the behavior of the surviving Inuit on the deaths of members of the party, particularly the behavior of Nuktaq on the death of Atangana. Boas "secured" this account, for he was sensitive enough not to intrude on their privacy at such a time. The account was secured from "an attendant (speaking Eskimo)," probably Esther Enutsiak. The report movingly details how Nuktaq attempted to follow traditional Polar Inuit custom in mourning his wife.

Boas wrote:

> When informed that his wife was dying, Nuktaq picked her up and carried her out of the house into the barn. . . . When informed she was dead, he asked whether she was still breathing, or quite dead. When sure of the latter, he prepared to see

her. He put on fresh underclothes, dressed fully, putting on coat, hat, and gloves, and asked for a cord, which he tied below his hips, outside his trousers. He also stuffed his left nostril with paper, and taking hold of his coat on both sides, walked out to the corpse. He was followed by his adopted daughter and Uisaakassak, his prospective son-in-law.

The report continued:

When they entered the room in which the corpse was, Nuktaq began to talk to the body, speaking fast and in a very low voice. . . . After a while he approached her. . . . With one hand he lifted up the blanket covering her, and passed his other over her body from her forehead to her heart. Then he took her by the shoulder, and shook her hard, telling her to remain where she was. He also spat on her forehead three times, telling her to wash herself. . . . He ordered her to stay where she was until he took her away. He reproached her with [*sic*] being an angakkoq and not being able to cure herself, and added, "I am sure I shall die myself." He said to her that, if there were anything she desired, she should appear to him at night in his dreams, and he would satisfy her, but that she should not come near him at other times. He ordered her to stay where she was buried, and to trouble no one, nor to follow him when he was kayaking. . . .

Finally they left the room. The others went out first, and then he followed, going backward until he was outside the door.

For the next five days, Nuktaq did not leave the house. . . . He wore his hat and coat all the time, and did not move about. For two nights he sat up in bed after the others were asleep, talking. After these two days, when informed that his wife had been buried, he no longer wore his hat, except when he was moving about. . . . During these five days he would not leave his room. He had all his food brought in to him. He demanded his meat rare or raw. . . . He drank no tea or coffee but only water. . . .

After these five days, the mourning observances were less strict. Early on the next morning, before sunrise, he left the house with his daughter. . . . He wore the cord he had worn on the day of the death, and as he went out, he made a scratch on the porch with a short stick at the place from which he started. Then they walked about the house twice without stopping . . . going in a course opposite to that of the sun. . . .

The following day he again took a walk exactly like the preceding. . . . A few days later he walked a little farther—as far as the barn—and on returning made three scratches on the ground. . . .

On the tenth day after the death, he was very anxious to see the grave. He said that on the tenth day after the burial the grave was always visited, and again ten days later. He said that this was necessary and was much troubled at not being able to go. . . .

Throughout this period the observances were similar to those of the first five days, though less rigorous. Both the men moved about little, and put on their hats whenever they did. Nuktaq went outdoors but rarely, and when he did, wore his gloves. . . . He also refused to have his hair cut. None of the party went outdoors after dark. . . . They all had their own cups, knives, and plates, and were careful to keep them separate. . . . He would do no work, nor make anything, such as kayak or sleigh models. He said that he would not do this until several months had passed. . . .

Before her death, Atangana had requested that, when she was buried, the stones should not be put too close together, for fear that she might not breathe. She did not want to be buried under the sand, and wanted no coffin. She asked, moreover, that no clothes be put on her, except a shirt . . . and that her face remain uncovered. Nuktaq asked whether this had been done, and requested that she be buried as she would have been at home.

The dead woman was not mentioned, even an allusion to her . . . excited his disapproval. All her property was either removed or destroyed at Nuktaq's command. He ordered everything to be thrown away or burnt, and her cup and plate to be broken. By accident a part of her dress remained in the room in which she had been, and her husband never entered that room.

The scientists at the American Museum of Natural History were embarrassed. It was one thing to bring primitive people from a far-off land to study them for a year. It was another to have members of the group dying there, almost in front of the prying eyes of New York's newspapermen. Eleven days after the death of Atangana, the *New-York Tribune* announced in a headline that the Inuit were "Going Home to Greenland." The accompanying article featured an interview with Boas.

"When you found they were sick so much, didn't you think of sending them North again?" asked a reporter.

"Yes," replied Boas, "but there was no opportunity to send them. There were ships going north as far as Newfoundland and Labrador, but that would not have been anywhere near their home, and we could not land them in a strange country. When Lieutenant Peary starts on his trip this summer, he will take them back with him. They are all fond of him, and were delighted at the prospect of coming here last summer."

But where was Peary? From the time the Inuit had arrived in New York, he had never come to see them. Nor is there any record of him having inquired about their welfare. Upon hearing of the death of Qisuk, he sent a brief telegram of condolence to the museum: "Deeply regret Eskimo's death. Confident everything was done. Entire responsibility mine." He made no public statement.

This man, who loved the attention of the press so much, was a publicity hound only when that attention could be favorable to him. But this fiasco he had created could in no way show him in a good light. He would be called inhuman for having brought this group to a land where unaccustomed illnesses ravaged their vulnerable bodies, which had been so strong and healthy in the starkness of the north. Critics would say he should have known; he should have realized that the germs of civilization would wreak havoc on the unsuspecting Inuit. Hadn't there been an epidemic before—in the Cape York region in the winter of 1895–96, a sickness that spread rapidly among the tribesmen, racking their bodies with chills, fever, and a constant hacking cough before death mercifully claimed them? Weren't some of the victims the very people whose graves Peary had subsequently ransacked, and whose bones were in the museum? Wasn't it true that this sickness had probably been brought that summer by the members of the Peary relief expedition aboard the *Kite*? And didn't Peary know that some of the Inuit had begun to say, with a black kind of humor, that each year now they would become sick even at the first sight of a ship?

Peary knew all this and more. It was certainly unfortunate, but this attempt to secure the attention and congratulations of scientists and the public had backfired; it was just as well for him to step aside and let the American Museum of Natural History bear the brunt of criticism. Jesup, of course, must not be seen in a bad light, but Peary was confident that he would not. The man had become a multimillionaire by being smart, not foolish. Let Boas make the public statements and deflect the probing questions of the press. Peary would wash his hands of the entire business. Besides, he was busy. He was involved now in something far bigger than anything he had ever attempted before.

In the spring of 1897 the navy had grudgingly granted him a five-year leave of absence, arranged through President William McKinley himself, to launch a major expedition to the North Pole. He was busy now planning for it, and its success could not be jeopardized by six— then five, then four—Inuit.

Peary, it turns out, wasn't the only one who apparently wanted out. On March 31, 1898, Wallace wrote to Jesup to say he had suggested to Boas that the remaining four Inuit be taken to the countryside, where, Wallace said, he could provide better care. Wallace had a place in upstate New York and could arrange for their care there for a cost of twelve dollars per week. He added: "I would like very much to be relieved of the personal care of them, and respectfully ask that some arrangements be made whereby I might be relieved of them."

Jesup noted on the bottom of Wallace's letter, "This matter is left with Wallace and anything he should decide to do I shall approve."

Wallace had a dairy farm in Lawyersville, a hamlet near the village of Cobleskill in mountainous east-central New York, about 160 miles from the city, and it was to this farm that Nuktaq, Aviaq, and Uisaakassak were moved in April. Everyone hoped the clear mountain air would help them regain their health. Minik was over his illness and remained behind in the city, living temporarily at the home of Jesup.

While in Lawyersville, the Inuit lived in a long, low house across from the local church. The house was owned by Wallace, who recruited a local woman, a Mrs. Snyder, to care for the Inuit.

The people of Lawyersville were perplexed by what they saw in their midst. They were rural folk, and few had traveled far from home. Yet they were certainly used to strange goings-on at the Wallace place—the previous spring a boa constrictor escaped from a cage there, disappeared into the forest, and had never been found. And they had certainly heard of "Eskimos"—the local paper referred to them occasionally in reporting the travels of Peary and others. But why bring Inuit to Lawyersville? The two adults spoke no English and insisted on wearing their heavy fur garments as they trudged about the park between their house and the church in the growing warmth of an approaching summer. The townsfolk knew that two of their number had already died in New York City, and, hearing the coughing of these three, they would not be surprised if these Inuit went the same way.

The villagers did not have long to wait. Nuktaq died on May 14. Soon, *The Cobleskill Index* reported that his adopted daughter, Aviaq, was "very ill of consumption" but that "a lad named Uisaakassak is also at Lawyersville. He is healthy."

Within ten days Aviaq died. Uisaakassak moved into an old shed near the church. The paper reported: "He had refused to return to a house in which an adult had died, in keeping with an Eskimo custom."

On May 25 Wallace wrote again to Jesup, saying, "Only one of the Eskimos now remains in the country [Lawyersville] the other two having died. It is very difficult to keep him there contented." Wallace said that he would have Uisaakassak returned to New York City, to the care of Matthew Henson, who was looking after the ship *Windward* for Peary. For the next month Uisaakassak lived with Henson aboard the *Windward* at her dock in the Hudson River off Canal Street.

When Peary arrived and told Uisaakassak that he was finally about to head for home, Uisaakassak "jumped about the deck and danced with glee, every few minutes stopping, however, to mop the perspiration from his brow with a most disgusting look." He complained to the reporters who were present that "the sun was burning the back of his neck and making him ill, and he hoped he would soon be where there was no sun as cruel as the American [sun]."

Henson acted as interpreter for the crowd of well-wishers who boarded the vessel shortly before her departure. One of them pinned a miniature American flag on Uisaakassak's cap and an American shield pin on his coat. Uisaakassak, in sign language, thanked the donor and through Henson added that "he would always keep it to remember America by, although he did not like this country a bit. It was too warm, and there was a great lack of walrus meat."

The *Windward* departed for Greenland on July 2. Minik remained in America. The Wallaces had taken a liking to the little orphan, and Jesup, with whom the boy had lived for a short time, had decided that they should keep him.

In May 1898 Robert Peary was putting the finishing touches on two thick volumes describing his Arctic expeditions to date and outlining his plans for the future. He told in detail of the heist of the meteorites and the interest they held for the world of science. But there was not a word about the removal of six Inuit from their homeland.

Nuktaq and Qisuk were mentioned, to be sure, in the context of their faithful service to Peary as dog drivers and hunters in the north.

But the book was silent about their coming to America. Instead, at the end of a lengthy appendix on the "Smith Sound Eskimos," Peary waxed nostalgic for his beloved north and its people. "As I sit here writing now I can see them," he wrote, ". . . and many a familiar face rises in memory." Then, among those he listed he mentioned "Qisuk, or the Smiler, the walrus killer," and "Nuktaq, my faithful hunter and dog driver." He spoke of them as if they were still alive, living healthily in Greenland, patiently awaiting his return, although Qisuk had died three months earlier in Bellevue Hospital and Nuktaq had passed away that very month.

Conveniently ignoring the tragedy for which he was responsible, he concluded his wistful piece of deception: "Fortunately for them, with no possessions to excite cupidity, with a land in which no one but themselves could conquer a living, they are likely to be left in peace, to live out the part appointed them by the Creator, undisturbed by efforts to understand the white man's ideas of God, of right, of morality, and uncontaminated by his vices or diseases, till the 'Great Night' ends forever, and the 'Great Ice' dissolves in the convulsions of the last day."

In *Snowland Folk*, a children's book he wrote later, Peary falsified the record even more. He told of the summer voyage on which he had secured a meteorite; and in one brief passage, he wrote: "Among the tribe was a good-natured Eskimo, Qisuk, nicknamed the 'Smiler,' whose little boy afterwards came to the United States." Thus Peary acknowledged that Minik, who still lived, came to America, though he failed to mention that it was at Peary's behest, and he did not mention Qisuk's tragic trip at all.

1. Minik and Aviaq with the artist Albert Operti (seated beside Minik) and others on the *Hope*.

2. Minik and Uisaakassak
photographed together
on the *Hope* in 1897.

3. Qisuk   4. Aviaq

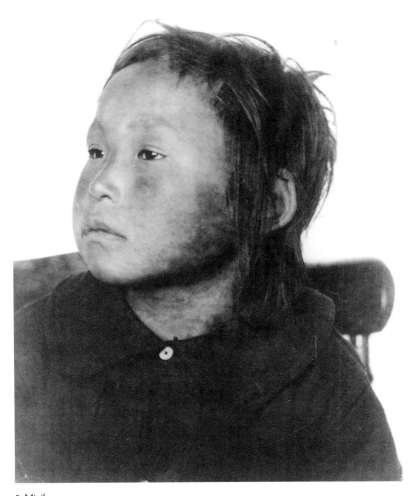

5. Minik

6. Nuktaq

7. Atangana, Nuktaq's wife

8. Uisaakassak

9. Qisuk in New York City in 1897.

10. A bust of Minik, from a cast made in 1897 at the American Museum of Natural History.

11. A bust of Qisuk, from a cast made in 1897.

12. A bust of Nuktaq, from a cast made in 1897.

13. A bust of Atangana, from a cast made in 1897.

18. Robert Peary

19. Robert Peary

20. Peary and a group of Polar Inuit aboard ship.

21. Peary with dogs on the deck of the ship.

22. Matthew Henson

23. Minik and Marie Peary

24. Peary's daughter, Marie, The Snow Baby.

25. Minik in 1899.

26. Minik and his foster brother, Willie Wallace, 1898.

27. The Reformed Church of Lawyersville, where Minik attended Sunday school in his early years in America.

28. The house in Lawyersville where Minik and the other Polar Eskimos were cared for in 1898. Nuktaq and Aviaq died in this house.

29. Minik and his foster mother, Rhetta Wallace, with an Alaskan Eskimo girl, "Zaksriner," and her foster mother, Miss Meagher, an artist at the American Museum of Natural History.

30. William Wallace

31. The house at Wallace's Cold Spring Farm.

32. Minik in Lawyersville, New York.

5

Minik, the American

In New York City, Minik lived with William and Rhetta Wallace in their comfortable home in the Highbridge area of the Bronx. It was a well-to-do neighborhood in a hilly section of the city along the Harlem River, an area lined with private homes, fine restaurants, and hotels. The Wallaces' son, William Jr., nicknamed Willie, was eleven years old and had become the Inuk's constant companion.

Rhetta Wallace took a special interest in Minik, for he was someone she could care for in place of the couple's daughter, Maretta, who had been born in the summer of 1895 but had lived only a year. Minik had been seriously ill in the spring of 1898 while the other Inuit had been dying in New York and Lawyersville. But after a long convalescence he made a full recovery. A healthy red glowed through the dark skin of his cheeks, and he had regained his strength.

William Wallace, employed at the American Museum of Natural History, was one of the most trusted employees of Morris Jesup, the president of the institution. Wallace had started work there in 1886 as a clerk, when he was thirty-one. He was ambitious and eager to please the demanding Jesup. He advanced quickly in the museum and within three years had become superintendent of buildings, the position he held in 1897, when he was one of the first museum officials to meet the Inuit. At the museum, Jesup turned over the care of the Inuit to Wallace, though he maintained a kindly interest in the party. Jesup had confidence in Wallace's ability to handle this situation in the same intelligent way that he had handled many other difficult tasks for Jesup.

When Nuktaq, Aviaq, and Uisaakassak were moved to Lawyersville in the spring of 1898, Minik had remained behind in New York.

After a short stay at the Jesup home, he moved in with the Wallaces. It was thought he would eventually be sent back home to Greenland when Peary left for the north again that summer. When he first went to the home of the Wallaces, Minik was broken in spirit and in health. He cried most of the time and "lived in mortal fear of having to return to the museum." The Wallaces quickly fell in love with the little orphan, embraced him as their own, and decided that they wanted to keep him. When Peary departed for Greenland on the *Windward* in July, Minik remained behind in New York. He had become one of the family and the Wallaces treated him as they did Willie. He grew particularly attached to Mrs. Wallace and told her one day, in his halting English, "Minik's father is gone, but Aunt Rhetta is here—Minik no cry more ever."

Jesup was instrumental in William Wallace's decision to take Minik into his family. In 1898 Jesup held a consultation with Wallace and his wife and told them that if they would take charge of the boy, he would compensate them for the expenses incurred. In a letter in August of that year, Jesup confirmed the agreement, while urging that Wallace "give Minik a name" and suggesting that he legally adopt the boy. There is no indication that Wallace ever did legally adopt Minik, but from that time on the boy was known as Minik Wallace. He took the middle name Peary.

In New York he was from time to time the subject of attention in the newspapers, often on the feature pages of Sunday supplements. This was a time when large numbers of immigrants were coming to the United States and becoming integrated into American life, and newspapers reflected a vision of America as a land of opportunity. Most of the articles were mildly racist in tone—one story was headlined "Taming a Little Savage"—and stressed how lucky Minik was to have been taken from the "dreary region" that was his "barren Arctic habitat" and how fortunate he was to be growing up in America. Another story began, "If there is one small boy in this city who . . . has reason to be thankful for a decided change in his circumstances which occurred about a year ago, that boy is Minik." Another chimed in, "Born in a land where life means nothing more than a mere physical existence, he has been brought by accident into an American home to enjoy all that that means." And one went so far as to claim that "he is an American now . . . and President McKinley is hereby notified that he can expand to Greenland if he wants to, on the strength of Minik's residence [in New York]."

One story, more sensitive than most, concluded, "We hope that this little ward of the United States, a guest from the far-away Northland, will grow up to a manhood that will combine the best qualities both of his land and of our own." Another, more chilling in its conclusion, called Minik "an experiment, and a promising one, in the effects of civilization upon one of the least known aboriginal races."

Minik quickly became aware of the unique interest he held for New Yorkers. Indeed, he had his first taste of their curiosity a few days after his arrival in 1897, when the curious had prostrated themselves on the sidewalk to peer through a grate into the basement windows of the American Museum of Natural History to catch a glimpse of the Inuit. He grew accustomed to seeing articles about himself in the papers and eventually came to regard interviews, as he said later, as "one of the ordinary duties of life."

As his command of English improved, he grew fond of telling the reporters tales of adventure in the north. One noted that he was "rather guarded and conservative in his statements," and he preferred to tell stories of his own choice, rather than directly answer questions from prying reporters. Perhaps many of his listeners thought the stories to be tall tales, but they were not unusual episodes in the life of an Inuit boy:

> Once my father had a very good dog. One day it fell into a big—
> very big—crack in the ice. Then my father say to me that I go
> down after the dog. My father tie a rope around my shoulders,
> and then they let me down into the big crack in the ice. I tie the
> rope around the dog, and the men pull us both up, so we have
> saved the dog.
>
> My father let me drive his dogs. . . . I drive ten dogs. One day
> I drive the dogs, and they see a fox, and they run away, very

fast—I could not hold them. Then the sled hit against a big piece
of ice—big as this room—and tip over, and I am thrown out.
The ice hold the sled, so the dogs could not run anymore, and
Nuktaq came and caught them.

We play hide-and-seek over the snow in the winter. We hide
behind the big pieces of ice. But we always have to watch, or
the bears might come and catch us. We have always four boys
together, so some can call if the bears come; one boy is never
alone. The bears are white, like the ice, and we do not see them,
and they come softly.

Life in New York was completely different from the life Minik had
known as a child in Greenland—with many a building in the city
housing more people than Minik's entire tribe—but Minik adapted to
it well. He made friends easily. He was kindhearted, affectionate, and
said to be "never better pleased than when he is able to do a favor for
some of his friends."

In the fall of 1898, at the start of the school year, Minik remained
at home. The Wallaces, overly protective, were concerned that
his health might fail again, and they wanted him fully recovered
before he was to begin his formal education. They enrolled him in
Sunday school, however, so his introduction to American education was gradual, albeit with a touch of religion. In January 1899,
when students returned to school after Christmas break, he finally
enrolled in the Mount Hope public school in the Bronx, where he
proved to be a good pupil. The Wallaces also engaged a tutor to help
him with English after regular school hours. Arithmetic, Minik said,
was his favorite subject. "I learned to read and write and to know
grammar and fractions and lots of other things," he reported years
later when summing up his school experience. At the graduation
exercises of his public school in June 1899, the principal noted that
Minik had been "a faithful pupil" who had "remarkable aptitude for
learning, and is fast catching up with the pupils who had several
years' start of him."

Minik hated to get out of bed in the morning. Once up, however, he was happiest outdoors. He loved sports, especially football—one report described him as "uncommonly sturdy"—and riding a bicycle Wallace had bought for him. With Willie as his inseparable companion, he also learned to skate and ride ponies. One of his favorite hobbies was catching snakes.

When a reporter asked if he had ever been cold playing hide-and-seek among the icebergs of northern Greenland, Minik replied that only his cheeks got cold, but that he often felt deeply chilled in New York, where winter's humidity is greater. Summer, obviously, was even more problematic. Mrs. Wallace was once quoted as saying, "He doesn't like to be too warm, and sometimes when he gets heated playing out of doors, he just stops and takes off some of his clothes and lays them down by some stone wall, and then he goes on playing. He has lately lost, in that way, some underclothes, his overcoat, and a sweater."

Minik often visited William Wallace at the American Museum of Natural History. Employees there greeted him with "handshakes, smiles and familiar pats on the back" as he would make his way to Wallace's office on the fifth floor. These visits were part work and part pleasure. The anthropological department, with Franz Boas in charge, was interested in the boy for social and scientific reasons. Minik had, after all, been brought south in the interest of science. The department's artist made a tinted clay portrait head of him, and Boas and a few others interested in the Inuit language made a point of talking with the boy to learn what they could of the speech of the Polar Inuit. But there was no one with whom to speak the Inuit language at home, and Minik, unfortunately, began to forget his native tongue.

He felt at home with the museum's Inuit exhibit, much of which was Polar Inuit material brought south by Peary. A reporter observed that Minik "can impart information concerning Esquimau folk and their life to Mr. Wallace and others. He can go to the Esquimau exhibit, identify every article that Lieut. Peary brought down with him and tell the name and history of the stuffed Eskimo dogs." He enjoyed looking through the pages of Peary's most recent book on his Greenland expeditions and identifying the people and places that illustrated it.

Minik was eager to please those about him, but he occasionally resented some of the attention he was given, especially when he was made a living exhibit in that hated basement of the museum. He would sit on a bench among Inuit exhibits and answer questions from Mrs. Wallace and recount stories of Greenland adventures, while children swarmed and squirmed about, often not paying much heed to him or his tales. Rhetta Wallace noted that, in contrast with the stories told in this artificial setting, "in the quiet of his own home Minik can tell some very interesting tales of the Arctic Circle."

Despite this regular involvement with things northern, Minik did not seem to be homesick for his Arctic—except on one occasion when he told a reporter, "I am going back north and be a chief like my father." He usually said that he did not want to return to the north. He was, of course, a mere child, but the novelty of life in America had not worn thin, and the Wallaces were a doting and supportive family.

In the summer of 1899, Herbert Bridgman, secretary of the Peary Arctic Club, an organization of Peary's enthusiastic boosters, told Wallace that he wanted to take Minik north with him on a summer supply voyage for Peary. "If Minik still retains his native tongue, he might be of considerable use as an interpreter," Bridgman said. Wallace replied that Minik had been ill again for some time and that his health was too delicate for such a trip. When Bridgman went north, he took a package of photographs of Minik to share with the Polar Inuit.

Although Minik was not yet ten, Wallace, Jesup, and others gave some thought to what work he should prepare himself for as an adult. Jesup had agreed to pay for Minik's care and education "with a view to preparing him for northern work." Knowing Jesup's interests, it is likely that he envisaged Minik someday returning to his people as a teacher and missionary. In fact, an article claimed that Minik was "being educated by Mr. and Mrs. Wallace, with a view of sending him as a missionary to his people." Another news story concluded that "with such foster parents as Mr. and Mrs. Wallace and with such kindly and generous men interested in him as Morris

K. Jessup, he is sure to be assisted in attaining any position which
he can reach."

As for Minik himself, he decided that he liked New York. "I want to
stay here," he said, "and when I get to be a man, I want to be a farmer
and grow things. All Esquimaux just love to grow things because in
our country nothing grows. We think it is fine to see a tree or a bush
or a flower."

The house in Highbridge was only one of Minik's homes in those early
years in the United States. The other was the Wallaces' summer place
in Lawyersville.

In 1885, a year before he joined the staff of the American Museum
of Natural History, William Wallace had married Rhetta Guffin, who
came from an old Lawyersville family. By 1892 he had purchased property in the area and established a large dairy farm and an icehouse for
refrigerating milk shipments. By 1896 it was an impressive operation;
in that year one shipment along to Binghamton, New York, amounted
to five thousand quarts, requiring a whole railroad car for transportation and six tons of ice for refrigeration.

Wallace's dairy operation was not confined to Lawyersville, for
he also owned a farm in East Windsor and another in Newburgh,
where he raised Brahma cattle. Business was good, so good that in
November 1897 *The Cobleskill Index* reported that "Mr. Wallace has
more orders for milk than he can supply." The following year he leased
another local farm to stock with cattle, and in 1900 he bought one
more local property.

Earlier, in 1893, Wallace, for the hefty sum of two thousand dollars,
had bought a historic house that had once been a popular inn, and he
converted it to his home. Within six years he also owned a boardinghouse in the village of Cobleskill.

All this was done while Wallace maintained his employment at
the museum in the city. He had built up an impressive business on
a part-time basis. He looked forward to the day when he could quit
the museum, live full-time in Lawyersville, and devote all his attention to his expanding business empire. He was confident that day was

not far off, for in April 1898—the same month that three of the Inuit were taken to Lawyersville—he and his wife transferred their church membership from Park Presbyterian Church in New York City to the Reformed Church of Lawyersville.

William Wallace was well known in the area. The local newspapers had generally referred to him as "Superintendent of the American Museum of Natural History," giving the impression that he was an administrator or a scientist, rather than superintendent of buildings. It was a misconception that Wallace did nothing to correct and may even have fostered, for he liked the prestige that the title accorded him. The papers regularly noted his comings and goings between Lawyersville and New York. Here was a man who had made good, an outsider to be sure, but one who had married a local girl and had done well for himself.

Wallace became known also as a local philanthropist, and the newspapers devoted even more attention to this aspect of his activities in and around Cobleskill. On one occasion he presented, on behalf of the American Museum of Natural History, four large double exhibition cases to the county historical society. In May 1899 he announced his intention to deed a site, part of one of his properties, to the local church for the building of a parsonage. On Children's Day in 1898 he presented to the Reformed Church a beautiful bookcase and over one hundred carefully selected volumes in honor of a boy, Dwight Guffin Karker, one of his wife's relatives, who had recently died. The newspaper, *The Cobleskill Index*, concluded its report of this generosity with the statement, "Mr. Wallace is the children's friend, and he is always making them happy with some generous gift."

In June 1899 Wallace announced the Wallace Prize Debate, to be held as part of the commencement ceremonies at the local school. He offered a fifty-dollar prize. The general subject, announced in advance, was "The Extension of Our National Domain." But the debate was to be extemporaneous, so the specific subject to be argued was not revealed until the big night. To promote the event and explain the ground rules, it was announced: "Mr. Wallace believes that it does a young man more good to stand squarely upon his feet and express his own thoughts even imperfectly, than it does to copy the thoughts of others and weave them into a polished oration."

Perhaps Wallace had done some soul searching as a result of the disastrous consequences of Robert Peary bringing six Inuit to the United States to enhance his own reputation as a benefactor of science and as a polar explorer, for the specific subject that Wallace announced that night was: "Resolved. That it is contrary to the true policy of the United States to acquire far distant territory."

Rhetta Wallace and the children passed their summers on the Wallace's Cold Spring Farm, and these were exceptionally peaceful times for Minik and Willie. Mrs. Wallace knew everyone in the area and was related to many of them, so Minik and Willie were never short of places to go and people to visit. Minik became known in Lawyersville and on the streets of Cobleskill, where he made friends as easily as he had in New York City.

The mountain air was good for Minik. He felt more at home in this high country between the Adirondacks and the Catskills than he had in the city. These mountains, though not snow-covered in summer as were the mountains of northern Greenland, were nonetheless not choked with people as were the man-made mountains of skyscrapers and apartment houses in the city. Here he was free, or at least as free as a doting foster mother would allow him to be.

There were still the lessons to attend to, of course. The Wallaces hired another English tutor for the boy, and during extended periods in Lawyersville, Minik was enrolled in the local school. Sometimes he skipped class. He loved to steal away and head down to the local streams, where he could swim and fish. He was known to catch fish with his bare hands and to eat them raw on the spot. In Lawyersville he and Willie were also able to indulge one of their favorite pastimes, catching snakes. The locals looked on Willie's passion for snakes with disfavor—the boa constrictor that had escaped from the Wallace farm in the spring of 1897 had never been found.

Minik also attended Sunday school at the Reformed Church and every night was expected to kneel beside his bed, bow his head, and say his prayers, including the traditional "Now I lay me down to sleep."

One evening he tried to avoid performing this nightly devotion with the excuse that he was too tired. The Wallaces' maid insisted, however, and the prayer was said. The next night he showed some ingenuity, for "when he started for bed he was heard murmuring softly to himself all the way upstairs and even after he began undressing. Finally he ceased, looking much relieved, and, glancing up roguishly at the maid who was superintending the process of retiring, he remarked sententiously: "See Lizzie, pray said!"

Even in Lawyersville, the Wallaces could not resist the occasional temptation to show off their little Inuit charge. On Children's Day in early July 1898 he was present at Sunday school and sang a song in his native tongue, one usually sung upon the death of an Inuk. And at the annual Cobleskill fair that year, the fair's president introduced him to a crowd as "the Eskimo who lives on the Wallace place, in native costume."

For William Wallace, now in his early forties, life was going well. He had a good position at the American Museum of Natural History and an impressive home in New York City. In Lawyersville he had businesses and respect. A stable family and church connections rounded out the life of this man so much admired by Morris Jesup, his superior at the museum, and by the good Dutch farmers of Schoharie County. This was, indeed, the good life.

For Minik, too, life was like a dream. He shared the Wallace home as their son, unofficially adopted, and was treated just as was Willie, the Wallaces' own boy. He had many friends in New York and in the mountains. His command of the English language was progressing and he was able to make himself understood wherever he went. The scientists at the museum maintained a kindly interest in him, and if that interest was self-serving, he was not aware of it. Life, indeed, was idyllic.

6

The Wallace Affair

On November 20, 1900, *The New York Times* carried a short item in small print in its section on legal decisions, a report that revealed that three judgments totaling $2,745 had been filed in city court against William Wallace. The news item revealed that Wallace had been sued by a business called the Hurricane Isle Granite Company.

Someone at the museum noticed the item and left a copy of the newspaper, with the article marked, on the desk of a fellow staffer, Professor Albert Bickmore. The professor clipped the section and took it immediately to Professor Henry Fairfield Osborn, another museum official, who then handed it to Morris Jesup. The museum president was concerned and asked Bickmore to meet with Wallace to determine the accuracy of the *Times* report.

A few days later Wallace, at Bickmore's house, was shown the newspaper and asked if the report were true. The meeting was a cordial one between two colleagues who had worked together at the museum for over a dozen years. Wallace acknowledged that he had incurred this indebtedness with Hurricane Isle Granite for work on his farm in Lawyersville.

The dairy had not been successful of late, and Wallace was tight on cash. He added that he had recently paid off six hundred dollars of his debt to the company from his salary and would shortly pay off the balance with a loan on a life insurance policy. Soon, he assured Bickmore, he would be entirely free of financial woes. Bickmore asked if he owed money to any other parties, and Wallace replied that he did not.

Bickmore, however, was unconvinced; he felt, as he put it later, "somewhat anxious" about Wallace's financial affairs. Remembering that he had often seen Wallace and a contractor named Cockerell in conversation at the museum, Bickmore arranged a meeting with Cockerell to learn what he might know about the *Times* report. When Bickmore read to Cockerell the account of judgments against Wallace, Cockerell replied that he feared that Wallace's debts would amount to as much as twenty-five thousand dollars. Bickmore was astonished. He asked if Wallace owed Cockerell money, but Cockerell was evasive.

A few days later, though, Cockerell called on Bickmore to convey more information. He mentioned other problems and financial irregularities of Wallace's, including a failure to pay thousands of dollars owed to one of the museum's carpentry contractors, and an eight-thousand-dollar debt to a private estate. He added that "there was usually a long delay" in the transmission of bills from Wallace's office for work done at the museum to the office of the city's controller, who paid the bills for the museum, a public-private partnership.

Cockerell added that he personally paid Wallace a kickback of one thousand dollars to get him to pass along bills totaling thirty thousand dollars that he was owed.

If Bickmore had been concerned earlier in the week, he was now speechless. He composed a lengthy statement detailing what he had learned about "our friend Mr. Wallace" and sent it to Jesup. It was one thing for Wallace to mishandle his own money, but quite another to mismanage the museum's.

Jesup, meanwhile, had begun his own investigation. A week after the *Times* report, a Mr. J. C. Cady of the architectural firm Cady, Berg, and See, the museum's architects, had written Jesup a brief note saying that Wallace faced financial problems while "engaged extensively in the milk business" in upstate New York, because of the "dishonesty" of one of his business associates.

That was enough for Jesup. He asked Wallace for a complete report of his activities and his handling of museum accounts. When the report was presented, Jesup was unsatisfied and angry. "I have just seen your report," he told Wallace. "Your statement is not satisfactory and does not cover the requests made in my letter." He said he was "deeply grieved" by Wallace's conduct.

On January 11, 1901, William Wallace, under suspicion and pressure, resigned from his position at the American Museum of Natural History, and his resignation was accepted without question.

Wallace's troubles were far from over, however. When George Chesley, a carpenter who had been owed money, heard of Wallace's departure from the museum, he became concerned. He had been engaged by the museum for several years, principally to build display cases. Since 1896, Chesley claimed, Wallace had borrowed amounts totaling $9,965 from him "on the pretext that it was to be used to carry on the business and work of the museum."

Wallace had paid back most of the money, Chesley said, but still owed him almost three thousand dollars.

The museum's lawyers were guarded in what they would reveal to the press about the Chesley claim, with one lawyer stating only, "I can say nothing as to whether Mr. Wallace did or did not borrow money from contractors, but I can say that neither he nor any other employee of the museum had any right to borrow money from any contractor."

The museum, meanwhile, broadened its probe into Wallace's management of museum funds. There were allegations that contractors overcharged for both work and materials, and that several projects received a green light from Wallace without the required approval of the museum's more senior officials.

Investigators traveled to Cobleskill to determine if museum funds and personnel had been employed there for Wallace's personal business ventures, including projects at the farms and the rooming house. Wallace claimed that no museum money had been used at these enterprises. But the investigation did not bear this out. The carpenter, Chesley, had worked at Cobleskill for four months during the summer of 1900. The museum had paid him for three months but found that he had been doing museum work for only one month; the rest of the time he had been working for Wallace personally. Another museum employee had drawn museum wages for a month at Cobleskill but "spent all of the time working on the private property of Mr. Wallace." One admitted to spending six or seven days there, at the museum's expense, bringing in Wallace's hay.

Why would the museum even have any of its employees at the farms in the first place? The answer was bizarre and an indication of the special trust Jesup had put in Wallace to perform far more than the normal duties of a buildings superintendent.

Behind the house on Wallace's Cold Spring Farm was a steep embankment fronting a spring. At Wallace's suggestion the museum had established there a facility referred to as the "macerating" or "bone-bleaching" plant. Animal specimens were brought there to be cleaned and scraped and prepared for museum exhibition. The natural flow of springwater allowed the operation to be performed cheaply and cleanly. The operation was an official undertaking of the museum, done with the full knowledge of its chief administrators.

It was in this bone-bleaching operation that the museum's employees were thought to have been working, while instead they spent much of their time working for Wallace personally. There also were reports of museum tools and equipment being misappropriated. A small engine, for example, had been taken from the museum for installation at the bone-bleaching plant, but was used instead at Wallace's creamery.

By the summer of 1900, Wallace was overextended and desperate. Residents of Lawyersville remembered that that summer he had brought a dead elephant to Cold Spring Farm to be cleaned so its skeleton could be mounted at the museum. But even that enterprise involved fraud. Wallace had claimed the animal was a baby elephant that he had purchased in Philadelphia for the museum. In fact, the elephant was neither from Philadelphia nor a baby. Museum officials learned from a former employee who had gone to Lawyersville to attend to the beast that the elephant was old, had been owned by a circus, and had died in Madison Square Garden. It also was clear that Wallace had overcharged the museum for the work.

The museum's cursory investigation indicated serious mismanagement of its financial affairs. Jesup went immediately to the president of the park board, the city controller, and the mayor to apprise them of the situation. He also informed the museum's executive committee; in a letter to it he described William Wallace, whom he had previously always praised as a dedicated and devoted employee, as "merely superintendent of the Museum building, his position being substantially that of a head janitor."

A more exhaustive investigation ensued. In midsummer, with that probe complete, Jesup wrote a long letter, marked PRIVATE, to professors Henry Osborn, his former assistant and current second vice president of the museum, and Hermon Bumpus, current assistant to the president, to alert them to a crisis in the affairs of "a great institution and cause."

The museum had thought that its financial controls were foolproof, but in the construction division—which, curiously, included the preparation of specimens—Wallace had found the loophole that he exploited so well. Construction expenditures went directly to the city's park board for approval, thereby avoiding scrutiny by the museum's own financial officers. The records came back for Jesup's cursory approval, but he blindly trusted his employees to have prepared accurate and honest invoices and, as he later admitted, automatically approved all claims for payment by the city's controller.

Wallace had been ordering goods and services at inflated values by using maintenance account order-book slips for payment by the city from the construction account. Favored contractors paid kickbacks to both Wallace and the museum's chief architect, who was in on the scheme. Jesup had been guilty of carelessness, and as a result the city's money, though not the museum's, had been misused.

Now Jesup had to admit that Wallace had been dishonest. It hurt him, a man who thought so much of his ability to accurately judge another's character, to have to write,

> Wallace, a trusted servant, for twenty years, turns out a dishonest man. I did trust him with entire confidence, and no doubt was cast on his character until about the time Professor [Osborn] came as Assistant; he was always faithful, attentive, loyal to duty, working early and late, he seemed to have the Museum's interest completely at heart, always at his post constantly, Winter and Summer, and almost the only one from whom at all times I could get information.

Jesup's first consideration, when faced with the evidence, was to ensure that the institution he had created remained blameless and faced no financial liability. A large number of contractors presented claims against the museum for work that had been ordered improperly and for which they had not been paid. Jesup and the city quietly paid off bills totaling nearly four hundred thousand dollars. The city's share was just over $322,000; Jesup personally paid $71,000.

Jesup was concerned, too, for his own personal reputation. The museum, after all, was an institution he had established. "The only mistake I have made," he wrote, "is in trusting and placing confidence in a man that I believed was honest, and trustworthy and loyal." He concluded his anguished letter to Osborn and Bumpus on a frank note: "I am not strong in body or mind just now: this trouble has un-nerved me."

7

Scam

The kickbacks that Wallace received were never fully identified, but they probably were substantial. It was possible that Wallace had been embezzling, skimming a little at a time for years, perhaps since 1892, when he purchased his first Lawyersville property. Then, desperate for money when he found himself overextended, he had let the whole affair get out of hand.

His behavior raises two questions: How could Wallace think he could get away with the scheme? And why did the American Museum of Natural History not press charges?

One answer to both questions is that the museum desperately wanted to avoid bad publicity. Jesup had always gone to great lengths to protect the institution he had created from any public scandal—that's why he had bailed the museum out by paying some contractors with his personal funds. Were civil or criminal charges to be pressed against Wallace, it's likely that a scandal of an even more odious nature would develop. For Wallace knew of unsavory activities, besides his own, that had occurred at the American Museum of Natural History, and Jesup and his advisers knew of them, too. They, and Robert Peary, were directly involved in them.

Robert Peary was engaged in a lucrative business dealing in Arctic furs and narwhal and walrus tusks, which he acquired in one-sided, self-serving trade arrangements with his Inuit. (Some years later a crew member of the supply ship *Erik* swore that "most of the time Peary and Matt Henson . . . were busy trading with Eskimos and making big profits on the fur and ivory and giving the Eskimos very little . . . coffee, biscuits and candy.") The Inuit did not complain, however. To them, the items Peary brought, including knives and guns, were a godsend, for there was no trading store in their area, and the whalers on whom they had come to depend for many items regarded as necessities were coming less frequently because the population of bowhead whales had decreased dramatically.

Peary benefited immensely from his lopsided trade arrangements with the Inuit. But to do so, he had to get his furs and ivory into the United States. He used two fronts to accomplish this: the American Museum of Natural History and the Peary Arctic Club. Morris K. Jesup was, conveniently, the president of both organizations. Peary also had a sales agent in America to sell some of his Arctic goods.

The explorer had worked hard to earn a reputation as a museum benefactor and a man of science. But he had worked just as hard to cover the circuitous route he had devised for getting material, perceived by the public as Greenland gifts, into the museum while at the same time being paid handsomely for it.

The trail of Peary's furs and ivory led from Greenland to New York, usually via St. John's, Newfoundland. Some shipments were consigned as specimens for the museum, so that, as scientific objects, they would not be subject to import duty. Once they had arrived safely at the museum—often with fanfare, for they were presented as generous donations—many of the materials would be released secretly to the Peary Arctic Club. The club then would give the items to Peary's patrons in return for donations to the Peary cause or release the furs and artifacts to Peary's sales agent.

Sometimes his deliveries went directly to the club. In 1898, at the beginning of his four-year expedition in northern Greenland, Peary sent a note from Cape York to the Peary Arctic Club on the returning supply vessel: "I send the president of the Club . . . two bundles of narwhal horns, seventeen in all."

Ten years later, he was still involved in this lucrative trade. In 1908 Peary confiscated a collection of two hundred fox furs, an unspecified amount of walrus ivory, and "two or three bundles of narwhal horn" from a cache at Neqi, Greenland—items owned by Dr. Frederick Cook, by then his rival in polar exploration.

Frederick Cook was an accomplished, and later, controversial, explorer. He graduated in medicine from New York University in 1890, at the age of twenty-five. The following year he joined Peary's first expedition to northwestern Greenland, as surgeon, and earned Peary's praise for his "unruffled patience and coolness in an emergency." He practiced medicine only sporadically after that, interrupting his practice often to lead or participate in other expeditions. Two of them were largely tourist voyages to Greenland in the summers of 1893 and 1894, and he served as doctor aboard a Peary relief expedition in the summer of 1901. He was made a Chevalier of the Order of Leopold for his lifesaving work on the Belgian Antarctic Expedition, a poorly supplied venture that spent two winters in the ice. In 1906 he claimed the first ascent of Alaska's Mount McKinley, an achievement later clouded by controversy.

Cook earned the everlasting enmity of his former friend and commander when he launched a secretive expedition in 1907 to reach the North Pole ahead of Robert Peary.

The material that Peary appropriated in 1908, which Cook later valued at approximately ten thousand dollars, was sent first to St. John's, then to New York on the *Erik*. The newspaper publishing a story about the shipment, *The Brooklyn Daily Eagle*, was unable to discover any official record of it reaching the club, only a statement from officers of the club that "a consignment of goods was sent down by Peary, and that it passed through the Custom House."

This was deliberately misleading. The club, in its statement, had falsified the routing of the shipment. The old ruse of using the American Museum of Natural History as an intermediary had been used again. In the fall of 1908, Herbert Bridgman, secretary of the Peary Arctic Club, received a note from a museum official regarding that shipment. It read: "We shall be very glad to receive the material consigned to the Peary Arctic Club by Commander Peary. . . . It will be all right to have the entire consignment sent to the museum, and after examination, we will forward to Mr. Crane [of the Peary Arctic Club] such material as he may desire."

Just a year earlier Peary had written directly to the museum on still another deal: "Among the material sent up from the '*Roosevelt*' some time ago, were a number of walrus tusks of various sizes. . . . These tusks can be of no value as specimens for the museum, and they will be of distinct value as souvenirs . . . and I shall be indebted if you will kindly give instructions to have them gathered up and sent over here to the Grand Union Hotel."

Though impossible to verify, Cook would later allege that Peary and his friends had made over a million dollars in trading over the course of Peary's Arctic career.

Jesup, although he was president of both organizations, expressed some concern over the fact that material that he sometimes would have liked for the museum ended up at the Peary Arctic Club. In June 1907 he directed his museum secretary to write to club secretary Bridgman the following note: "He [Jesup] feels that in everything received by the Peary Arctic Club, the Museum of Natural History should have priority of choice."

Peary benefited from the sale of not only animal specimens, but human as well.

In 1896, the year before he brought Minik to America, Peary brought to New York the skulls and other skeletal remains of several Inuit—people he had known by name—who had died in an epidemic the previous winter. The remains presumably were to be used for research and display. The museum's records show that Peary did not donate these specimens to the museum; instead, the museum purchased them from him.

Financially, though, the biggest prize of Peary's Arctic career would be the Cape York meteorites. If the reward for bringing them to the museum was to be substantial, he thought it was worth taking time to lay the groundwork properly.

Peary had acquired two of the meteorites in 1895 and the third, the most difficult to obtain, two years later. He had decided when he discovered them that they would belong in the American Museum of Natural History. In 1898 he wrote, "From the dazzling May morning in

1894, when Aleqatsiaq showed me how his grandfathers had removed fragments of the iron and fashioned their rude knives, I felt that these unique meteorites deserved more than to be simply ranged in order among so many other inert masses of iron in some great collection." He had set the stage for their acquisition by taking the artist Albert Operti as his guest on his voyages of 1896 and 1897 to plan a worthy museum setting, one that would have all the Cape York meteorites displayed with scenes from the lives of the Inuit. He concluded a two-volume book he wrote on his first five northern expeditions with a sentence claiming that the Cape York meteorites were "peerless and unique among all the meteorites of the world."

Once collected and taken to New York the meteorites were displayed in the American Museum of Natural History. The public understandably believed they had been a gift from a man dedicated to the cause of Arctic science. And Peary did nothing to disabuse anyone of that notion. What the fawning public did not know was that Peary viewed the meteorites as simply a long-term loan to the museum. He intended someday to be paid for them.

In 1907 Peary was still negotiating with Morris Jesup over the sale of the meteorites, which already had reposed at the museum for a decade. Jesup's letter to Peary on the subject is instructive because it illustrates the manner in which the Peary trail to the museum was often covered: "I have offered the three meteorites now at The Museum to a friend, to be offered to another friend, the same for purchase at fifty thousand dollars, to be presented to the Museum." Failing that, he stated that "the Museum of Natural History shall be the resting place of these meteorites, and that [if] no outside person can be found to purchase them at the price you name; that your desire is that I have them at the price that may be agreed upon between us, for presentation to the Museum."

Jesup, indeed, was never easy to deal with when being solicited directly for money. But Peary had learned how to humor him, and over the years Jesup, while never being a soft touch, kept Peary's interests to the fore while ensuring that the explorer remained properly grateful.

"A friend of a friend" had been offered a chance, for fifty thousand dollars, to become a patron of the museum, and the money, were it forthcoming, would go straight into Robert Peary's pockets.

But the friend of the friend did not take up Jesup's offer. And to Peary's dismay, in January 1908, while still negotiating the meteorite deal, Jesup died. With Jesup gone, and Peary busy organizing what would be his final expedition to the north, it was Mrs. Peary who was left to take up the challenge of cashing in on the meteorites.

In a letter to the museum's new president, Henry F. Osborn, Josephine Peary was uncharacteristically blunt in describing her claim and her financial need: "I think it only fair to state that the meteorites are my property, and that the money obtained for them will not be expended in Arctic exploration. It is all I have with which to educate my children in the event of anything happening to my husband. Of this Mr. Jesup was cognizant, and he approved entirely my keeping the proceeds as a nest egg."

The Pearys had constantly stressed, both to Jesup and to their other patrons, that they were folk of modest means, living on the kindness of benefactors, while Peary devoted all his energies toward his altruistic polar goal. A year later, however, a few weeks after Peary had claimed the conquest of the North Pole, Mrs. Peary somehow managed to buy ten thousand dollars' of US Steel bonds, a tidy investment for a woman claiming to live on the largesse of friends. Later that year she completed the sale of the meteorites to the American Museum of Natural History for fifty thousand dollars.

William Wallace knew the details of the early years of these schemes involving the museum, Peary, and the Peary Arctic Club. He had been involved in them himself, in a peripheral way, though he had never benefited financially. As the trusted servant of Jesup, he had been responsible for ensuring that some of the routine matters of the scams worked. He had received the material consigned to the museum by Peary from the Arctic, and it was he who had rerouted some of it to the Peary Arctic Club. And he knew where much of it had gone from there. All around him at the museum, Wallace had seen a misuse of museum funds and influence.

He had watched as Peary continually coddled Jesup and established an unwarranted reputation as a generous benefactor of the museum. Envious, he had developed a love of the grand gesture and a desire to share the lifestyle of those with whom he associated in New York. The businesses in Lawyersville and Cobleskill would be his vehicles to the lifestyle he craved. His philanthropy to the local institutions in and around Lawyersville paled beside the largesse of Jesup, the man he pathetically, perhaps subconsciously, tried to emulate. Yet it was a start. He could justify, to himself at least, the appropriation of funds in New York for his own use. It wasn't museum money, in any case, that he was using; rather, it was kickbacks from dishonest contractors, and he had convinced himself that he had not betrayed the trust of Morris Jesup. It was his own scam, less exotic perhaps than that of Robert Peary, but he hoped nevertheless that it would allow him to eventually leave the museum and live the good life of which he dreamed in the clearer air of Cobleskill.

But unlike Peary, Wallace had been exposed. And when Wallace was caught, his boss, Jesup, was merciless. Four days after Wallace's resignation, Jesup had him back in his office for an interview. Jesup had heard reports that Wallace had threatened to make certain unspecified disclosures, and Jesup wanted to know Wallace's intent. Wallace denied he would tell all, but a month later the museum's lawyer, who had met with Wallace's counsel, remarked in a memorandum to Jesup that "at present Wallace seems to have the idea that we need him."

Wallace always maintained his innocence. And despite the weight of the evidence against Wallace, the same museum lawyer, reflecting on the whole affair nine years later, commented: "I shall have to say . . . that I am far from clear that Wallace was dishonest. The impression upon my mind was of a man of routine and narrow training and gifts finding himself in a place of large unrestrained power with the expenditure of large sums of money, and with the result, owing at least in material part to vanity, that his head was turned and that he enjoyed the idea of exercising this power without regular and precise communication with Mr. Jesup."

Wallace's threat that he might publicly disclose his knowledge of the transactions that had taken place and were still occurring among the museum, Peary, and the Peary Arctic Club was serious. He had something on Jesup. But Jesup had something on Wallace as well. The threat did not succeed in letting Wallace keep his job. It did, however, help keep him from jail.

8

"Destined to a Life of Tears"

The Inuit, first welcomed by the museum, soon became a source of contention.

Among the matters investigators considered while probing Wallace were the "bills paid by the museum in connection with the Greenland Eskimos." They totaled $1,022, a pittance in comparison with the museum's other expenses, but still something over which to wrangle. Of this amount, $418 had gone directly to Wallace for board of the Inuit and their nurse, and $202 had been spent on autopsies and undertakers' expenses. The balance, $402, had been spent on clothing, medicine, and the salary of a nurse. All expenses were incurred from February to May 1898.

Once the investigation into Wallace's affairs had commenced, the museum became reluctant to reimburse him for the care of the Inuit. A $190 bill for clothing resulted in the supplier suing Wallace personally. A dentist from Cobleskill sent in a claim for twenty-two dollars for treatment of the Inuit in April and May 1898, a bill Wallace paid with his own money.

Four of the Inuit had died, and one had returned to Greenland. If they had not been the responsibility of the museum, in whose interest Peary had brought them to America, then whose financial responsibility were they? More to the point, who would pick up the tab for Minik? Peary was back in the far north, and was unavailable and unwilling to help. He had hardened himself against any connection with the distasteful episode he had created. According to him, the Inuit were the museum's responsibility. But from the date Wallace left the museum, the institution acknowledged no further financial interest in the Inuit who had been there or in Minik, who remained.

Jesup, it seems, had broken a promise.

Jesup had encouraged William Wallace to take Minik into his family, and had urged him in an 1898 letter to "give Minik a name." In that letter he also agreed to pay Wallace whatever was needed for Minik's support.

But Jesup now wanted no part of Wallace. The suggestion was put forward that Minik be taken from the care of the Wallaces and sent to a New England private school, but the Wallaces balked at the idea. Rhetta Wallace had had no idea of her husband's financial wrong-doings, but she was sticking by him, and the family remained together. As far as she was concerned, Minik was an integral part of that family and she would not hear of him being taken away. Now, strapped for funds, Wallace appealed to Jesup for money to support the boy. Wallace requested compensation for his previous care of Minik and the continuation of the support that Jesup had promised. He received neither.

In April 1902, after receiving Wallace's letter asking support for Minik, Jesup wrote to his secretary, John Winser, saying, "You probably know something of the relations between Mr. Wallace and this boy, which commenced about February 1900, or possibly before that time." Having gotten the date wrong, perhaps intentionally, by more than a year, he asked his secretary to inform him of "anything in your mind or memoranda that relates to this boy and Mr. Wallace's custody of him, and how it came about."

Winser replied to Jesup with a terribly garbled chronology of the events surrounding the bringing of the six Inuit to America, the deaths of most of the party, the return of Uisaakassak to Greenland, and the assumption by the Wallaces of the care of Minik. He told Jesup that he had "never heard you speak in any way that would indicate that you would be responsible for his maintenance," although the record showed that at least on one occasion Jesup had sent Wallace fifty dollars for the boy. Winser went on to remind Jesup that there had been a great deal of scientific interest in Minik, and Wallace was insisting that "you had requested him to care for the boy as Mrs. Jesup wished to see the results of the experiment as to what civilization could do for such a child."

Jesup found in Winser's sycophantic reply what he wanted to hear. He juggled Winser's information around in his mind and convinced himself that neither he, personally, nor the museum bore any liability for Minik. His mean-spiritedness toward Wallace was justified as far as the museum's financial affairs were concerned, but ignoring Wallace's appeal for help for Minik was unconscionable. With Minik, Wallace was doing only what he had been asked to do—caring for him and expecting support from Jesup for that care. Jesup would not hear of it. Like Peary, Jesup washed his hands of the affair. Minik was on his own with the Wallaces.

Mercifully, for Minik and the Wallace family, word of Wallace's disgrace did not reach the small communities of upstate New York. The Wallaces continued to live in New York City, but with Wallace no longer busy at the museum, the family was able to spend longer periods in Lawyersville. Wallace was in deep financial trouble, but he managed to hold his shaky business interests together for a bit longer. *The Cobleskill Index* became uncharacteristically silent on his affairs, for there was no longer money for the flamboyant philanthropic gestures Wallace had enjoyed making. But if the paper was silent about the sudden lack of gifts to the local church, school, and historical society, it was silent, too, on the misfortune that Wallace had brought upon himself in New York City.

For Minik and Willie, the opportunity to spend more time in the mountains was a joy. They remained free during the summers to wander the hills and pastures of the Wallace farm. The farm was quieter now with no museum employees there and the macerating plant no longer operating, but that only added to their sense of freedom and well-being. Some things didn't change. Willie continued to bring snakes to the farm, and the reptiles continued to escape from their cages and startle the good people of Lawyersville. Minik continued to indulge a passion for soft drinks and was well known to everyone on the streets of Cobleskill.

Minik's health remained a cause for concern for the Wallaces. In the spring of 1903 he became severely ill and was taken to Fordham

Hospital in New York City, where it was feared he might have tuberculosis, a chilling thought given that four of his kinsmen had died from the ailment. Doctors discovered that he had enlarged glands of the neck, and he underwent minor surgery. He recovered and was soon playing baseball and football with his many friends.

Rhetta Wallace's health was an equally grave concern. She was never robust, and by early 1904 she was suffering from heart disease and other ailments. The children had not been apprised of the severity of her condition. One day Minik returned from school and ran into the house calling for "Aunt Rhetta," when he was greeted by William Wallace, who admonished, "Hush, Minik—Aunt Rhetta is very sick."

Instinctively, this boy who had seen so much misery and death in his short life knew that Rhetta Wallace hadn't long to live. The expression of sorrow that had clouded his face after his father's untimely death returned. When Mrs. Wallace was confined to bed, he refused to go to school and rarely left her bedside. William Wallace observed that this "poor little fellow . . . destined to a life of tears" treated Rhetta Wallace much as Qisuk had treated him during his own illness.

With the end near, Rhetta beckoned loved ones to her side and whispered last messages to each. She turned her head to Minik and, smiling feebly, said, "Aunt Rhetta's last kiss is for her little Minik." The next instant, she was dead.

Rhetta's obituary described her as "a woman of kind heart and cheerful personality." Besides her bereaved husband, said the Cobleskill paper, she "is survived by one son, William Jr., and an adopted son, Minik, the Esquimo, whom her sympathetic heart loved as her own."

Rhetta died on March 29, 1904, and was buried in the family plot that William Wallace had purchased in the Cobleskill Rural Cemetery.

It had been a trying three years for William Wallace. Without the museum's salary to depend on, he discovered that his business empire was an empire only in his imagination. It could support him no longer. The debts piled up and creditors demanded payment. In the space of little more than three years, he had lost his job, his business,

and his wife. With the job had gone also a reputation for honesty and
trust built up over a period of twenty years of apparent devotion to
duty. With the business had gone his stature in the local communities
surrounding Cobleskill, and many of his fondest hopes. And with his
wife had gone his reasons for remaining connected with Schoharie
County at all.

He tidied up the few loose ends of his affairs in the area shortly
after his wife's death. For Wallace, now almost fifty years of age and
virtually destitute, the hopes and accomplishments of twenty years
had been mercilessly swept away. All that remained were shame and
embarrassment and the responsibility of raising two young sons.
There was nothing now to keep him in the picturesque and peaceful
hamlet of Lawyersville, for he would only grow to hate the community; it had brought him so much anguish and pain. He was a city
man, and big-city ideas had brought about his downfall. It was time to
start anew. Minik, now in his early teens, and Willie, seventeen, would
roam the familiar hills no more.

With the loss of his other property, Wallace had lost also his prestigious house in New York City. Leaving Cobleskill, he did not return
immediately to New York. What was there to return to? He took
Willie and Minik, whose own health was still not robust, and went to
Connecticut for six months. In the fall Wallace and Minik returned
to New York and took up residence at a hotel, the Hunter Island Inn,
in Pelham Bay Park on Long Island Sound. There were just the two
of them, for Willie had gone to live—temporarily, it was hoped—with
relatives in upstate New York.

For Minik this was almost as good as Lawyersville. He was an
outdoors boy at heart, vigorous despite the frequent illnesses he
suffered, and the two years they spent on Hunter Island saw his health
improve remarkably. He played football and baseball, became a profi-
cient swimmer and diver—finishing second in a swimming competition for boys eighteen years of age and under—and won two prizes
in a skating competition. He became an excellent horseback rider as
well as a crack pistol and rifle shot. He retained his passion for fishing
and took up caddying at the local golf course of Pelham Park, where

he "made a reputation for grit." He liked golf himself and won the trophy in the caddies' golf tournament there. He was cheerful and good-natured as usual, but he had developed a strong streak of independence. When the manager of the golf course ordered the boys to get uniforms, Minik refused and warned the other caddies that he would "thrash the first one who yielded." One of the other caddies, older and bigger, took him up on this challenge and "promptly got a whipping."

Wallace could no longer afford to pay for Minik's education and had to abandon his plan to prepare the boy for northern work, perhaps as a missionary or a teacher. A newspaper reported that Minik, fourteen years old, had "given up his idea of becoming an explorer and has embarked in the real estate business," working with Wallace, who had found a job selling property for a firm in the Bronx. Eventually Wallace and the boy ended up living in a crowded flat in the city, an apartment that was "like a prison to the wild spirited Eskimo."

From time to time Wallace appealed to Professor Bumpus, director of the American Museum of Natural History, for assistance in Minik's care. On occasion he swallowed his much-wounded pride and contacted Jesup as well. In 1904, as Wallace's world was falling apart, the philanthropist had made another well-publicized personal gift of two hundred thousand dollars to the museum. Surely, thought Wallace, he would provide a little support for the Inuit boy. But Wallace's efforts were to no avail. Minik had become an unwitting victim in a clash of personalities. Jesup despised the man who had betrayed his trust, and Minik, who lived with Wallace, would in no way benefit from the largesse of Jesup or the institution he controlled.

Wallace, for all his faults, was devoted to Minik and desperate for the means to provide him the life he had promised. "We had planned much for him," he wrote, "but our dreams seemed doomed to failure. Our only object had been his welfare and his success."

If gentlemanly approaches to Jesup had been to no avail, perhaps a more dramatic approach was warranted.

9

"Give Me My Father's Body"

By 1907 New York had largely forgotten about Minik. He continued his quiet, if impoverished, life with William Wallace. But everything changed on a Sunday in early January, when the *New York World*, Joseph Pulitzer's paper, carried a sensational full-page article in its magazine section. Amid pictures of Minik and an artist's sketch of the pleading boy, his arms outstretched toward the museum, the headline blared, "Give Me My Father's Body." The subhead read, "The Pathetic Story of Minik, the Esquimau Boy, Who is Growing Up in New York and . . . Who Now Wants Most the Bones of His Father from the Museum of Natural History."

The article shocked the *World*'s readership. It read in part:

> Minik, the Esquimau boy, longed for but one Christmas gift, but that one he couldn't have. He asked back his father's bones that he might put them in a quiet grave somewhere, where they could rest in peace forever.
>
> And Minik wept just a little, stoic that he is, when he found that it couldn't be.
>
> . . . Minik lives here in New York, despairing of ever seeing his people again. He is the sole survivor of six Esquimaux whom Lieut. Robert E. Peary brought here. . . . Four died, including Qisuk, Minik's father, and one went back again to the frozen north, glad to escape from the death and disease of New York.
>
> The scientists who were delighted to study leisurely the Esquimaux here in New York have long since forgotten these simple folk from the bleak Arctic. True, four of them died here, all of

tuberculosis, but not until these wise men had learned every-thing they cared to know.

And then, were not the corpses turned over to the doctors for very interesting dissections which added much to our knowl-edge on ethnological subjects? But, best of all, the perfect skel-etons were turned over to the American Museum of Natural History, up in Manhattan Square, where savants who wish to study Esquimau anatomy may do so quite comfortable.

And that is where the bones of Minik's father, nicely articu-lated, are now.

There too, is his precious kayak—his boat of skins—his gun and his knife and his Esquimau clothes, a most interesting exhibit. . . . Minik thinks that according to the American laws of inheritance these things ought to be his. He has heard at school, too, of fair play and the square deal, and he has in his mind an idea that he ought to be allowed to bury his father as the Chris-tians do, in some quiet country churchyard.

But an upstairs room—at the museum—is his father's last resting place. His coffin is a showcase, his shroud a piece of plate glass. No quiet of the graveyard is there; the noise of shuffling feet and the tap, tap of the hammers as the workmen fix up other skeletons, is ever present. And when the sunlight fades they turn on the electric lights so that Minik's father may not have even the pall of darkness to hide his naked bones.

Lieut. Peary has long since ceased to concern himself with little Minik, the Esquimau boy, and others who have assisted the boy have not continued the contributions which at first aided him.

". . . I can never be happy till I can bury my father in a grave, [said Minik]. It makes me cry every time I think of his poor bones up there in the museum in a glass case, where everybody can look at them. Just because I am a poor Esquimau boy, why can't I bury my father in a grave the way he would want to be buried?

"Our poor people are brought up to love their parents and their ancestors. Even the poorest of them up in Greenland can bury their father and their mother in a grave covered with stones. But I can't. And when a man dies his gun and his knife and his kayak always go to his son. Why can't I have my father's things?"

In February 1898, when Minik's father, Qisuk, lay dying in Bellevue Hospital, an official from that institution wrote to Franz Boas at the museum, "I hardly believe Qisuk will survive the night. The body will, I suppose, belong to the Museum of Natural History or Mr. Peary, and they can, of course, do anything they wish with it." Minik was eight years of age. Had he been older and able to read, he might have seen reports in the newspaper two days later, after his father's death, under the heading "The Esquimau's Body" and the prophetic subhead "Trouble Over the Dead Eskimo." The American Museum of Natural History and Bellevue Hospital were fighting over Qisuk's remains.

But by that evening the situation had been resolved. The paper reported: "The disposition of the body was adjusted last night. It was agreed that students at Bellevue should make such use of it as possible in the dissecting-room, and that the skeleton should then be mounted and preserved in the Museum of Natural History."

But Minik could not read, nor could he even understand more than a few words of English. So he was easily deceived.

Had he not been at a funeral for his father after Qisuk's death in Bellevue? Had he not stood in the garden of the American Museum of Natural History on a cold February evening with a group of scientists and museum employees and the only man the Inuit could speak through, Matthew Henson, and seen his father buried there? How then could his father's skeleton be in a glass case in the museum? With his own eyes, wet and weary from the tears of his father's death, he had seen his father laid to his final rest there in that peaceful garden.

Even had Minik been older and able to read, it is unlikely he would have chanced to see the dry scientific report prepared in 1899 by the anthropologist Alfred Kroeber, one of those who had studied the Inuit while all six were yet alive. Kroeber acted under the direction of

Boas and with Esther Enutsiak as interpreter. He continued to work with the Inuit through the time of their illnesses, their residence at Bellevue, and the deaths of Qisuk and Atangana.

The report included a section written by Franz Boas on the Inuit manner of mourning their dead. It contained a startling admission implied in one word in brackets in the section dealing with the death of Qisuk. Boas reported that Nuktaq insisted, some time after Qisuk's death, that Minik "visit the [supposed] grave of his father, and instructed him how to act."

The "supposed" in brackets is Boas's. For, incredible as it may seem, the scientists at the American Museum of Natural History had staged a phony funeral for the benefit of Minik.

Strange reasons were given for this fake funeral. Were they contrived after the fact? Was the bogus service a genuine expression of kindness toward an unsuspecting Inuit boy, but a stratagem that eventually backfired? William Wallace was later to provide an explanation, but somehow it failed to ring true:

> It is an Eskimo custom for the nearest relatives of the dead to see that they are properly buried or pay the penalty with their own lives. So the four Eskimos told Minik they would kill him unless he went to the hospital, claimed the body of his father and saw it interred.
>
> Minik went to the hospital . . . but there the scientists had turned the body over to the museum.
>
> Then Minik went to the museum with a demand for the burial of the body.
>
> At first there seemed no way of appeasing the child son of the dead man. Finally this scheme was hit upon. A fake burial was authorized for the benefit of Minik.

This implausible reason for staging a fake burial stretches credulity. One can hardly imagine a grief-stricken Inuit boy of eight, speaking no English, petitioning a New York hospital or museum for the burial of his father's bones. Nor can one put much credibility in the belief that the other Inuit would have killed Minik had he not succeeded in having his father buried. True, Kroeber reported that infanticide was common among the Polar Inuit and that "when a woman dies who has a child that she is still carrying in her hood, it is buried with her," but Minik was hardly an infant. The report claimed, too, that "when Qisuk died, leaving a son, Minik . . . without a mother, Nuktaq offered to kill him," but there was no indication that this offer was placed in the context of arranging for Qisuk's burial. This explanation, if plausible at all, is probably the result of a misinterpretation. If so, it was a misunderstanding with tragic consequences.

From Peary, Kroeber had learned some of the characteristics of an authentic Polar Inuit funeral, and he quoted the explorer in his report:

> On the death of a man or woman, the body, fully dressed, is laid straight upon its back, on a skin or two, and some extra articles of clothing placed upon it. It is then covered with another skin, and the whole covered in with a low stone structure. A lamp with some blubber is placed close to the grave; and, if the deceased is a man, his sledge and kayak, with his weapons and implements, are placed close by, and his favorite dogs, harnessed and attached to the sledge, are strangled to accompany him.

From his own inquiries, Kroeber learned much the same and added:

> When a person is dying, he is removed from the house, when possible. . . . The mode of burial is as follows: A hood is put on the corpse. It is then carried on the back to the burial-place of the settlement, which is not far away, the corpses being laid down next to each other with their heads away from the sea. The body is then surrounded by stones, and covered with flat slabs.

The scientists at the American Museum of Natural History decided to duplicate this primitive funeral as best they could on the museum

grounds. Years later, William Wallace would recall the bizarre
ceremony:

> That night some of us gathered on the museum grounds by
> order of the scientific staff, and got an old log about the length
> of a human corpse. This was wrapped in cloth, a mask attached
> to one end of it, and all was in readiness.
>
> Dusk was the time chosen for the mock burial, as there was
> some fear of attracting too much attention from the street,
> which might invite an investigation that would prove disastrous.
> Then, too, the boy would be less apt to discover the ruse. The
> funeral party knew the act must be accomplished quickly and
> quietly, so about the time the lights began to flare up Minik was
> taken out on the grounds, where the imitation body was placed
> on the ground and a mound of stones piled on top of it after the
> Eskimo fashion.
>
> While Minik stood sobbing by, the museum men lingered
> around watching the proceedings. The thing worked well. The
> boy never suspected, and when the grave was complete he made
> his mark on the north side of it. You see that is the Eskimo way.
> They think that the mark prevents the spirit of the dead coming
> back to haunt them, and the mark is always made between the
> home of the living and the resting place of the dead. At that time
> Minik was living at my place in Highbridge.
>
> When he got back to the other Eskimos, he told them he had
> seen his father buried, and they were satisfied.

By the time Wallace recounted this tale, he was certainly no friend
of the American Museum of Natural History, and one might suspect
that he fabricated or embroidered the tale to discredit his enemies at
that institution. Such is not the case, however, for there is verifica-
tion of the bizarre event from another source, none other than Franz
Boas himself. In 1909 Boas, by then at the Anthropology Department
of Columbia University, confirmed to a reporter that the burial had
occurred much as Wallace had described. The purpose of the burial,

Boas claimed, was "to appease the boy, and keep him from discovering that his father's body had been chopped up and the bones placed in the collection of the institution."

Boas didn't only confirm the story of the fake burial, though; he defended it. He said that he saw "nothing particularly deserving severe criticism" in the act. "The other Eskimos who were still alive were not very well, and then there was Minik, and, of course, it was only reasonable to spare them any shock or uneasiness. The burial accomplished that purpose, I suppose."

The reporter questioned the right of the museum to claim the body of a man whose relatives were still alive, but Boas responded, "Oh, that was perfectly legitimate. There was no one to bury the body, and the museum had as good a right to it as any other institution authorized to claim bodies." But, protested the reporter, did not the body belong rightfully to Minik, son of the deceased? "Well," came Boas's reply, "Minik was just a little boy, and he did not ask for the body. If he had, he might have got it."

The same reporter questioned Dr. Huntington of the College of Physicians and Surgeons at Bellevue Hospital, who said that the brain of Qisuk was in preserving fluid at the college and that an autopsy had been performed at the school in accordance with an agreement with the museum.

What was William Wallace's involvement in this sordid affair? After the story broke, the museum staff attempted to deflect criticism of the institution itself and implicate Wallace as a main, if not *the* main, perpetrator of the whole event. Penciled on the top of a museum memorandum from 1907 is the notation, "Wallace made effort to get skeleton for museum and for burial."

But the museum was hampered in its efforts to lay blame on Wallace by the fact that the events had occurred a decade earlier, and Wallace—and another player in the story, Boas—had left the institution in the interim. They were no longer there as big obvious targets. Neither remained on friendly terms with the museum—there had been enmity and petty jealousies between Boas and the museum's new director prior to Boas's departure. As a result, when it came to questions about the mock burial, neither Wallace nor Boas shied away from giving damning interviews to the press, and the museum was in no position to muzzle them.

On paper, at least, Wallace was superintendent of the museum buildings, but memos under his signature suggest he was often asked to do tasks beyond the normal scope of that job. His superiors often expected him to serve as the museum's agent and negotiator on matters totally unrelated to the building. Thus, when a dispute arose between the American Museum of Natural History and Bellevue's College of Physicians and Surgeons over the disposition of Qisuk's body, Wallace, according to newspaper accounts, came forward to say Peary had left the Inuit in his care and that he, therefore, had a right to claim the body. Wallace, on behalf of the museum, told reporters the institution wished to have the body dissected and the skeleton mounted as part of a study.

This, of course, all occurred before Minik had become so dear to Wallace and his family. Later, with the benefit of hindsight, Wallace came to consider his earlier conduct reprehensible.

When Nuktaq died at Cobleskill, Wallace again was asked to perform duties beyond that of a buildings superintendent. He reported by memo to Jesup that "Dr. Boas requested me to have the body sent to New York. . . . I followed Dr. Boas [sic] request in regard to the matter of the final disposition of the body."

Wallace's name turns up often in the fiasco over the Inuit bodies. Looking back in 1909 on the grisly events at the bone house in Lawyersville, when the Inuit bodies were prepared for the museum, Wallace claimed a subordinate role. "We were only acting under instructions from the museum authorities," he said. "It had all been arranged that the bones should be prepared for exhibition and they had to be cleaned."

One anonymous reporter for *The New York Times* seems to have known, in 1898, the fate of Qisuk's body. He wrote, "Now they talk of removing his flesh and making an anthropological specimen out of his poor bones! Nobody seems to have asked the other Eskimos what they think of this plan, or with what emotions they contemplate the possibility that they, too, may be put to the same highly scientific usage." No other reporter at the time seems to have stumbled upon the plans to deflesh Qisuk's body, so it came as a surprise when the whole story was revealed over a decade later. The simple fact was that nobody—or not enough people—cared. The *Times* reporter summed it up poignantly when he wrote, "There seems to be nobody to weep for Qisuk the Eskimo."

Before he died, Nuktaq expressed concern at not being able to go see the grave of his wife, Atangana, on the tenth day after her death. It was fortunate for the museum that he had been too sick to leave the cottage at Highbridge when she died, for its scientists had not heeded any of the woman's last requests. Immediately after her death Atangana's body also was spirited away to the College of Physicians and Surgeons, where her brain was removed for study and an autopsy was performed.

But Nuktaq insisted on seeing her grave. And so, incredibly, even though it was weeks since her death, the museum planned another fake funeral. "We have to fix up a grave for Nuktaq tomorrow," Rhetta Wallace told a reporter in late April. "He refuses to go to the country until he can go through that ceremony over his wife's body, which is also at the museum; so we'll have to satisfy him as we did Minik."

The bodies of Atangana, Nuktaq, and Aviaq all followed Qisuk through the College of Physicians and Surgeons and then the Wallace bone house before arriving at the Osteological Department of the American Museum of Natural History. Aviaq, the child, was the last to die, so there was no reason for the museum to even consider a fake funeral for her to impress or appease immediate relatives or the press.

10

"In the Interest of Science"

D r. Aleš Hrdlička was one of the scientists who studied Minik and the five other Polar Inuit in New York. Hrdlička was born in Bohemia but immigrated to the United States as a young teacher. After earning a degree in medicine in New York City, he interned at the State Homeopathic Hospital for the Insane, where he compiled data on the body shapes of abnormal individuals. He became interested in American Indians and thereby was drawn gradually from medicine to the young science of anthropology.

Hrdlička's main interest in his new discipline became the collecting of skeletons and skeletal material, and he went about it with zeal, building up one of the world's largest skeletal collections for the Smithsonian Institution in Washington. Hrdlička—or "Hard Liquor," as he became known to friends—scoured the world seeking to add to the geographic and racial coverage of that collection. Franz Boas described the man as "evidently possessed of an incredible capacity for work, and of a wonderful energy."

He was one of the first to examine the Inuit after their arrival in New York, and he saw them often during their illnesses. Yet his interest in them cannot have been the same as that of Boas or Kroeber, folklorists and ethnologists, for to a physical anthropologist obsessed with the collecting of skeletons, one brief but final breath separates a human curiosity from a scientific specimen. In the spring of 1898 Hrdlička found an opportunity with the deaths of four of the Inuit in a space of two months to perform his studies. Of them, he wrote, "These six individuals the writer was able to examine during life and, in one instance, immediately after death; he further secured and described the brain of one of the men and made a preliminary report on the others. . . . Finally, he was able to examine the skeletal remains of the four who died, as well as several additional skulls and skeletons collected in . . . the Smith Sound region by Mr. Peary."

Perhaps the final indignity for Qisuk was the publication of Hrdlička's article "An Eskimo Brain" in 1901. The identity of specimens usually remains unknown, but this one was denied the dignity of anonymity, for the article began: "The brain in question is that of Qisuk . . ." The article contains two photographs, which Minik mercifully never saw; they were labeled "Qisuk's Cerebrum (Dorsal Aspect)" and "Qisuk's Cerebrum (Basal Aspect)."

In the late nineteenth century, anthropology, as a science, was still in its infancy. It had not completely shaken off its early preoccupation with phrenology, an aberrant pseudoscience holding that the conformation of the skull was indicative of mental faculties and character. Phrenologists had busied themselves acquiring skulls from a broad spectrum of humanity. Theirs was a time when heredity, rather than society, was thought to account for most human behavior, and so the skulls of murderers and other social misfits were compared with those of intellectuals in the hope that the differences that were assumed to exist would reveal information to account for the social behavior of the original wearers of those heads. National jingoism also permeated this pseudoscience, and so the skulls of people of different races and nationalities were compared and judgments pronounced on which race or which national group was the more advanced.

Physical anthropology at the time of Hrdlička's early work had advanced little past phrenology. He and his colleagues collected the skulls and skeletons of people from across the world. The specimens they secured were cataloged, studied, measured, described, and compared. Indeed, physical anthropologists of the day measured unceasingly in the vain hope that mere quantifying would lead to an understanding of the nature of humans.

It is easy, with the hindsight of more than a century, to look back on the work of these early anthropologists and disparage both their activities and their attitudes. Yet Hrdlička, like his colleagues, was not a "gaunt and dedicated decapitator," drooling with scalpel and calipers in hand at the prospect of another severed cranium on his dissecting table. If his passion for collecting skeletons bordered on obsession, it is because he was a man dedicated to his work, one who intended to leave his discipline a richer field than he had found it.

It is simple to characterize these men as unfeeling, dispassionate scientists who cared little for the human consequences of their work. But it is wrong. Although that was the stereotype of the early physical anthropologist, most of these men did care. It was their interest in human beings that had drawn them to the science of anthropology in the first place. They and their colleagues in cultural anthropology— men such as Boas and Kroeber—were proud of their liberalism and open-mindedness. They would have been hurt deeply had anyone suggested that they were, at heart, racists.

They were, nevertheless, products of their times, and the intellectual and cultural traditions from which they had emerged were permeated throughout with an insidious bigotry. The endemic prejudices of the late nineteenth century were racist and sexist. Anthropologists, along with the man on the street, generally believed men were superior to women, and whites to blacks. The Inuit had inspired intense scientific and popular interest because they had been able to eke out a livelihood, and at the same time develop a rich culture, in the world's most hostile environment. They were remarkable, but they were not white, and that fact alone marked them, too, as inferior.

An eminent historian of science, in a compassionate evaluation of the work of such men, has suggested that, from our vantage point, "it is a little unfair . . . to criticize a person for not sharing the enlightenment of a later epoch, but it is also profoundly saddening that such prejudices were so extremely pervasive."

The bones and brains that gather dust on the shelves of the back rooms of the world's great museums were acquired in the spirit and hope of human enlightenment and betterment. Undoubtedly a great deal of valuable knowledge has been derived from their study. The scientists did not murder to secure specimens; the original owners of these human parts were usually unaware that their naked bodies would be dissected by strangers in the name of science, and in most cases no harm was done.

In most cases. But with the six Inuit from Smith Sound, science went too far. It was one thing to collect human parts in the far-off corners of the world. It was quite another to bring living specimens, human exhibits, from those far-off corners to entertain the public and allow the scientists of America to do their work in comfort. Was this fieldwork when the field was brought to the scientist? Science had briefly become a sideshow in 1893 when people from all over the globe were exhibited at the World's Columbian Exposition in Chicago. Boas had been chief assistant in anthropology at that world's fair, at which Inuit from Labrador had been exhibited. Had he not learned anything from the deaths of many of that fair's "exhibits," including some of its Inuit, whose bodies then became part of the permanent collection of the Field Museum established there? Yet he had encouraged Peary to bring more of these naive and unsuspecting people to America, to New York City, in the interests of his science.

Had it been worth it? Boas's only published statement on the scientific results of the study of the six Polar Inuit is remarkably brief: "Many things heretofore unknown have been learned regarding their language, their traditions and their personal characteristics. Casts of their heads have been made for the museum."

Peary, as usual, had profited from bringing these people to the United States. But Boas, Kroeber, and Hrdlička had profited too, for their young careers each received a boost with the publication of their research on the Inuit. Four Inuit paid with their lives for this meager addition to scientific knowledge. Moreover, it had necessitated a bizarre and misguided cover-up: a phony funeral on the lawn of the American Museum of Natural History, to impress an eight-year-old boy. Men of science were both involved in and implicated in this macabre event.

The truly profound harm, however, would be done almost a decade later when the cover-up was revealed and young Minik experienced the trauma of learning the truth of his father's funeral.

Inuit from Greenland were not the only victims of the museum's zealous collecting. In 1899 the museum's staff was still busy acquiring Inuit bodies. An eleven-year-old Alaskan girl, one of twins brought to New York by Captain Miner Bruce, a fur trader, had died of consumption in Mount Vernon Hospital. The *New-York Tribune* reported that the body would be sent to Columbia University, where it would be preserved and turned over to the Museum of Natural History "as a specimen of the race," there being no relatives to claim it. A letter to the editor in the newspaper questioned the legitimacy of such an act:

> It would be interesting to know by what authority Columbia College assumes to take any such course.
>
> While it is true that our law permits a person to direct the manner in which his body shall be disposed of after death, there is no intimation that this poor Esquimau child ever gave any such direction.
>
> "Except in the cases in which a right to dissect is expressly conferred by law," says section 306 of the Penal Code, "every dead body of a human being, lying within this State, must be decently buried within a reasonable time after death." And the same statute imposes the requirement of burial in respect to the remains of a human body after dissection.
>
> There can be no authority to turn the body of this Esquimau girl into a mummy and place it on exhibition in the Museum of Natural History, unless it be derived from the girl herself during her lifetime.

Columbia University responded to this charge with a statement issued by Dr. Bern B. Gallaudet, a clinical lecturer and specialist in anatomy, who said: "We think the body of the girl will be an interesting study—an Esquimau, you know—and we would like to examine the internal organs to see how they compare with those of persons reared under other conditions and in other climates. Just what will be done with the body I don't know, but we . . . can do what we please with it."

Boas, then holding down the double role of lecturer in physical anthropology at Columbia and curator at the American Museum of Natural History, arranged the transfer of the body from Mount Vernon Hospital. He had reported succinctly to the museum in a memo a week earlier, "Little Eskimo girl died in Mt. Vernon. I have secured skeleton. $15." Now he commented, "Before Captain Bruce went away he told me, the children being sick at the time, that if either died, the college might have the body for scientific purposes." Boas concluded that "the body will probably be preserved after it has been examined," adding the phrase, a favorite of his friend Peary, "in the interest of science." To Dr. Gallaudet he sent a terse memo: "I am sorry to see that the papers are making so much fuss. Skeleton to be transferred to Mus."

Several years passed between the death and phony burial of Qisuk and Minik's discovery that the bones of his father were on display in the American Museum of Natural History. During those years, as Minik grew up as a loved member of the Wallace family, William Wallace kept the terrible secret of Qisuk's fate from the boy. He regretted his involvement in the whole disgusting affair and he dreaded to think what opinion his foster son would form of him should he chance to become aware of the truth. Then, finally, Minik did learn the truth. Wallace tells the story:

> The newspapers had found out that the bones of his father were in the museum, and though they never knew of the fake burial or the bone cleaning in Cobleskill, they printed stories about the skeletons. At school Minik was thrown in contact with other children, and naturally they talked to him about the Eskimos. Eventually he learned that he had not witnessed the burial of

his father's remains, but he kept it to himself for a long time. We noticed that there was a change coming over him, and then one day we learned its cause.

He was coming home from school with my son Willie one snowy afternoon, when he suddenly began to cry. "My father is not in his grave," he said; "his bones are in the museum."

We questioned him and found out how he had learned the truth. But after that he was never the same boy. He became morbid and restless. Often we would find him sitting crying, and sometimes he would not speak for days.

We did our best to cheer him up, but it was no use. His heart was broken. He had lost faith in the new people he had come among.

Minik's own version of his discovery of the fate of his father is more dramatic, but less truthful: "Unexpectedly one day I came face to face with it. I felt as though I must die then and there. I threw myself at the bottom of the glass case and prayed and wept. I went straight to the director and implored him to let me bury my father. He would not. I swore I never would rest until I had given my father burial."

11

"The Very Pitiful Case of Minik"

Four days after the publication of the *World*'s article in January 1907, William Wallace wrote to Morris Jesup about financial assistance for Minik. On two occasions the previous summer, he pointed out, he had met with Hermon Bumpus at the museum to discuss the original agreement between himself and Jesup, but he had gotten no satisfaction from the museum director, for Bumpus claimed that the "Esquimaux matter was fully settled." As far as Bumpus was concerned, no agreement had ever been made. The Inuit had been brought to New York as wards of the US government, Bumpus insisted, and as for Minik, Wallace had simply picked him up from the street as a vagrant—a startling admission from a museum official.

In his letter, Wallace argued that Jesup's letters to him from years past, and payments, although totaling a meager two hundred dollars, did not bear out this contention. Rather, he felt, Professor Bumpus was "simply carrying out your unkindly feelings, which I can not accept." Wallace told Jesup that his petty actions were unbefitting "a gentleman of your standing" and asked two concessions: the return to Minik of his father's personal belongings and of his body for burial, and financial assistance for Minik's education, for "it requires more means than I have to provide."

The letter contained also just the slightest hint of blackmail: "You too well know, Mr. Jesup, that any part of the collections that were received by the United States Government from the steam ship *Kite*, which I fitted out under your direction, was paid for indirectly to Mr. Peary."

The *World*'s article sent the staff of the American Museum of Natural History shuffling through ten-year-old files to ascertain the status of Minik. They had hardly begun the task when another article appeared, this time in the prestigious *Washington Post*.

A New Yorker by the name of Roswell Chester Beecroft had called at the White House on January 11 and had had an audience with President Roosevelt's secretary, William Loeb Jr., in the hope of enlisting the president's aid in providing a proper education for Minik. Loeb had heard his guest out and, according to the *Post* article, had promised to bring the matter to the president's attention. He had also asked Beecroft to prepare a complete statement on the subject. Beecroft was quick to oblige; he prepared a lengthy report.

That statement began, "I beg to call your attention to the very pitiful case of Minik . . ." Whereas the *World*'s article had discussed simply Minik's interest in getting his father's body from the museum, Beecroft's statement referred to that only in passing. The letter was, instead, a reasoned plea for financial support for Minik and for his education. He described Minik as "a National guest and a National prisoner" and claimed that "his condition is rapidly becoming a National disgrace." He characterized the boy as "the most abused and helpless individual within its [America's] jurisdiction."

Beecroft was equal to the task of trying to get a fair shake for Minik and letting the right people know of the boy's plight. A former child actor and a graduate of the American Academy of Dramatic Arts, Chester Beecroft was from a middle-class family—his father worked in publishing, and two brothers were lawyers. By 1907, at the age of twenty-five, he was a professional publicist associated with the Hotel Astor and a motion picture company, but he stressed that his "only interest in Minik is a humane one." He had met Minik three years earlier, before the death of Rhetta Wallace, and since then had maintained a kindly interest in him—one newspaper account referred to it as a "particular and peculiar interest." He had become concerned about the deterioration in the boy's condition since Rhetta's death.

William Wallace was, he knew, devoted to the boy—too devoted perhaps, for he had struggled alone to ensure that Minik was given proper schooling when others who had once been interested in Minik had defaulted on their obligations. By early 1907, though, Wallace had lost almost everything. He was poor, with a marginal job working as a foreman over a gang of laborers making improvements to the New York subway. He had had to give up the house in Highbridge, and Minik lived with him in a small city flat. The lad was "meagerly clad" and, despite Wallace's heartfelt efforts, "improperly cared for." His education had been abandoned.

Beecroft was concerned about the boy's physical surroundings. Minik was in his midteens, and his character was "still forming, and, indeed, is probably now in its most critical state." Pointing out that one aim of the scientists who had first expressed an interest in him was to learn the effects of civilization on an Inuk, Beecroft stated that "if he is allowed to grope about in the unwholesome atmosphere of the slums, with cigarette-smoking boys and gambling, swearing men as his daily examples, it can scarcely be hoped that he will ultimately turn out a polished gentleman."

Beecroft outlined the circumstances under which Minik and five of his countrymen had been brought to New York by Peary. The government of the United States bore no blame for Minik's desperate situation, Beecroft suggested, but he hoped it would still provide help, because, after all, Minik had been brought to America by "an officer of the United States." While it was true that Peary had washed his hands of the matter immediately after he turned the Inuit over to the museum, Beecroft reminded the president that the Inuit, whom he characterized as "gentle, kind and hospitable," had "received Peary warmly, welcomed his people, provided shelter, food and the dogs and guides that made possible the explorer's sledge dash toward the pole."

He continued, "It would be reasonable to expect that Mr. Peary, if only out of a sense of gratitude for their valuable service, would make it his duty to see that [Minik] . . . was properly provided for."

But he added, "Peary showed no indication of living up to that responsibility and, if he would not, the government should."

Beecroft alluded to the Wallace affair at the American Museum of Natural History. He claimed that the museum was neglecting Minik because of the bad relations it had with Wallace, and that Minik was suffering because of his continued association with the man. But

Minik had not defrauded the museum. And the financial scandal that had so embarrassed the museum's officers six years earlier was, in any case, not Beecroft's concern; his concern was for Minik's welfare.

He continued: "What private griefs these gentlemen may have had, or what quarrels or disagreements may have come up, between any of them and the man who adopted and cared for Minik, I do not know; but I am certain that they furnish no excuse for the shameful neglect of the boy. . . . Were these men not quite human?"

As a literate young man, Minik had told Beecroft that he admired President Roosevelt and his domestic program called the Square Deal. He had asked Beecroft if he did not think the president would give even an Inuk a "square deal" if he knew how unfairly that Inuk had been treated. Beecroft assured Minik that the president would see that he was treated fairly, and it was this suggestion of Minik's that inspired Beecroft to bring the matter to the White House.

Beecroft closed his long statement on an optimistic note, expressing confidence that "right shall at last be done."

Two days after the appearance of the article in *The Washington Post* and the composition of Beecroft's outline of the case, a curious event occurred. William Wallace wrote personally to Roosevelt's secretary, Loeb. His letter was brief and negated much of what Beecroft had passionately requested. Wallace claimed that he had never asked Beecroft to request the president's assistance, and, he said, "I would thank you, if you will kindly not bring the matter before President Roosevelt. Mr. Morris K. Jesup of this City is interested with me in this little lad from the far North, and we hope some day, he may be of great service among his people at Smith's Sound."

To Loeb's office this must have been a confusing turn of events. In any case, it was not something Loeb was going to blindly lay on Roosevelt's desk without first investigating. To an experienced political aide, this was more than the social or simple charitable matter it appeared on the surface; this was a political matter. And it could well become a political liability. Morris Jesup was a man of influence, and the institution he had built in New York was prestigious. The museum founder and president had impeccable political connections in that city, and he could influence votes. He was to be treated carefully.

Peary, too, was not to be treated lightly. He had just returned, on Christmas Eve 1906, from his latest Greenland expedition, which, though unsuccessful, was the first trip with the specific purpose of reaching the North Pole. Jesup had provided a considerable amount of funding for that voyage, on the condition that Peary raise the rest. To do this, Peary had solicited money from the wealthy through a dignified pamphlet that outlined the importance of conquering the Pole, a brochure with a statement from Roosevelt himself. "No better—and I may add, no more characteristically American—work could be done than Peary's efforts to go to the Pole," the president had written.

The ship Peary used on that voyage was one he had designed himself, a vessel custom-made for ice work. Launched in March 1905, she had been christened the *Roosevelt*, with the president's consent, a sign of Peary's care in ensuring that people in high places would continue to look kindly on his expensive polar obsession. Peary's attempt to reach the North Pole had failed, but he had achieved a new "farthest north" and was already making plans for his next voyage.

Yes, this was more than a social matter. Loeb knew he had better look beneath the surface of this affair before acting. He contacted the American Museum of Natural History for comment. The matter was handled by Benjamin Strong, the private secretary to Jesup, who dealt with all of the president's affairs, both within and outside the museum. The *Washington Post* article was unfortunate, Strong thought, but it had already been published, and there was little he could do about that now. But the letter from Wallace to Loeb was perplexing. The longer Strong studied it, the more he thought it out of character for Wallace to write such a letter. Perhaps, he thought, Wallace had not written it at all.

Sometime after the death of Rhetta Wallace in 1904, William Wallace had remarried. The previous summer the new Mrs. Wallace, the widow of a former museum employee, had written Bumpus, and that letter was on file. Strong compared it with Wallace's letter to Loeb, for both letters were handwritten. The handwriting was identical.

Moreover, Wallace's signature on the letter to Loeb did not match his signature on any other letters on file.

So Mrs. Wallace had written the letter to Secretary Loeb asking him not to bring the Minik matter before the president. But why? One can only guess. Perhaps she thought that her husband and Chester Beecroft were going just a little too far in championing Minik's cause. She may have thought that Wallace should wait a bit longer in the hope of possible results from his letter to Jesup, written only four days earlier. Perhaps she resented Beecroft's involvement altogether and the public attention that was being thrust upon the family as a result of the sudden revival of popular interest in Minik. Or perhaps she resented Minik himself, for it is clear she did not show the same affection for him as had Rhetta. Her reasons are unknown. But when Benjamin Strong discovered that she had written the letter purporting to have been written by Wallace, he advised both Bumpus and Loeb.

In Washington, apparently, the bogus letter went no farther than Loeb's desk, but Beecroft would later claim that he had met the president personally and that Roosevelt had called the museum's actions an outrage and the Minik affair a disgrace. But Beecroft also would claim that "afterward we learned that Capt. Peary . . . had influenced Mr. Roosevelt to pay no attention to Minik."

When Bumpus received from Strong a copy of the Wallace disclaimer and the information that it was not in Wallace's hand, he contacted Franz Boas on January 19 in an effort to learn for himself the circumstances under which the Inuit had been brought south. This cannot have been a pleasant task for Bumpus, for he and Boas had never gotten along well. When Boas had been curator of the museum's Department of Anthropology, he and Bumpus had often complained, through petty letters, about the interference of each in the other's work, and Jesup had been expected to act as referee. Jesup had usually sided with Bumpus. For that matter, relations between Boas and Jesup had often been strained. By midsummer 1906 Boas had left the museum and gone to Columbia University. He apparently gave Bumpus no information at all.

Bumpus met Peary in the Grand Union Hotel in the city to discuss the matter. Peary was at the time still basking in the limelight of the publicity surrounding his recent return; he could not be bothered with the Inuit matter, for he had not devoted more than a passing thought to it since 1898, when he had deposited Uisaakassak safely home on the shores of Smith Sound. Moreover, he was now engaged in a flurry of activity planning his next expedition to the north, which he hoped, vainly as it turned out, would get underway that very summer. He did offer the implausible information that he had brought the Inuit to New York at their own "urgent request" and that Minik had been urged to return in 1898 but "absolutely declined, presumably on Wallace's or Mrs. Wallace's instructions."

Bumpus was by now simply confused. He was at a decided disadvantage in handling any of this matter because he had not been at the museum when the Inuit were brought there and had only just joined the museum staff when Wallace was fired in 1901.

The museum director finally checked with the museum's lawyer, who advised him to "do nothing whatever about the case except to keep all papers on file."

In the midst of all this, Wallace wrote Jesup yet another letter, this one in his own hand. In it he told Jesup that his friends were "insisting that I lay the matter before the President [Roosevelt]," but first he felt he should receive some reply from Jesup to his earlier letters. Once again he called attention to Jesup's letter of August 1898, in which he had asked Wallace to "give Minik a name," and later correspondence between the two in 1902. Strong received this latest letter from Wallace at Jesup's business office. It is clear that Strong had been keeping much of the Minik matter from Jesup, and it is doubtful if the aging Jesup ever saw any of this 1907 correspondence on the subject.

Strong, though, did contact Bumpus immediately, suggesting that "the President [Jesup] should be informed of the exact state of the case and that it should be done orally and promptly." Bumpus suggested that Strong inform the museum's legal counsel of the recent letter, but also advised him that the lawyer had already disapproved of replying to any letters from Wallace.

Bumpus did not comment on the advisability of informing Jesup. Jesup at this time was in ill health. Perhaps for this reason his staff kept unpleasant matters such as this from him. But if Jesup was not informed about the exact state of affairs in early 1907, he nonetheless knew that there was one Inuk remaining in the United States who had been brought there at the request, official or otherwise, of his institution. Five years earlier he had corresponded with Wallace briefly on the subject over his own signature. Moreover, with the attention the Minik Wallace matter was given in the press in 1907, Jesup could not have remained totally ignorant of the situation.

And there the museum left the matter, save for one small malicious act a month later. The new Mrs. Wallace—Pamela was her first name—was the widow of Jenness Richardson, one of the leaders of the museum's first field expedition, in 1887, a trip to Montana financed by Jesup, to collect bison specimens for exhibit. Richardson's son also happened to be a museum employee; he followed in the career of his father as a taxidermist. But with the events of early 1907, the museum decided that it could scarcely afford to have any member of the Wallace family in its employ, so in a terse letter in mid-February, Bumpus informed Jenness Richardson Jr. that his employment would cease at the end of the month. "You are not adapted to the work of the museum," he wrote. The museum had been cleansed of the Wallace affair.

That same month Jesup, ever solicitous of the welfare of the explorer who had placed his name on the most northerly cape of the world, committed twenty thousand dollars to Peary's next expedition.

12

"A Hopeless Condition of Exile"

William Wallace probably never realized that Jesup was not receiving his letters directly. When he had been at the museum, he'd had direct access to Jesup, and it probably never crossed his mind that since he'd left, some of Jesup's employees, especially his private secretary, Benjamin Strong, had begun to act as a shield between the aging Jesup and the public. Wallace's letters and his other efforts at reaching Jesup in 1907 were to no avail. Even were he to receive Wallace's entreaties, Jesup would have been impervious to any solicitations for funds to provide for Minik's education or support.

Nonetheless Wallace continued his sporadic efforts. In an interview he remarked:

> I am unwilling to believe that Mr. Jesup has treated Minik and myself so without having what he believes to be some good reason. I feel quite certain that he has been misled by someone. . . . Mr. Jesup was kind to Minik at the Museum, and it was his own suggestion to finance his care and education with a view to preparing him for Northern work. This he has failed to do, and I am at a loss to understand his action, or rather his lack of action, unless, as I said, he has been misled and influenced by someone whose personal interests prevent him from allowing justice to be done.

That person, Wallace suggested, was Peary. He continued:

> As far as Peary is concerned, he soon found out the extent of the wrong he had done in bringing the poor Eskimos to this

country, and tried to get himself out of the matter as quickly as possible. During Minik's stay at the Museum and his later illness, Peary never visited him. Since that time he has simply ignored the boy, and once, when Peary was living in a New York hotel, I took Minik to see him and received in answer to our card that he "did not wish to see us."

Both Wallace and Beecroft had some definite ideas about what type of education Minik should receive to prepare him for an eventual return to the North. Neither suggested a conventional approach. Beecroft felt that special tutoring was necessary, while Wallace proposed that an informal group of physicians, scientists, and teachers should be appointed to "ascertain how far it was possible to carry his education so that no stone should be left unturned to fit the boy for the northern work he desired and seemed made for." Wallace said that if his continued guardianship of Minik was the only obstacle to having his education assisted, he would give up all claim to him. Beecroft took up the subject in his overture to President Roosevelt. The only tangible result of the efforts of both Beecroft and Wallace was a suggestion from the White House that Minik apply to the Carlisle School in Pennsylvania, a residential school for American Indians. Minik refused this offer; he wanted preparation for a return to the Arctic, and he thought, quite rightly, that he would not receive this in a school whose avowed purpose was the acculturation of native people.

Wallace was impoverished by this time, although he was employed—the construction gang over which he was foreman was working on the subway ventilation system at Union Square. Minik, as he grew older, came to blame himself for Wallace's circumstances. He could not have known the details of the Wallace affair at the museum that had culminated in Wallace being fired in 1901; Wallace certainly would not have volunteered any information on this episode in which his own dishonesty had been discovered.

In his own tortured mind, Minik blamed all that had happened since 1901 on himself: "I can't be a burden on Uncle Will any longer," he said in a story that appeared in a Hearst paper, the *San Francisco Examiner*. Its publication twenty-five hundred miles from New York shows just how significant and captivating editors considered the Minik saga to be.

The report continued:

> He has lost his position, lost his money—he is miserably poor, and slaves like a laborer, all for me. He is the only man who has ever been kind to me, and see how I have repaid him. I have made him destitute. For three years I have wanted to leave him and go to work to help him. I am willing to do anything. Each year he has said that the ones who are making us suffer would relent and do what is right and fair; but the condition remains just the same and will always be the same while I stand in his way.
>
> If I cannot work or make those who are responsible for my being here do something, I can at least go away off to the Canada woods and lose myself and give poor Uncle Will a chance. But before I go I want to make the Museum give me my father's body to bury, and his canoe and gun to keep. If they don't give them up, I will sue them just as soon as I come of age. But think of my father being down there to be stared at and laughed at all that time. I would try to punish Mr. Peary and Mr. Jesup and Prof. Bumpus, only I want them to see how well Uncle Will has brought me up, and how much more just a savage Eskimo is than they are. . . . Here I am, a prisoner in this country.
>
> Everything, my home, my father, all has been taken from me. I ask that they pay back Uncle Will what he has spent on me, return my father's body, and give me a preparation for northern work. I can support myself then.

On January 22, 1908, Morris K. Jesup died at the age of seventy-seven. With him died William Wallace's hope of any support for Minik. Over the years—it was only a few months less than a decade since Jesup had written Wallace in 1898 with a pledge of assistance—

Jesup had contributed a grand total of two hundred dollars for Minik's support. He left behind an estate valued at $12,814,894. To his wife, he left over nine million dollars. Another million went to the museum and one hundred thousand to the Presbyterian church he attended. Of the sixty-one benefactors, only three were blood relatives. The rest were institutions and individuals. Minik was not among them.

The efforts of Wallace and Beecroft were directed not only at securing money for Minik's education, but also at getting the release of Qisuk's bones from the museum so that they could be turned over to Minik for a proper burial. Wallace was not as involved in this as was Beecroft, for Wallace bore a continuing shame over his role in the phony funeral of Qisuk and the deception of the unsuspecting Minik so many years earlier. Although Wallace knew that the boy bore him no malice, he was averse to taking a strong public stance in the matter of Qisuk's remains. It was better to let Beecroft handle most of this, along with Minik himself, for Minik was now in his late teens, articulate, and able to state his own wishes and demands.

The man who had to shoulder the responsibility at the museum and respond to Wallace's and Beecroft's efforts was Bumpus, a zoologist and the museum's director since 1900. He had the misfortune to be saddled with a name that conjured up a Dickensian vision of a bumbler, which perhaps fit the stereotype of the absentminded professor. Unfortunately, reality largely confirmed any suspicion.

Hermon Bumpus was described by a biographer as a man of "exceptional charm of manner, with dynamic, tireless energy and exuberant vitality. He had . . . an exceedingly lively creative imagination, which he relied upon, rather than tradition, habit or counsel, to direct his course of action." Yet few of his colleagues at the museum shared that opinion. Indeed, in 1910 the president of the museum, Jesup's successor, Henry Fairfield Osborn, would force Bumpus's resignation as a result of his nasty dispute with a recently appointed professor over questions of authority, a dispute the museum dubbed the Bumpus Affair. In the investigation of that scandal, Osborn solicited testimony from many of the museum's staff as proof of Bumpus's incompetence. One colleague described the director as "temperamentally unfit to govern the Museum" and listed his qualities as "uncontrollable temper . . . quick to be overbearing and discourteous . . . inordinate vanity, bad faith . . . quarrelsomeness, jealousy . . ." He went on to list his personal characteristics as "very autocratic . . . very unsystematic . . . untruthful and unreliable . . . imperious in his treatment of certain curators and employees."

This was the man from whom Minik sought understanding and assistance, and from the outset Bumpus resented the demands on his time that investigating the Qisuk matter would take. He felt it was unfair that he should be expected to have or find the answers to questions about happenings at the museum before his tenure, but he tried time and again to cover his ignorance of these matters with evasive statements. He bore no bad feelings toward Minik personally but resented the interest in Minik that drew reporters to his door and caused his name to be bandied about in the newspapers.

After Minik discovered that his father had not been buried but was instead a museum exhibit, Wallace had gone to the museum to discuss the matter with Bumpus. This was in the summer of 1906, a good half year before the *World* broke the story of Minik's unhappy experiences in the United States. Beecroft and Minik had also visited the professor that summer at the professor's home in New Rochelle. Bumpus had insisted on having his lawyer present. He was an administrator who took personally any criticism of an institution with which he was associated, and so he took great pains to deny that he was in any way responsible for Minik's position—even though no one suggested that he was. He listened attentively to the story told by Minik and Beecroft and expressed some sympathy for the boy. He promised the immediate return of Qisuk's body, and of his canoe and gun. He promised, furthermore, to take up the matter of Minik's education with Jesup as soon as Jesup returned from his country home. But nothing came of either promise. Wallace called Minik's "pleading for a Christian burial for his father's bones . . . pathetic in the extreme." Minik's people had always been unstinting in their assistance to American explorers, and he felt that "out of gratitude the boy's plea for a Christian burial should be granted."

When the *World* broke the story of Minik's unhappy experiences in the United States in January 1907, Bumpus had been interviewed about the events. His brief comment covered the gamut of his ignorance:

> If all these things happened, they were before I came here as director. I have heard that Mr. Wallace has cared for the boy Minik, but to my own knowledge no formal request has been made for the bones of Minik's father. We have hundreds of skeletons here, and I do not even know that the one he wants is here now.
>
> Should Mr. Wallace or the boy make formal application for the skeleton to the trustees it will be presented to them at the regular meeting and acted upon as they see fit. Those Eskimos were wards of the United States, and whatever was done for them here was done of pure generosity. That is all I know of the matter.

In April 1909, when Minik's demands for the return of his father's body were once again very much in the news, the museum's secretary, a Mr. Sherwood, said that he did not know of any request having been made for the body of Minik's father, "the skeleton of which is still in the museum."

But five days later, Bumpus expressed himself as being "thoroughly mystified" by the entire story. If the skeleton of Minik's father were in the museum, he asked, would somebody kindly show it to him, and as for the man's belongings, Bumpus claimed to know nothing about them. "As for his father's body," he blustered, "I know nothing of it. He made no demands on me for it. . . . We have no bodies here. We have a great mass of Arctic curios in the museum, which Peary brought with him on one of his trips, and it is barely possible that the sled and gun of the boy's father are among the collection. If so I do not know of it."

Bumpus showed himself a master of semantics, if nothing else, by the fine distinction he insisted on making between the body and the bones. When asked if the skeleton was in the museum, his reply was always that no bodies were kept in the museum. Thus he denied the existence in the museum of Qisuk's body—from whose bones the flesh had been removed so many years before at the bone house in Lawyersville—while ignoring the question of whether the museum had the skeleton.

But the *New York Evening Mail* reporter who was pursuing this inquiry was as persistent in his efforts to discover the truth as Bumpus was in evading it. The reporter went to Bumpus's enemy, Franz Boas, then a lecturer in physical anthropology at Columbia University, who lost no opportunity to make Bumpus look the fool:

"Dr. Bumpus . . . has had some hesitancy about admitting the presence of the bones in the museum," the reporter began. "Are they there?"

Boas replied, "Of course they are."

Asked whether, in his opinion, Minik had had a fair deal from the museum, Boas refused to comment, suggesting that Dr. Bumpus should be asked to speak on that matter.

The reporter visited Bumpus once again and remarked that "he seemed inclined to talk about anything and everything except the skeleton of Minik's father." The interview, which he described as like a game of hide-and-seek, was printed:

"Are the bones of Minik's father in the museum?" Director Bumpus was asked.

"I don't know where they are," was the reply.

"Are they not on exhibition in a glass case?"

"No, they are not."

Then Dr. Bumpus was asked where the body of the Eskimo boy's father was.

"The body is not in the museum."

"Are the bones in the museum?" asked the reporter.

"Well, if they are, I don't know exactly where they are now," replied the director.

"Was not the skeleton of Minik's father brought here after his death in a New York hospital?"

"Minik's father did not die in this museum. He never came here while he was alive."

Dr. Bumpus finally admitted that he had a faint recollection of some of Minik's father's bones having been brought to the museum, but he declared he did not know whether they were still there.

"Who would know if those bones are in the institution?" Dr. Bumpus was asked.

"I suppose I would, if anybody."

"Well, don't you know?"

"No, sir, those bones were never on exhibition."

Dr. Bumpus was reminded that that was not the question.

"If you should order the curator that has charge of the skeletons to hunt up the bones of Minik's father and told him that if he didn't find them in fifteen minutes he would lose his job, do you think he would make good?"

"Well, yes, I think he could find them all right."

That Bumpus changed his story about the bones many times is shown from Minik's later comment: "I asked Dr. Bumpus for my father's bones when I grew older, and he told me first he didn't know where they were. Then he said I could not have them for they belonged to the museum. I tried many times, but it was no use."

By this time Minik was no longer living with Wallace. In his belief that he was responsible for the problems of the Wallace family, he had left the home, although he continued to feel an emotional bond with William Wallace. For a time he lived with Chester Beecroft at the Hotel Astor, and then he took a room of his own at Alliance House, a boardinghouse on Forty-Fourth Street. This was hardly a fit environment for an impressionable young man. There was no parental authority, save for the kindly and intermittent influence of Wallace and Beecroft. There is no evidence that Minik was ever in any trouble, but he certainly became streetwise.

Although he loved the outdoors and rough-and-tumble sports, he still frequently became ill, and in November 1908 was in Fordham Hospital with pneumonia; for a time he was not expected to live. Illnesses had often interfered with his schooling, but by now he had left school and was sporadically employed. At one point Wallace found him a job working as a laborer on the construction of the Sixth Avenue subway.

Chester Beecroft remained most concerned about Minik's environment. Beecroft was an avid outdoorsman and often took Minik on camping trips outside the city. On these trips Minik would typically wander off alone for hours. On his own walks Beecroft would sometimes encounter him, sitting in a secluded spot and staring blankly into the forest. On these melancholy excursions into the woods, Minik would contemplate running away. He fancied escaping to the wilds of Maine or Canada. Either would be an ideal place to try to put behind him the life that had become so sad in the city. He would no longer burden his friends, and perhaps, with time, he could forget his traumatic experiences.

When he was alone in the woods, his thoughts often returned to Greenland. He did not belong in New York and had come to believe that he would never adapt. Greenland was a distant childhood memory. He had scant recollections of his early years—it had been a decade—and when he thought about them, his thoughts were in English, for he had forgotten his native language. Nonetheless, he wanted to go home.

Early in 1908 Minik heard that Peary, who had been delayed a year in his departure for northern Greenland, would be leaving for the north that summer. Minik determined to go with him. It proved impossible for Minik and Wallace to obtain an audience with the explorer, however, for Peary seemed intent on ignoring the boy. But, Minik thought, perhaps Professor Bumpus could be of assistance. He visited him at the museum with a request that the professor approach Peary for permission for Minik to go north with him. Bumpus noted only, "I attempted to do this but failed."

On June 23 Wallace wrote to Peary: "Minik is very anxious to visit his people in the far north, and I beg to ask if you can allow him to accompany you on your trip. . . . Kindly let me know by Minik if you can grant his earnest request."

Three days later Peary replied. "I have your letter of June 23rd, and while I would like to please Minik in this matter, I regret that my ship will be too crowded for me to take him this summer. Some other summer, when I may be going north . . . I shall be very glad to give him an opportunity to see his people. Or, if he is very anxious to get some news from up there, I shall be glad to try and send him back a kayak or sledge or whatever he may most desire."

This was a crushing defeat for Minik. There was no way for him to return to Greenland except with the consent of Peary, for no other vessels would be going that far north.

Minik's response was, "If you expect to find the Pole this time, there will be no need of a future trip. . . . You found room enough to bring me . . . here . . . Why can't you take me back?"

A newspaper commented, "The plight of this poor Esquimau is . . . most pathetic. . . . He was brought here from Greenland in the interest of science. He has served his purpose, and American scientists have cast him adrift. A parallel case probably does not exist the world over. It would be difficult to imagine a more hopeless condition of exile."

By chance, a Danish newspaper specializing in items of American interest, the *Dansk-Amerikaneren*, picked up an item on Minik's plight from the *New York World* and published a story that attracted the notice of the Danish Ministry of Foreign Affairs. That ministry wrote to the Danish consulate in New York with a request for more information on Minik, whom it regarded as a Danish subject, since Denmark had jurisdiction over at least part of Greenland.

The consul tried several times to meet with Minik, but each time the appointment was postponed by Wallace "under one or another pretense." In early September, Minik went to Syracuse for a short vacation, and during his absence the consul met with Bumpus, Boas, Wallace, and several others who knew something of the young man's past.

33. Minik, dressed in Inuit costume in Lawyersville, New York, about 1900.

34. Minik, standing outside the Augustin Hotel, Cobleskill, New York, about 1904.

35. Professor Bickmore in his study at the museum.

36. Franz Boas, who asked Peary to bring a Polar Inuit to America.

37. Morris K. Jesup, president of the American Museum of Natural History.

38. Dr. Hermon Carey Bumpus, of the American Museum of Natural History.

39. Herbert L. Bridgman

40. Capt. Bradley S. Osbon,
of the Arctic Club of America.

41. The first newspaper article to describe Minik's attempt to have his father's body released from the American Museum of Natural History was published in *New York World*, magazine supplement, 6 January, 1907.

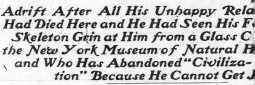

The Pathetic Appeal of Little Mene Wallace, Who Was Brought to New York "in the Interest of Science," Turned Adrift After All His Unhappy Rela...

WHY ARCTIC EXPLOR...

Had Died Here and He Had Seen His F... Skeleton Grin at Him from a Glass C... the New York Museum of Natural H... and Who Has Abandoned "Civilization" Because He Cannot Get J...

By Mene Wallace, Last Survivor of Peary's Wretched ...

What They Did to This Eskimo Boy "in the Interest of Science."

Little Mene in His Very Earliest Days, with the Bicycle Mr. Wallace Bought for Him.

Peary's Daughter in Eskimo Costume.

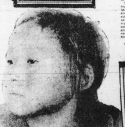

Mene as He Looked When Peary Found Him.

The Meteorite Peary Brought from the Arctic.

The Eskimo Boy Nine, Pleased with Clothing of Civilization.

42. The most sensational of all articles to appear on Minik in American newspapers was entitled "Why Arctic Explorer Peary's Neglected Eskimo Boy Wants to Shoot Him." It appeared in the *San Francisco Examiner*, magazine supplement, 9 May, 1909.

PEARY'S NEGLECTED ESKIMO BOY WANTS TO SHOOT HIM.

His Eskimo Garments of Fur, He Was Dressed When He [Taken] from Greenland.

SKELETON OF AN ESKIMO PRESENTED BY ROBERT E. PEARY

"What would Mr. Peary do if he was walking through the museum and suddenly came face to face with the skeleton of his father staring at him from a glass case?"

How the "Scientific Subject" Struggled Against His Destiny.

Mene's Father, Whose Bones Are Now in the Museum as an Interesting "Scientific Exhibit."

43. Vesta Tilley, the actress who befriended Minik.

VESTA TILLEY.

44. Vesta Tilley dressed in male attire for the stage.

45. Herbert Bridgman and Josephine Peary, in Sydney, Nova Scotia, 1909.

46. Frederick Cook, who claimed to have reached the North Pole before Robert Peary.

47. The mission station at North Star Bay under construction, 1909. The supply ship *Godthaab* is seen in the bay.

48. The completed mission station at North Star Bay, August 1909. On the left is the mission-aries' house, on the right a warehouse. In the background is the mountain, Uummannaq, later to be known as Mount Dundas and also as Thule Mountain.

49. Polar Inuit at Uummannaq, July, 1909.

50. An Inuit man, Ittukusuk, and his sister, Kassaaluk, outside a summer tent at the Inuit village at Uummannaq, July 1909.

51. Three Polar Inuit hunters. *Left*, Maasannguaq, aged about 45; *center*, Ittukusuk, aged about 24; *right*, Ulloriaq, aged about 35, at Uummannaq, July 1909.

52. Arnarulunnguag, Navarana, and Inugaarsuk, three Polar Inuit women. Arnarulunnguaq married Minik's first cousin, Iggiannguaq; Navarana was the wife of Peter Freuchen; Inugaarsuk was Minik's first cousin, a daughter of Amaunnalik.

53. Inuit children at the mission and trading station at Uummannaq, July 1909.

54. Soqqaq, the Polar Inuit
shaman, who took Minik into
his home at Uummannaq in
1909. Photographed before
1898.

55. Eri, son of the shaman,
Soqqaq in 1909. Eri is about
35 in this picture, taken in July
1909.

56. Qaaqqutsiaq, son of Eri and grandson of the shaman Soqqaq, at Uummannaq, July 1909. Qaaqqutsiaq was one of the Inuit who talked with the author during his research on Minik.

57. Two Polar Inuit women. Standing, Arnaruniaq, aged about 21; seated, Inalliaq, aged about 24.

58. Uisaakassak, who went to America in 1897, shown on a Peary expedition in Greenland.

59. Uutaaq, who led Peary to his farthest north, taught Minik Inuit travel and hunting methods.

The information the museum's staff, both past and present, provided the consul was brief and in part incorrect. The consul reported to Copenhagen that in 1897 Wallace, on Jesup's instruction, had

> made room for the Eskimos in the basement of the museum, where they remained for not longer than two days, after which they were moved to a large, bright room on the top floor. It must be pointed out immediately that the basement was not an ordinary basement, but a large room in the huge museum building, without any excess of humidity, and that the Eskimos did not remain there any longer than absolutely necessary, and were given the best of care. That winter there was an influenza epidemic in New York, and all the Eskimos became sick and were transferred to Bellevue Hospital, where they probably were infected with tuberculosis, if they had not already been infected on board ship. At any rate, after they had been released from the hospital and taken to a farm in the country, the sickness developed rapidly and all the members of the little colony died except the boy Minik.

Uisaakassak had apparently disappeared from the memories of the museum staff.

Both Boas and Bumpus admitted that Qisuk's body had been autopsied and his skeleton kept, but they denied that it had ever been exhibited. Nor would they accept any responsibility for Minik's trauma on learning the fate of his father's body, claiming to the consul that "the boy would never have known anything about it had Wallace not told him and impressed it upon his sick and half-civilized imagination."

Museum officials convinced the Danish investigator that William Wallace was merely generating publicity over Minik's circumstances as part of his "systematic campaign" to get back at the institution for his dismissal, although the consul felt no doubt that Wallace loved the boy deeply and had cared for him well as long as he could.

Upon Minik's return from Syracuse the consul was finally able to have a private interview with him. Minik talked of his desire to return to his home in Greenland, but the consul doubted that his wish was based on serious thought. "He has heard so much about his own homesickness," the consul wrote, "that he believes himself that he has such a burning longing." The Danish government had been considering intervening in the case and sending Minik back to Greenland, but Dr. Boas recommended against it, "at least for the time being," for no apparent reason.

The consul disagreed with the scientist, however, reasoning that "down here, he will hardly become any more than half-civilized," and recommended that if the Danish government did decide to send him back to Greenland, it should consider sending him first to southern Greenland where he could relearn the Inuit language (albeit a markedly different dialect from his own) before continuing north.

The consul promised to monitor the case carefully and report any further developments to Copenhagen.

13

The Polar Plan

In early January 1909 the Arctic Club of America met for its fifteenth annual dinner at the Hotel Marlborough in New York. The club, a loose affiliation of men interested in the Arctic and its exploration, had been founded by those who had gone north in the summer of 1894 on Dr. Frederick Cook's disastrous *Miranda* expedition, an accident-ridden tourist voyage to Greenland. At the outset, the vessel had collided with two or three small craft while leaving its pier in New York, was later holed by an iceberg off the Labrador coast and had to return to St. John's for repairs, and finally struck an underwater reef and sank off Sukkertoppen, Greenland. When they returned to America, the survivors of that adventure—there had been no loss of life—agreed to meet once a year to perpetuate the friendships they had made on their Arctic cruise. The club had gained more members in the fifteen years since its formation. They were all successful men, but were more down-to-earth than the super-rich of the secretive Peary Arctic Club.

Professor William Brewer, who was retiring as president—he had held the post since the club's formation—and Admiral Winfield Schley addressed the meeting. In 1884 Schley had achieved fame when he found and rescued the remnants of a party under Adolphus Greely, who had gone to northern Ellesmere Island on a scientific expedition, part of the American participation in the first International Polar Year. Only seven of Greely's twenty-five men were alive when Schley reached them. Now, a quarter of a century later in New York, Brewer and Schley spoke enthusiastically about the expedition they were planning to send out that summer in search of Dr. Frederick Cook, one they hoped would have happier results. The explorer Cook had gone north in 1907 as a rival to Peary on his own search for the North

Pole and had not been heard from since. The Arctic Club of America's proposed expedition would be headed by Dillon Wallace, himself an explorer and survivor of an expedition into interior Labrador in 1903, on which his partner, Leonidas Hubbard, had lost his life. His story of that expedition, *The Lure of the Labrador Wild*, became a best seller. A second Labrador trip, in 1905, resulted in another popular book, *The Long Labrador Trail*.

Minik was in attendance on that January night. He was often invited to the club's meetings, and sometimes he was asked to come dressed in his furs. These events were exhibitions of sorts, too, but more private and respectful than his earlier exhibitions at the American Museum of Natural History. Minik listened with rapt interest to the plans for the Cook relief expedition, for the club had already agreed that it would give him passage back to Greenland on that voyage.

It was no secret to club members that Minik had formulated some ideas of his own about the North Pole. He read voraciously everything he could lay his hands on about the Arctic, and particularly the expeditions that had gone to his part of the Arctic, northwestern Greenland, in search of the Pole. He concluded that neither Cook nor Peary nor any other white explorer would ever reach the top of the world because their methods were all wrong.

But Minik had gone a step further. He had conceived a plan for an all-Inuit expedition to the Pole. William Wallace once claimed, "Our . . . object had been to educate him to be an explorer, for it had always been his theory and ours that if anyone reached the pole it would be an Eskimo." This was the "northern work" that he would undertake.

Minik explained his plan with cutting sarcasm for the methods used by the most recent spate of Arctic explorers. His frankness must have made the northern veterans in the club's membership and the supporters of Robert Peary—for he had his admirers in this club as well—cringe:

> The explorers who are trying to find the North Pole now don't
> know how to do it.

They fit out nice comfortable ships, take along a number of useless passengers to eat up their provisions and sail as far North as they can in one summer and passively wait until they are frozen in. Then they while away a winter eating up their provisions until summer comes again, when they make a so-called "dash," in which they sometimes cover as much as a mile a day, going as far as they can in half the summer. The other half of the summer is taken up in beating it back to their ship before the Arctic winter [arrives and] becomes too severe. Then they return to the United States in a blaze of glory, announce that the Pole is to be discovered "not yet, but soon," and start out on a long and profitable lecture tour, telling why they failed and how they will surely succeed next time.

The North Pole will never be discovered in such a way. The man who finds it will go as far as he can in one season and make a permanent camp there until the next season. Then he will continue on his journey, and in such a way he must succeed. That's what I want to do. Not only do I want to be the first man to find the Pole, so that the honor will go to one of my own race, but I want to explore the vast unknown tracts of Greenland, which contain more country unknown to man than any other land.

Such blunt criticism of Arctic explorers was unheard of in the Peary era, especially from an eighteen-year-old youngster. The press, in the business of creating heroes for an expansionist-minded America, had lapped up almost every detail of Peary's experiences in the Arctic, and seldom was a critical comment printed. But it had not always been so. Those with long memories might have recalled a time, over three decades earlier, when even the prestigious *New York Times* had speculated on the mysterious attractions of the far north in an article that recalled the names of American explorers Elisha Kent Kane, Isaac Hayes, and Charles Francis Hall, and British naval officer George Nares, all of whom had famously wintered in the Arctic in the 1800s:

The record of recent Arctic exploration is exceedingly monotonous. The expeditions of Kane, Hayes, Hall, and Nares, succes-
sively started with well-equipped vessels, ostensibly to reach
the North Pole. They stopped at Upernavik, in Greenland, long
enough to send word home that they were in excellent spirits,
and confident of success, and then proceeded up Smith's Sound,
in order to go into winter quarters in the neighborhood of the
eightieth degree of latitude. As to how the explorers passed their
time while in winter quarters, we have, of course, only their own
testimony, but we all know that not one of them ever reached the
Pole. On the contrary, they uniformly returned at unexpected
periods, with the report that on reaching eighty-two degrees
of latitude . . . they found further progress impossible, and so
returned home. . . .

It is impossible that this sort of thing should go on indefinitely without invoking the suspicions of the long-suffering and
credulous public. The time has come when people will insist
upon knowing what is the attraction, which makes most officers so anxious to go into winter quarters in Smith's Sound.
Their pretense of wanting to go to the North Pole is altogether
too transparent, and their excuses for returning home without
having achieved their professed object are suspiciously contradictory. Kane and Hayes asserted that they found an open polar
sea, which they could not cross because they were unfortunately
unprovided with the proper boats. Hall said that instead of an
open polar sea there was a nice overland road to the Pole, over
which he promised to travel in sledges, but as he died before he
was quite ready to return home, he avoided the task of explaining why his promised sledge journey was not undertaken.

As for Capt. Nares, he informs us that he did not go to the
Pole because in so doing he would have been obliged to cross a
frozen sea, where the ice was only 160 feet in thickness. What
his precise weight is we are not told, but even if he weighs four
hundred pounds, the ice was thick enough to bear him. The
English people may not be very familiar with ice, but they cannot

help knowing that ice 160 feet thick can be crossed, with reasonable care, by even the heaviest naval officer in the service. . . .

When four successive expeditions spend a winter in Smith's
Sound, and return with the report that they could not reach the
Pole because there was too much ice or too little ice, or because
there was an open polar sea or because there was not an open
polar sea, intelligent people cannot avoid the conclusion that
there is something in this business which is kept from them,
and will demand to know the true reason why explorers are so
anxious to spend a winter in Smith's Sound.

At the Arctic Club of America dinner, Minik met another man of
some northern experience and interest. This was naturalist Harry
V. Radford, who was to leave shortly on a northern expedition, and
whom the Arctic Club presented with a flag to carry with him.

Minik listened with great attention to Radford's impassioned talk
about his plans. After the meeting, the young man approached the
explorer. Would it be possible, Minik asked, to accompany him north
on his expedition and return to his people in that way? But it was
not possible. Radford's destination was northwestern Canada, and
there was no way of getting to Smith Sound from the area in which he
would be traveling.

Radford was impressed with the boy, however, and with his seemingly rational talk about an Inuit expedition to the Pole. But, asked
Radford, if Minik's polar expedition were to be a success, and if Minik
were to be of service to his people after he had achieved the Pole,
shouldn't he learn to use surveying instruments and the compass
and be trained in the sciences before he left? Radford, by chance,
was a graduate of New York City's Manhattan College, a Catholic
college with a preparatory school run by the Order of Christian
Brothers, and he suggested to Minik that he could arrange for the
young man's acceptance at that institution. Minik now had to decide
whether he would, in fact, go north with the Cook relief expedition
in the summer of 1909 or postpone his trip indefinitely and resume

his education. He told Radford that he wanted a few days to consider the proposition. It was difficult to choose between his longing for the home he no longer knew and his desire for learning, but two days later, when he came to see Radford, it was to tell him he had opted for schooling.

He put his decision in the context of his long-term desire to both reach the Pole and serve his people:

> I would like to return to my people and see if I could help them. I have never forgotten my people although I have not seen them since I was taken from my playmates when I was six years old. . . .
>
> My people, they always have tried to help the white man reach the Pole. White men have not reached it, principally because the Esquimaus will never tell the white man all they know. The Esquimaus don't know today what Commander Peary is looking for. He isn't able to explain it to the Esquimaus. They have no knowledge of geography. They see his ship and think it from some fairyland filled with crackers and coffee.
>
> Now, I think I can find the Pole, after I get my civil engineering knowledge. First, I will go back to Greenland and learn my language again. My people would tell me things they would tell no white man about the best way to reach the North Pole. They don't know how great a thing it would be to find it, but I can tell them all that and make them understand that the only way to reach the Pole is to hunt for it until we find it. Too much time is spent now by explorers coming back to this country to tell people how cold it is up there and how they had to buck the ice. The Esquimau knows it is cold up there, but he is used to it, and he doesn't know anything about writing books about the north. He doesn't know how to lecture. I can learn how to read instruments so that I can know when I have found the Pole, and the Esquimaus will stick to me until I do find it. There is a lot of time lost in coming back to this country to talk about the ice.

Radford introduced Minik to a Brother Peter, president of Manhattan College. Minik told Brother Peter of his plans and ambitions with the same conviction with which he had spoken to Radford, and the brother was so impressed that he promised Minik free tuition through both the preparatory school and the college, in a course of studies specializing in civil engineering and astronomy. His education to date had been sporadic, interrupted often by illness, and finally it had been terminated because of William Wallace's financial circumstances. However, Brother Peter was sufficiently confident in Minik's abilities, on the basis of a single conversation, to tell him that he would be enrolled in one of the high school classes and that Minik should take some employment outside of his regular school hours to pay for his board and incidental expenses. He could start almost immediately, for the second semester would begin on February 1.

Radford was pleased. He commented, "I have known Minik only a few days, but have every confidence in him. I do not think it is too much to say that he may be a veritable Moses among his people—or, should we say, a Peary?"

Minik grimaced. "Just let it rest at Minik," he said.

14

Runaway

inik's experience at Manhattan College was neither pleasant nor successful.

Shortly after he enrolled in February 1909, he was off for a considerable time during another of his recurring bouts of pneumonia. This was his third serious attack in the past few years. When he had recovered sufficiently, he returned to school, but he found that he hated it. He later explained, "I cannot bear the confinement of . . . a school class room—it makes me deathly sick in a few days."

Even at Manhattan College he was a curiosity. The newspapers had gotten wind of his acceptance. When William Wallace accompanied Minik to the school on the day of enrollment, they found many of the students waiting on the campus to welcome him. But Minik wanted to fit in to the student body like any of his classmates, and this display of interest, well intentioned though it was, made him uncomfortable. He felt he had become "more or less a freak to those about me. It was so at Manhattan College, and I saw it could never be different. So much for me."

While in school, he continued to live on his own in Alliance House on West Forty-Fourth Street, and he visited Chester Beecroft often. His surroundings were hardly conducive to good progress at school, but Beecroft tried to keep a fatherly eye on him and ensure that he maintained his studies.

Minik made one last effort to get his father's bones from the museum for burial, but failed again. With this failure he became severely depressed, and once again he wanted desperately to be anywhere but New York City.

In January he had been optimistic that he would return to the

Arctic in the coming summer on the Arctic Club of America's Cook relief expedition. The plans for that voyage under the explorer Dillon Wallace had been announced in the city papers that month—they were proposing to charter the *Jeanie*, a small but sturdy Newfoundland fishing schooner. But Minik had put aside his intention to accompany that voyage when Radford had counseled him to attend Manhattan College instead. He could, of course, drop out and take the Arctic Club up again on its offer of passage. It would be a little humiliating, but if nothing else he was now inured to humiliation and setbacks. Still, two questions were gnawing at his mind.

The Arctic Club had "promised" to take him north on its expedition if he wanted to go. But would they? He had heard promises before, and nothing had come of them. And there were strong Peary admirers within the club. Peary had refused to take him back north in the summer of 1908. Might not Peary's supporters object to the Arctic Club taking him back this year?

But the more important question was this: Would there be a Cook relief expedition at all? It was expensive to outfit an Arctic expedition. It was now March, and the Arctic Club of America was not having the success it needed in getting public subscriptions to help finance the trip. The wealth of club members could not match that of the men of the Peary Arctic Club, and so they could not pay for the charter themselves. They were on the verge of scrapping the entire plan. In fact, they had gone so far as to send a letter to a Dundee, Scotland, firm, owner of one of the few whaling ships that still frequented the fished-out waters of Baffin Bay, offering a substantial reward—most of the donation money they had succeeded in getting—to any whaler that would bring home Dr. Cook. Minik was well aware of all of this because Beecroft had told him. And Beecroft knew it because he, too, had planned to go north with Dillon Wallace that summer. And so Minik's depression was more severe than normal, for if the Cook relief expedition did fall through, he would have no way of returning to Greenland at all.

In late March, while Beecroft was out of the city, there was a student strike at Manhattan College. Realizing he would not be missed at the school's morning roll call for several days, Minik packed his few belongings in a single suitcase and left the city on a Monday evening. He had five dollars with him.

He headed first across the Hudson River to Newark, New Jersey. On April 3, while still there, he wrote Beecroft a letter and left it with an acquaintance to be mailed after his departure. When Beecroft received the letter it bore an April 7 postmark. It read:

> When this reaches you I will be well on my way as it will not be mailed for three days.
>
> No matter what happens, I won't forget what you have done for me, my good friend. You made a brother of me when all the others that were responsible for my being stolen from my own country failed. There was no reason why you should have been so kind to me when you just happened to meet me, but you have a big heart and understand what the others can't.
>
> I don't see any chance in New York, and I don't want to be a burden to you any longer. You would go on helping me . . . and I feel horrible about it, so I am going away to give you a chance. They won't give me my father's body out of the museum, and they never keep their promise, so I am disgusted and will leave it all if I can. You and Mr. Wallace have been true friends, and I would die for you, but I won't stay and bother you.
>
> Never mind where I am. I am just working North. I am homesick and disgusted and when Commander Peary . . . told me he had no room for me on his ship, I lost hope; and then when Prof. Bumpus, of the museum, refused to give me my father's body so that I could bury it, or give me even his sled and gun, I gave up believing that your Christian belief, which was taught me, was meant for a poor Eskimo. After all, my own people are more humane and kind, and I am going home; your civilization has done nothing but harm for me and my people. Good bye.

William Wallace opened a similar letter.

When Beecroft received his letter he immediately wired the police of various towns he thought Minik might pass through, asking them to detain the young man if they found him. Beecroft suspected that Minik was heading for Ottawa. Sometime before Minik fled, Beecroft had received a letter from Harry Radford, and from it he knew that Radford was in Ottawa making the final preparations for his trip into the Canadian northland. Minik knew that Radford's trip would take him to northwestern Canada, far from the northern part of Greenland that he wanted so desperately to reach. But perhaps he would try to accompany Radford anyway. Perhaps he had decided that any north was better than the existence he was suffering in New York. Or perhaps he merely intended to visit Radford briefly to borrow a little money to continue his trek, with the ultimate goal of reaching Greenland.

It was possible, too, Beecroft thought, that Minik was trying on his own to reach Brigus, Newfoundland, the home of the seagoing Bartletts, the family of sealers that had provided so many captains and crew members to Arctic expeditions. If he arrived there he might try to secure passage on a northbound vessel. This possibility frightened Beecroft, for he knew that, except for a Cook or Peary relief voyage, no Newfoundland ships were likely to go as far north as Smith Sound. "If Minik is making for Newfoundland and he succeeds in getting passage further north," he said, "I am afraid that he won't get much nearer to his home than a point about 800 miles distant."

He added, "I want Minik to return to his home, but I want him to go in the right way."

In fact, Beecroft found it impossible to speculate, beyond sheer guessing, on the boy's destination, for the young man remained deeply depressed and confused. He wanted to reach Greenland, but what direction was Greenland from New York? It was north, of course, but by what circuitous route could he reach it?

On April 9 Minik arrived in the small town of Deposit, New York, about 160 miles northwest of New York City. He knew that Chester Beecroft had a brother, Will, living there, and that evening he appeared at Will Beecroft's door. He was wearing an old overcoat and sweating profusely; he had no suitcase or, indeed, any belongings with him. He spent the night with Beecroft and left the following morning with two dollars given to him by Beecroft and ten dollars borrowed from another man. When Minik left, he told Will Beecroft that he was heading for Albany, where he thought Chester was on a business trip.

He passed the following night, a Saturday, in the Crandall Hotel in Binghamton, and from there he continued to Albany. The state legislature was in session, and on Monday evening Minik visited the assembly and secured a floor pass from the Speaker of the House. He had been to Albany once before to visit a legislator in the hope of getting assistance for his education and in securing the release of his father's bones, but he had failed on both counts. This evening was a final attempt to reopen the matter, but he received no encouragement. Upset, he left the statehouse and went to the home of Maggie Arned, who had been a servant in the Wallace home for years and had cared for Minik when he was a child.

But the next morning he was off again. He went to the village of Schoharie, near Cobleskill, the area of his boyhood bliss. But no sooner had he arrived than he realized there was nothing to draw him there anymore, and he abruptly left for Troy, a city near Albany.

Chester Beecroft, in the meantime, had been busy. His brother had called him, concerned after Minik's departure, and told him about the boy's intention to visit Albany. Beecroft called several people he knew were acquainted with Minik, and he followed his tracks all the way to Troy, where he lost the trail. There was nothing left to do except return to New York City in the hope that Minik would change his mind and contact him.

Beecroft figured that if Minik was definitely trying to escape his circumstances and not be found, he was doing a mighty poor job of it. He had visited people whom Beecroft knew were his acquaintances, paid a call to Beecroft's own brother, and gone briefly to the area of his youthful summers. This young runaway was leaving an obvious trail, which suggested to Beecroft that he was crying out to be caught.

Beecroft was incensed that the neglect of Minik by the museum and the Peary Arctic Club's members had driven the boy to such desperate and futile measures. He let the New York newspapers know about the runaway, and he pulled no punches in telling the press exactly what he thought of society's shoddy treatment of Minik. "The treatment which has been accorded this child by men who, besides being learned scientists, hold reputable positions in society, is not barbaric, it has been inhuman," he was quoted as saying.

And was it any wonder Minik had abandoned the Christianity that had been the religion of the devout Morris Jesup and the other men who could afford to patronize Peary but could not manage to send one young Inuit boy to school? "Everywhere Minik looked for help," continued Beecroft, "he got none. Old men and women patted him on the head and told him to love Jesus and have faith in God; but as far as giving him a real lift was concerned, they had nothing in that line to offer. He asked for bread, and he got a stone."

Minik knew Beecroft well enough to know that, with his superb connections, he would have contacted the authorities to be on the lookout for him. Small and swarthy in complexion, he knew, too, that as one of the few Inuit in America he was conspicuous. And so he trekked farther northward cautiously. In the daytime he slept in barns or any other structures offering protection from the cold spring weather. At night he walked or rode freight trains. He begged food along the way and worked a day or two on farms in return for a square meal and a bed for the night.

At the Canadian border he was mistaken for a Chinese. He was detained but applied his usual charm and was released after a few hours.

By the time he reached Montreal, Minik was half starved and ill. He spotted a partially sunken derelict boat in a river. The vessel's cabin was still above water, so he crawled in and slept. It wasn't comfortable, but it was at least safe, and he was exhausted. He remembered, "When I woke up, I was so stiff I could not stand. I was sick, too, and oh, so hungry. I lay down in the driest spot, and slept again. For three days I stayed on that boat, and I thought I was dying. It was there I decided to kill myself."

Finally he had enough strength to leave his damp refuge, and he made it to a cottage nearby. There a woman gave him a sandwich, and he wrote another letter to Chester Beecroft:

This is probably the last letter I will ever write. I know that you will feel awfully bad when you read this, but I must let you know. Please forgive me, and this will be the last favor I will ask of you, who have always been my big, kind brother.

I guess I will never swim with you or camp with you, or sail with you, or suffer with you again. You see, Dob [his nickname for Beecroft—it meant "dear old Beecroft"], I worked my way up here, and you can guess how hard it is to work your way, or beat your way as far without money, and many a day I have been hungry, and many a night I have cried. Now I am in Canada, and am sick and weak, and have no more strength to fight off this awful want to die.

What is the use, Dob? I can't get to Brigus in time now to catch a whaler, and if Capt. Moses Bartlett is going to run the relief ship for Dr. Cook, I will be too late to catch him, even if I could keep well to make the trip.

You can't know the sad feelings I have, Dob. No one can know unless they have been taken from their home and had their father die and put on exhibition, and be left to starve in a strange land where the men insult you when you ask for your own dear father's body to bury or to be sent home.

These are the civilized men who steal, and murder, and torture, and pray and say "Science." My poor people don't know that the meteorite that they used till Peary took it fell off a star. But they know that the hungry must be fed, and cold men warmed, and helpless people cared for, and they do it.

Wouldn't it be sad if they forgot those things and got civilized and changed kindness for science? I can't get home to them, but I can die. I remember that you told me that the sure way to get revenge is to be unlike the one that hurts you. I am going to do that now. I am going to die smiling at Peary and Prof. Bumpus, and the scientists and others in the Government that you know.

Good-by, dear Dob. If I don't find some health and some way positive to get me home by next Monday I will kill myself. I will wait just long enough, not just because I am afraid, but because

I want to use up every chance first; but Monday will be the last, and you know that I will keep my word.

Good-by, dear friend. Two things I have to be thankful for. One, because I was educated enough to write this letter to tell you. The other is that I knew you. Tell them to let my people alone to live the way nature made them to live.

When they are perfect themselves, then let them tell everybody else that their way is the only way. If you ever get a chance, warn my poor people against proud hypocrites and save what few are left. Don't cry for me, Dob. Be glad. Stay like you were to me, and don't get like the rest.

The rich build homes for cats, but who offered to even let me work? Only you and Uncle Will.

My last word will be thanks. On Monday, Dob, good-by, good-by, good-by.

This melodramatic letter was not a suicide threat. This was a pathetic plea for help from a boy deeply traumatized. Elsewhere Minik had written, "Think of the injuistice [sic] of it all. Think of that burial of stones or a piece of wood instead of what I thought was my father's body. When I found out, can anyone imagine what I felt?"

Beecroft received the letter at the Hotel Astor. About the same time he was handed a telegram from William Wallace. Wallace had gone to Lynn, Massachusetts, where he knew that Minik had friends, in the hope that Minik would contact them. He did, and Wallace telegrammed the information that Minik was in Montreal, confirmation of the letter Beecroft had just received.

Some of the New York newspapers had published articles about Minik's flight, and Beecroft had allowed them to print Minik's first letter to him. Vesta Tilley, an entertainer on Broadway, had read the letter and, sympathetic, she publicly expressed her indignation at the way the young man had been treated. Miss Tilley was a lady of means. Although she used the stage name Vesta Tilley, she was in fact Lady Matilda Alice Powles de Frece, the wife of Colonel Sir Walter de Frece, a former member of the British Parliament. She had initially made her reputation on the stage as a male impersonator, but at the time she took up Minik's cause, she was playing the lead role in *My Lady Molly* at Daly's Theatre. Through Acton Davis, editor of *The New York Sun*, she met Beecroft and offered to defray the cost of his search for Minik. Now, with Vesta Tilley's money, Beecroft left for Montreal.

Beecroft had earlier telegraphed police in Montreal to be on the watch for Minik. In fact, they had already found him once, but Minik had convinced them that he was a Native American from the nearby Caughnawaga Mohawk reservation. This ruse was successful, so Minik decided to employ it again. He met a man named William Green and told him that he was one of the native athletes who was to participate in a marathon race on May 24 in Quebec City. But he lacked the train fare from Montreal to Quebec, so Green gave him six dollars to buy his ticket. He also gave him a letter of introduction to a priest in Quebec City who would look after him upon arrival.

After Minik stepped off the train in Quebec City—a few hundred miles closer to Newfoundland—the priest took this bedraggled Inuit traveler to a boardinghouse for a much-needed rest. Even had he been a Native American athlete, he was certainly in no position to compete in a marathon. And it was in this boardinghouse that Beecroft, through good luck and connections, found him.

With the characteristic understatement with which he often closed his stories, Minik summed up his adventure. "I went to a boarding house," he said. "I was very sick. As I was lying in bed, who should come in but Mr. Beecroft. I was glad to see him, and here I am."

Beecroft brought him back to the Hotel Astor and to the questions of eager newspapermen. Minik was in poor health, disillusioned, and bitter. But he made time to explain his position to the reporters:

> I left New York six weeks ago determined to get home to my people. Mr. Beecroft and Mr. William Wallace had done all they could for me, and I was tired of waiting for the Arctic Club to send me back. I beat my way by foot and on freights to Montreal, and realizing that I could not get North in time to reach Capt.

Bartlett's whaling expedition, I made up my mind to kill myself. I still want to get back to my people.

Yes, I had a hard time, but it was worth trying. There is nothing for me to do here. Nobody cared what became of me. I was a curiosity, that's all. And what good could I do by being that?

I was not strong like American boys, and I could not have worked, because I have pneumonia every little while. They would not take me back to my people. They had used me for what they wanted; they had stolen my father's body for their science. They did not want me any more, and it was too much trouble to take me back.

Vesta Tilley visited Minik at the hotel. Beecroft was now almost certain that the Arctic Club of America would not raise enough money for its Cook relief expedition. Both he and Miss Tilley thought that the US government must be called somehow to act in the matter of sending Minik home. Vesta Tilley promised that if the government would not do something for the boy, she would personally organize a benefit concert to raise money to send him back to Greenland.

But if anything was to be done, it would have to be done fast. It was now late May and the brief Arctic summer was rapidly approaching.

15

"An Iron-Clad Agreement"

After Minik had fled New York but before he had been brought back by Beecroft, the *San Francisco Examiner* printed the most sensational article yet on his plight. Illustrated with photographs and a sketch of Minik gazing in horror at his father's skeleton mounted in a glass case, it bore the title, "Why Arctic Explorer Peary's Neglected Eskimo Boy Wants to Shoot Him."

Based on interviews with Minik from before his disappearance, and with Wallace and Beecroft, the article gave a complete summary of the whole sordid affair.

In it, Minik posed these rhetorical questions: How would Peary like to have his daughter carried off to the Arctic and abandoned to the charity of some kindly Inuit? And what would the explorer do if he were walking through the museum and came across his own father staring blankly at him from a glass case? The article also quoted Minik as having said, "I would shoot Mr. Peary and the museum director, only I want them to see how much more just a savage Eskimo is than their enlightened white selves." This, coupled with the readers' knowledge that Minik was already trying to make his own way north, made another comment particularly relevant: "I can never forgive Peary," he said, "and I hope to see him to show him the wreck he has caused."

The report concluded provocatively, "And if he does meet Peary, what then may follow?"

Almost all articles that had been published about Minik were critical of the roles that Peary, Jesup, and the museum had played in his tragic life. Yet this was the only one known to have gotten a reaction in print out of the Peary family. Robert Peary was in the Arctic, but his wife, Josephine, saw the article and dashed off an enraged note to

Herbert Bridgman, secretary of the Peary Arctic Club, in which she said that she was "hopping mad" and wanted to know what could be done about the news feature. Bridgman contacted the American Museum of Natural History to ask what its reaction would be. But the museum maintained its remarkable consistency in the treatment of the Minik affair; its brief reply was that "our policy of paying no attention to these [reports] seems to be the wisest."

But more was to follow. It was as if Minik had saved up a final barrage of invective to heap upon the Peary forces and their sympathizers.

A few days after his return to New York, he told a reporter what he suspected may have been Peary's real reasons for refusing to take him north the previous summer. He said, "Peary suspected I would tell my people just how he and members of the [Peary] Arctic Club have treated me, and knew that if I did, he would never reach the Pole."

His friend Beecroft had earlier told a reporter from *The New York Times*:

> Minik is, you know, somewhat of an Indian, so he can hate, and I do not think he has any too much love for Commander Peary. Bearing this in mind, I am not so sure but that he has some scheme in mind to try and defeat Peary in his hunt for the North Pole. . . .
>
> If Minik were to tell them [the Inuit] of his treatment here they would, I think, believe the boy and do all in their power to hinder Peary. . . .
>
> I once heard Minik say, "If I get north and see my people before Peary gets there [the Pole], it will be the last move he will make in the north."

These comments are telling. They reveal far more than Minik's despondency and hatred for Peary, however. They show also that Minik and his well-intentioned adviser, Beecroft, really knew little about Inuit, how they thought, and the conditions under which they lived. They knew that Peary depended heavily on the Inuit—but that was no secret, for anyone could read it in the newspapers when Peary returned periodically to America in his brief flashes of glory. What they did not know was how heavily Minik's people in northwestern Greenland had come to depend on Peary, the man who single-handedly controlled the influx of trade goods into the district. The relationship that had developed between the Inuit and Peary, although uneven, was mutually beneficial, a very lopsided symbiosis. In assuming that the Inuit, no matter how sympathetic, would abandon Peary en masse, Minik and Beecroft underestimated the essential pragmatism of the Inuit, the one quality above all others that enabled them to survive as a people in one of the world's harshest environments.

Yet to the Peary forces Minik's claims, however implausible, were damaging just the same. They were getting increasing coverage in the press, and the public was slowly developing a righteous indignation at the treatment meted out by wealthy individuals to a helpless foreign orphan.

The articles of the previous few years had been ones in which Jesup and the museum were criticized and Peary merely mentioned—disparagingly to be sure, but only in the context of having brought the boy here in the first place. But the most recent coverage was rapidly turning it into a different matter altogether. With Jesup dead, Robert Peary, isolated in his Arctic domain, was now bearing the brunt of Minik's criticism. Mrs. Peary, the staunch protector of her husband's reputation during his absences, was genuinely mad and getting madder.

The Minik affair was becoming an embarrassment and, potentially, a liability. Neither Herbert Bridgman nor Mrs. Peary had any way of knowing if Peary had reached the Pole on his present trip, but of one thing they were certain—if he had not, he would want to try again. In that event, there would be money to be raised, and that meant politicians to be influenced. This Minik affair was a potential problem, for it could tarnish the public's view of Peary and perhaps hinder his efforts to raise the money to satisfy his polar obsession. Bridgman was well aware, too, that the Danish consul in New York had earlier expressed official interest in the treatment of Minik and was continuing to follow the situation and report to his government in Copenhagen. A serious formal complaint from the Danish government might adversely affect Peary's reputation in Washington.

Hence Bridgman and Josephine Peary turned over all the possibilities in their minds and discussed them at length. It was well that Peary himself was not in New York, Bridgman knew, for the explorer had a way of making intemperate statements in public when angry. Finally Bridgman and Josephine Peary concluded that it would, after all, be better if Minik were sent north to Greenland, so that the American public could, they hoped, quickly forget him. The task of raising money for a future Peary trip would be difficult enough without any unnecessary hindrances.

The Cook forces had failed to raise enough money through donations to charter a vessel to go to the doctor's relief. They had to throw in their lot—and their paltry thousand dollars—with Herbert Bridgman, who was now Peary's master strategist. Bridgman purchased the *Jeanie*, the small two-masted schooner of ninety-eight tons, the same ship that the Arctic Club of America had proposed to use for its voyage to relieve Cook. Her commander and a partner with Bridgman in her purchase was Captain Samuel Bartlett, uncle of the *Roosevelt*'s captain, Bob Bartlett. Samuel Bartlett, like all the Bartletts of Brigus, was an experienced sailor in icy waters and had been north for Peary on three previous occasions. This expedition, Bridgman emphasized, would not be jointly sponsored; it would be a relief voyage for Peary sponsored by the Peary Arctic Club. But the club agreed to accept the Arctic Club of America's money to inquire after, relieve, or bring back Cook.

General Thomas Hubbard, a former army colonel in the Civil War who was a wealthy contributor to Peary's expeditions, had replaced Jesup as president of the Peary Arctic Club. But Bridgman, still secretary and treasurer, was clearly the man with the most knowledge of Peary, the only member of the club to have actually been north himself, and the most capable manipulator of both the press and the public.

Bridgman was a most remarkable man. In 1909 he was sixty-five years old but powerfully built, with the sturdy chest and shoulders of an athlete. He had a large head and a luxurious, flowing mustache. His eyes, deep-set and probing, gave a look of brooding asceticism to his otherwise handsome face.

He had been in the news business all his adult life. In 1887 he had become the business manager, and later part owner, of the *Brooklyn Standard Union*. As one of the founders of, and three times president of, the American Newspaper Publishers Association, he found it galling that he was unable to influence his colleagues in New York to stop their troublesome coverage of the plight of Minik Wallace.

Behind an austere front hid a man with a passion for the exotic. He indulged it in travel. Bridgman had a reputation, well deserved, as both an explorer and a patron of exploration. He had a particular interest in the Arctic, although he explored also in Africa and other parts of the world. He first met Robert Peary in 1892 and had become an unwavering supporter. He went to the Arctic on Peary relief voyages on three occasions. In 1899, after he returned to the United States from the voyage of the *Diana*, he formally organized the loose club of gentlemen who had earlier been brought together by Morris K. Jesup as the Peary Arctic Club. While Jesup, until his death, had been president of that club and its wealthiest patron, Herbert Bridgman was happy to remain in the background, attending to details as secretary and treasurer. He was often simply described as Peary's press agent, and he didn't mind the description at all. He was an unassuming man who took his private pleasures in the respect of the wealthy and influential rather than the masses. He was a man of simple tastes, for when he died in 1924, his wife was surprised to discover that he was a millionaire.

Both Bridgman and Jesup were respected for their support of young people's interests. Jesup, indeed, had been a founder of the Young Men's Christian Association. What could have been their reasons, then, for maintaining their resolute opposition to any of the requests made by Minik and on his behalf for the return of his father's bones for burial and for assistance in securing an education? It may have been simply this: Jesup's and Bridgman's America was the land of opportunity for all who wished to seize it. The nation's population was still rapidly expanding westward, and immigrants were pouring in by the shipload to build America and their own fortunes. Bridgman and Jesup were both self-made millionaires. Was there any reason why Minik could not embrace their work ethic and become one, too? There should be no need for special treatment. People of other countries scrimped and saved for their passage to America. To live in the United States was a privilege. Why, they may have wondered, could Minik not understand that? Just being in America was enough!

Minik's friends had been agitating for the young man's repatriation to Greenland. But the Arctic Club of America's planned expedition under Dillon Wallace had fallen through, and there would be no way home now unless the Peary Arctic Club agreed to take him north. Bridgman and his colleagues had already decided that they would be happy to see the last of him. Perhaps it had been part of Minik's strategy to ensure that decision by launching his torrent of abuse at Peary through the press in May 1909. Mrs. Peary agreed, too, but she had her own concerns—after all, Minik was on record as saying he would like to shoot her husband. And so Bridgman determined to send him north—but there would be a few strings attached.

Bridgman and Beecroft met in early July and Bridgman, in complete charge, outlined the conditions for Minik's repatriation in a general way. He concluded the conversation by reminding Beecroft that "the conversation counted for nothing, and that I would make no commitment, except in writing."

He drafted an agreement that he proposed must be signed by William Wallace, Beecroft, and Minik himself before Minik would be allowed to travel on the *Jeanie*, and he forwarded a copy of it to Mrs. Peary for her approval or, for that matter, her disapproval, for "we are under no obligation in any manner."

On July 9, the day before his departure, Minik and his two closest friends in the United States signed what Bridgman referred to an "an iron-clad agreement."

There were actually two agreements. The first, signed by William Wallace, who was identified as "Foster Parent," and by Chester Beecroft and Minik Wallace, read:

Minik and his friends, guardians in fact though not in law, hereby agree that he will accept the discipline of the *Jeanie* and obey the orders of its captain; that he will land and remain at some point of call, agreed on by Commander Peary and himself, or in Commander Peary's absence by Capt. Bartlett and himself; that he will take on shore for himself and for his people only such arms, ammunition, and other goods as Commander Peary or Capt. Bartlett may approve, and that all claims of every kind against the *"Jeanie"* and her owners are hereby expresly [*sic*] and forever waived.

Wallace was made to sign an additional statement. It read,

Thirteen years ago I became the foster parent of Minik at the request of the late Morris K. Jesup, and as a parent I accept the kindly interest offered by H. L. Bridgman to allow Minik to again see his people in the far north, feeling that it will aid the boy and his people.

This statement, drafted by Bridgman, the late Morris Jesup's closest associate in the Peary Arctic Club, belatedly acknowledged what Jesup had steadfastly refused to admit, that Wallace had assumed the care of Minik at Jesup's request. Bridgman's eye for detail had not noted, though, that Minik had been in the United States for only twelve years, nor that for the first of those years Wallace was not his foster parent. But such details were of little consequence. The agreements were signed.

One further condition was exacted from Wallace. As Bridgman reported in a letter to Mrs. Peary, he had a telephone conversation with Wallace the night before Minik's departure, in which Wallace agreed that he would give the captain permission to examine Minik's baggage before the young man embarked for Greenland from St. John's, Newfoundland, and added that "Minik's feelings toward Peary and all of the Americans were kindest." One wonders why Bridgman bothered to extract hollow statements of loyalty and kind feelings from a young man who had no reason to feel anything but hatred toward Peary, for there was no chance that Minik or Wallace would disagree with anything Bridgman said at this point. One suspects it was a means for Bridgman to humiliate Wallace as much as possible. In his letter to Mrs. Peary announcing Wallace's concession, Bridgman added that he would ask Captain Bartlett "to avail himself of this permission to the fullest extent and endeavor to hold him, in Peary's absence, personally responsible . . . for anything that Minik may land."

Was this also a case of paranoia? What did they expect Minik to take with him? It seems that Bridgman and Mrs. Peary were concerned that Minik might actually try to make good on his threat to shoot Robert Peary. Peary had been in the north since the summer of 1908 and had no way of knowing the events that had occurred since then. He had been in the north through all the turbulent events of early 1909—Minik's unsuccessful flirtation with higher education at Manhattan College, the attempt to escape northward and homeward via Canada, the plea for help and understanding in the suicide letter from Montreal, and all the sensational press coverage that showed the world how Peary and his cronies had mistreated and neglected a helpless boy in a foreign environment. Peary would not even know that Minik was aboard the *Jeanie*, let alone that the young man had publicly stated he would like to shoot him. Bridgman, whose responsibility was to effect the relief of Peary, could not afford the possibility, however slight, that an unsuspecting Peary might be shot on sight by the Inuit boy he had ignored.

Bridgman sent Bartlett a copy of the agreements, with the instruction that he should transmit them and any other relevant facts on the matter to Peary as soon as he should meet him, although Bridgman added, "I will endeavor to cover the ground in my own letter to him." One can be sure that letter was lengthy.

A few days later, after Minik's departure, Bridgman would gloat in a letter to Mrs. Peary, "Minik Wallace still has no contract nor anything else signed by me. They all signed the memorandum of which I sent you a copy."

Josephine Peary sent her own letter to her husband via the *Jeanie*, and in it she vented her own concerns over Minik. "I hope you take Minik over your knee & lick him until he begs for mercy," she wrote. "On no condition allow him to return to the country [America]."

Since his return from Quebec, and his recovery under Beecroft's care at the Hotel Astor, Minik had been living with Wallace again, on Long Island. He had maintained his friendship with Vesta Tilley. She would later claim in her autobiography that "he had become my devoted slave, and both my husband and myself were loath to part with him. We rigged him out, and he left us in tears." He made a request to see his father's remains one last time before he went north, but his request was denied. "They say they are not on exhibition any more," he complained, "so I can't see them!" He spent the day before he left the United States at Beecroft's camp on Hunter Island, swimming and trying to relax.

Although he had just recovered from another attack of pneumonia, he showed a fighting spirit during his last visit with the press on the day before his departure. "You're a race of scientific criminals," he charged, giving his parting thoughts on America.

"I know I'll never get my father's bones out of the American Museum of Natural History. I am glad enough to get away before they grab my brains and stuff them into a jar!"

Incredible as it may seem, someone had, just before he was to leave, made the suggestion, duly reported in *The New York Times*, that he should "bequeath his brain to science for anthropological purposes." The *Times* could not seem to understand why Minik was shocked and offended by such a suggestion. The newspaper commented, obtusely: "To Minik, the polite request seemed chilling, and suggestive of early and sudden demise. He could not catch the scientific point of view."

Minik continued, "I sail north tomorrow, and I am tickled to death to get away. . . .

"About the only persons I regret to leave are Mr. Beecroft and the Wallaces, my foster parents. I don't know what I should have done, but for them. They have been most kind to me."

In overdone language, replete with stereotypes about both the north and his own people, he outlined again his plan, naive and pathetic as it was, to conquer the North Pole himself with an all-Inuit expedition:

> You Americans never will discover the North Pole. You are not physically constituted for the work. Only an Eskimo can live for any length of time up there.
>
> When I get back to Etah in the north of Greenland, I am going to organize an expedition of my own and go in search of the pole myself. I'll find it, too.
>
> You folks down here have done one thing for me. You have given me a scientific education. I understand navigation and the use of the sextant, so I'll know when I do reach the pole.
>
> My people will have many advantages over your polar expeditions. When the six months of darkness set in, your explorers have to go into camp and stay there until it grows light again. If they didn't they'd get lost. We are accustomed to the darkness and go straight ahead.
>
> We won't need to bother much about supplies, either. People who are brought up on blubber and fish don't worry much about canned peaches and other delicacies like that. We will be able practically to live on the country as we go along.
>
> The only reason the Eskimo hasn't discovered the North Pole is that he is not able to realize that the world is curious about it. He thinks Peary and the rest of the explorers are crazy.
>
> From what I have seen down here, I think I understand the restless spirit of scientific competition that drives you on. So I am going to get into the game myself.

While decrying the ability of Americans to find the Pole, Minik nonetheless struck a note of American patriotism in one statement. "To an Eskimo shall belong the honor of discovering the North Pole," he said. "I shall be that Eskimo. Carrying the American flag, I shall organize a party of my own people . . . and we shall find the Pole."

He didn't balk at talking to the press about the agreement he and his guardians had been forced to sign, either, and he put it in the context of his plan for a North Pole expedition: "It is this fact which caused the signing of the agreement never to return to this country, because other explorers are jealous and do not wish me to inform the world of possible success. This, however, will not deter me and the world will know what I discover."

Could he have done it? There is little likelihood that his plan could have succeeded. The sole interest of the Inuit in the North Pole was that Robert Peary paid those he trusted reasonably well in trade goods for their services as sled drivers and camp helpers. Other than that, they had no desire to reach the Pole. It is impossible that they would be persuaded to join Minik in such a senseless undertaking simply for bragging rights or the glory of their race.

Minik, though, was correct in stating that the Inuit suspected that white men, at least the ones they knew, were indeed crazy, with their single-minded quest for a remote geographic point. Although Minik could not have known it at the time, in April of that very year, his people's suspicion had been confirmed, they felt, when Robert Peary claimed to have finally reached the Pole in their company, and, to their utter amazement, there was nothing there! The Inuit would not partake in such a pointless expedition except for a just reward, and Minik most certainly did not have the means to pay them.

But to the meticulous Bridgman, Minik's boast was probably a cause for concern. Peary, as he had demonstrated repeatedly in his statements of virtual ownership over his "American Route" to the Pole, was easily threatened by the thought of competition, real or imagined.

Minik's bravado, his flair for publicity, and his apparent self-confidence belied a terrible insecurity. Four months earlier, as he trekked desperately northward in his futile attempt to reach the Arctic and live the life of an Inuk again, a perceptive newspaper reporter had asked, "But even if he gets there, can he do it? He has been in America since he was seven, and even though he is unfit here, it is probable that his life has made him equally unfit for that environment. If so, it will be his crowning tragedy and the crowning injustice of the heartless science that made of him a subject. He will be literally a boy not without a country, but without a place on earth."

The experiment begun by the museum's scientists and sanctioned by Jesup had been curtailed years before. It had drawn inexorably to its own sad close. As far as the museum and the Peary Arctic Club were concerned, the experiment would formally end on the following day.

Wallace bid farewell to Minik at Beecroft's camp on Hunter Island on the night before departure. He brought with him his son, Willie, Minik's onetime playmate in the halcyon days at Cobleskill. Now twenty-two, Willie was about to become a father—his young wife, Matilda, would give birth to their first son in only four days. Sometime after the death of Rhetta Wallace and the virtual collapse of William Wallace's world, Willie had gone to live with relatives. This tearful parting with Minik was also their first reunion in many years.

On July 10 Minik sailed from New York for St. John's on the Red Cross Line steamer *Rosalind*. The line had given him free passage. Once in St. John's he would transfer to the *Jeanie*. Bridgman was at the pier to see him off and, to be sure, to make certain that he left. It was not a pleasant farewell, but the Peary Arctic Club had to keep up appearances. Minik carried with him a few unlikely gifts—a set of dentist's tools given him by a dentist in New York, who had instructed him in their use, and a medical kit, a last-minute gift from a doctor.

Chester Beecroft remained suspicious of Bridgman's motives, even as the *Rosalind* steamed away. "They may balk on taking poor little Minik back to Greenland, fearing he may injure Peary," he told a reporter. "If he is left in St. John's . . . I shall go there and bring him back. He can always have a home with me."

Bridgman, never one to leave affairs half finished, wrote to Wallace that evening, "I bade Minik good-bye this morning on the *Rosalind* and was glad to see him looking so well and cheerful. I hope the journey will be agreeable and that he may ultimately be of real service to his people."

16

Return to Greenland

Minik had a three-week wait in St. John's before the *Jeanie* left for Greenland. There was nothing for him to do except wait for his departure in a local hotel, for Bridgman had arranged that Captain Bartlett would not take charge of him until the actual sailing.

The down-to-earth people of St. John's, unlike New Yorkers, had seen "too many Eskimos in their native state . . . to be very much impressed with one," but they did note with sarcasm that Minik could "smoke cigarettes, play billiards and drink brandy neat, along with other evidences of . . . higher education."

But there was one man in St. John's at the time who took a more compassionate view of Minik. He was a minister of the Church of England bound for the Canadian Arctic. His name was Archibald Lang Fleming, and he would later become the first bishop of the Arctic.

Fleming had arrived in the city in early July to attend to the outfitting of the *Lorna Doone*, a small fishing schooner that the Church had chartered for a voyage to Lake Harbour on Baffin Island. While there, he chanced to meet Minik. Fleming described the encounter:

> Shortly after my arrival in the city an immaculately dressed young man came up to me in the lobby of the Crosby Hotel where I was staying and said, "Excuse me, but are you the man who is going to the Eskimo in Baffin Land?" Almost before I could answer he surprised me by saying in a pleasant, soft voice, "I go back to my home in Greenland." I was startled and for a moment speechless. Before I had recovered and while I was still studying his face, noting his copper skin, brown eyes, black hair and high cheekbones, he smiled gravely and said, "I am Minik Wallace."

Fleming had heard of him and read of his troubles in the Canadian newspapers, but he was surprised to find him in St. John's, for in his mind he had associated him only with New York. Nonetheless he greeted him warmly. This was to be Fleming's first trip to the Arctic, and Minik Wallace was the first Inuk he had ever seen. The missionary took a kindly interest in him. "My surprise and delight at encountering him were very real," he wrote. "We soon became friends, and because Minik had nothing to do but await the arrival of the ship that was to take him north, he was glad to come with me on various errands when I was purchasing our supplies. He was very lonely and talked with great freedom about his experiences in New York."

Minik had had some second thoughts about leaving the south for the unknown of Greenland, especially since he, Wallace, and Beecroft had been forced to sign Bridgman's agreements. He was "discontented and even bitter," Fleming thought. In his tormented mind Minik had begun to look upon the move as an exile, not a repatriation. He had decided also that Wallace should share some of the blame for his travails. And he had started to fantasize, wrote Fleming, so that his life in New York, barely behind him, had begun to take on elements even more fantastic than what had already occurred. The sad and defeated William Wallace suddenly had become "Dr. Wallace," who was "just waiting for him to die so that his skull might be put in the museum alongside that of his father!" Vesta Tilley, the actress more than twice his age, whom he had met only in May, had become his girlfriend and constant companion.

Fleming felt sorry for this young man who was searching so obviously for friendship and love. The rough exterior was not convincing. Minik professed to be a cold, uncaring fellow, yet he sought out fellowship and the company of the missionary, helped him on his errands, and spent countless hours conversing with him. Behind the bragging and boasting that peppered his talk hid an insecure young man pleading for understanding. Fleming wrote, "My heart went out to him, but I found him hard and void of any love for his own people. This may have been understandable after the adjustments he had been required to make, but it was distressing. He was completely lacking in religious faith of any kind, whether pagan or Christian."

On July 30 Minik was at the dock to wave farewell to Fleming as the *Lorna Doone* bore the missionary out of the protected harbor of St. John's to begin his Arctic odyssey.

On August 3 it was Minik's turn. On that day the *Jeanie* finally sailed, the latest a ship had ever left for the High Arctic. Minik was aboard, taking with him "a fine assortment of the vices that are supposed to be necessary evils, which go with civilization."

Three weeks later, on Sunday August 22, the *Jeanie* was in Melville Bay off the northern Greenland coast. She was steaming ahead under dead reckoning. The fog was thick but now and then, when it lifted, Captain Samuel Bartlett could pick out familiar landmarks. It was important to recognize every significant feature of the shoreline in this treacherous body of water, the grave of so many experienced seamen. When the fog lifted late in the morning, a stretch of pack ice miles wide could be seen rafted against the shore to the east of Cape York. Bartlett gave the pack a wide berth and, picking his way delicately past some monstrous icebergs, passed Cape York and the crimson cliffs beyond it. Here icebergs were numerous as they calved off the three-mile-wide marble wall of the Pitugvik Glacier.

The weather remained clear. In late August the sun sinks lower in the sky as fall approaches, but at midnight it still skimmed the edge of the horizon. Coffee was served in the cabin at midnight, and no one felt like turning in, even though there was no real reason for staying up, except that the scenery was spectacular and the temperature pleasant.

Minik was the first to sight the *Roosevelt*. It was half past one in the morning when the distinctive rigging of Peary's specially designed Arctic ship came into view on the horizon. As the *Jeanie* drew near, the fur-clad figure of Peary could be made out on the bridge standing beside Samuel Bartlett's nephew, Bob, the *Roosevelt*'s master. The sailors, too, recognized one another, for they were all Newfoundland men, almost all from Brigus.

The two Bartletts decided to head for nearby North Star Bay where they could coal the *Roosevelt* in protected waters. The cargo of coal that the *Jeanie* carried for Peary was vital for him, for the *Roosevelt* had used up most of her fuel. The precious cargo of the *Jeanie* was what she awaited before making her departure for the south.

As the two vessels entered North Star Bay, kayaks appeared from the shore as the Inuit of Uummannaq hurried to discover the reason for the *Roosevelt*'s return and to inspect the unknown ship that accompanied her. Aboard the *Roosevelt* were several Cape York Inuit—"Peary's People"—on their way back to their homes. And on the *Jeanie* stood one small Inuk, frightened, back home at last, but feeling quite alone.

The Inuit were curious about this dark-skinned young man. He looked like one of them. But he was reticent about stepping forward and making himself known, for he could not speak a word of the native language. There were a few white men aboard the *Roosevelt*, however, who could speak the Inuit language after a fashion, and they explained to the curious Inuit that this was their long-departed countryman, the son of Qisuk, who had sailed south with Peary so many years earlier. This was the orphan Minik.

The Inuit from the *Roosevelt* came aboard the *Jeanie* to have a closer look at their young kinsman. Some of them had seen his picture from time to time when Peary had periodically returned from America. They called out his name and tried to speak with him, and were surprised when he appeared not to understand. They had never before seen, let alone imagined, an Inuk who could not comprehend his own language.

Harry Whitney, a sports hunter who had gone north on the *Erik* the previous year, and who would shortly leave for bear hunting on Ellesmere Island aboard the *Jeanie*, had picked up enough of the local language to make himself understood, and he tried to tell them that "Minik was now a '*qallunaaq*,' a white man." The Inuit wouldn't hear of it. Inuit did not become white men. If he was the son of Qisuk, he was one of them. Through signs, smiles, and gestures of friendship, they welcomed Minik home.

Before Minik went ashore to begin his new life, he gave a reporter traveling aboard the *Jeanie* a message to relate to Chester Beecroft. "Tell him to come up with his ship next year," he said. "Tell him to come with provisions for five years, and that we will find the North Pole." He entrusted a postal card addressed to Dr. Cook's wife to a passenger, and asked that it be mailed on the *Jeanie*'s return to the south and under no circumstances be given to anyone on the *Roosevelt* to mail.

He was teary-eyed when he left the ship. The reporter took note of his departure with these words: "Climbing down into the small boat, with the other Eskimos, whom he could not understand and who could not understand him, he turned his back on civilization and began the working out of his destiny with his own people."

The *New York Herald* correspondent aboard the *Jeanie*, Royal K. Fuller, noted the next day that, although Minik could not understand the language of the Inuit, "he soon fraternized with them and last night was again a full-fledged 'huskie,' sleeping in a *tupiq*."

Fuller also wrote, "Commander Peary has given to him two guns and an elaborate outfit, and when he gets his fur clothes, he will be one of his own again."

In another report, the correspondent said that Minik "made his peace with Mr. Peary when the ships were lying side by side at North Star Bay, and Minik received a shotgun, a rifle, ammunition for both, and complete outfit of good tools and supplies, which he declared was all he asked and which was entirely satisfactory to him."

These dispatches from the *Herald*'s correspondent cannot be entirely trusted. Before the *Jeanie* left St. John's, Herbert Bridgman, the master strategist, had put the finishing touches on what he referred to as a "scheme" involving the *Herald*. The paper had paid a thousand dollars for the privilege of sending its reporter aboard the vessel, and it accepted Bridgman's restrictions on what its man could report, agreeing that "upon junction with Peary [the *Herald*'s] representative will confer with him, and use, concerning the work of Peary and of the *Roosevelt*, only such material as Peary approves." This plan was important enough that it required Mrs. Peary's approval. Bridgman drafted a memorandum to her, and in a rather awkwardly written cover letter drew new attention to the third paragraph as being "of special interest." He explained, "Besides the obvious advantage to the owners of the *Jeanie*, I am rather inclined to think that the *Herald*'s man on the spot, with what I should be able to give him beforehand, would get 'the rights' of this whole Cook-Minik, etc. business, in a way which would be advantageous. . . . I have had the *Herald*'s formal assent to the scheme."

Bridgman's plan was designed, in part, to make Peary look charitable and ungrudging in his treatment of Minik.

The first thing Samuel Bartlett gave Peary was the thick letter he carried from Bridgman. It provided Peary with a complete rundown of everything that had transpired to date in the matter of Dr. Cook's preemptive polar expedition and Minik's steps toward repatriation. It suggested to Peary strategies for handling both. Before Minik left the *Jeanie* and was finally free of Peary, he was made to sign one more document:

> I hereby acknowledge the receipt from Commander Peary of the following items of supplies and equipment. The same being all that I have asked for and all that are needed to make me entirely comfortable.

The items listed were:

> 4 cases biscuit.
> 1 case tea.
> 1 case coffee.
> 1 case sugar.
> 1 case beans.
> 1 case oil.
> Salt and pepper.
> 1 double barrel 10 gauge shot gun.
> 1–100 loaded shells.
> 1 40-82 Winchester repeating rifle.

200 rounds ammunition.
11 pieces lumber for sledge, kayak and paddle.
1 pair steel sledge shoes.
6 dozen screws for same.
2 pieces lumber for harpoon and lance shafts.
250 primers.
1 hatchet.
1 saw knife—2 knives.
2 pair scissors.
2 files.
2 fox traps.
4 papers needles.
12 spools thread.
14 thimbles.
2 pair smoked glass goggles.
1 cooking pot.
1 cup.
1 plate.
1 bowl.
1 knife and fork.
3 pipes.
3 or 4 lbs. Tobacco.
2 dozen boxes matches.
1 sweater.

This, the final document in the humiliation of Minik, was Bridg-man's last thrust at the unfortunate young man and undoubtedly part of the plan to have the *Herald* make Peary look generous in his treatment of him.

But there was one other observer of Minik's return from America. This was an educated Greenlander, Gustav Olsen, who had arrived in North Star Bay on the Danish vessel *Godthaab* only a month earlier as the first missionary to the Inuit of farthest northern Greenland. Neither Herbert Bridgman nor Peary had any control over what Olsen wrote, and of Minik's return he made a brief entry in his diary:

On this day another small ship . . . arrived. It was the *Jeanie* and
had come from Newfoundland. . . . On that ship was an Eskimo
named Minik who was returning home. He was one of the ones
Peary had taken away when he was a child. He has completely
forgotten his language. He came ashore here, but we have seen
very little of him. He has only the clothes on his back.

17

An Inuk Again

The departure of the *Roosevelt* and the *Jeanie* marked the end of an era for the Polar Inuit. Robert Peary, who had dominated their lives for almost twenty years, would return no more. It was twelve years since he had taken six Inuit to New York, and in those years he had returned to northwestern Greenland on three major expeditions and had come to regard the area even more as his exclusive preserve.

Now, in 1909, he was claiming the elusive geographic point to which his ego had driven him. Peary had sought the Pole for almost two decades. In 1909, with the *Roosevelt* in her winter harbor at Cape Sheridan, farther north than any ship had ever wintered, Peary, accompanied by Matthew Henson and four Inuit, finally reached the top of the world by sled on April 6. At least that is what Peary claimed. He had no way of knowing that his rival, Frederick Cook, would shortly claim to have reached the North Pole a year earlier.

Cook had arrived in northern Greenland in 1907 and set out for the Pole in early February of the following year. He claimed to have reached his goal on April 21, 1908, accompanied only by two young Inuit men, but it took him another year to return to Anoritooq in Greenland, where he cached some supplies and began making his way to the south. The Arctic Club of America's aborted relief expedition, proposed for 1909, was, it turns out, not needed. Cook had traveled by sled and boat to Upernavik, south of Melville Bay, and taken passage on a Danish ship; he was well on his way to Europe by the time the *Jeanie* reached North Star Bay.

It was one thing to reach the North Pole, or claim to do so, but quite another challenge to be the first to tell the world about it. Cook won that race. The *Hans Egede*, on which he traveled, put in at Lerwick in the Shetland Islands en route to Copenhagen. From there Cook sent a telegram to *The New York Herald* on September 1, announcing his success. Peary wired his message of triumph to Bridgman and his supporters five days later from the Marconi station at Battle Harbour, Labrador.

Neither Peary nor Cook could have anticipated the controversy that would erupt in America, when both men's claims hit the press in September within a few days of each other. But Peary and his well-heeled supporters never wavered. Cook was a fraud, they claimed. He and his two Inuit sled drivers had never left sight of land. But the controversy continued. In the end, the claims of both men were suspect.

The Pole, Peary had written on an earlier expedition, would be "MINE . . . to be credited to me, and associated with my name, generations after I had ceased to be." In 1909 he was no less boastful when he wrote, "The Pole at last!!! The prize of 3 centuries, my dream and ambition for 23 years. Mine at last." He did not intend to share the credit with anyone. Yet if the Pole belonged to Peary, it belonged equally to Matthew Henson, of whom Peary had said, "[He is] as subject to my will as the fingers of my hand," and to the Inuit, Uutaaq, Ukkujaaq, Iggiannguaq, and Sigluk, whom he described as "my little brown children of the ice" and belittled with the backhanded compliment that "although they were not qualified to lead, they could follow another's lead and drive dogs much better than any white man." They were the ones who had brought him to his farthest north. Still, the glory would be Peary's.

With each return of Peary to northwestern Greenland, the Inuit had become more dependent on him, and he on them. With his usual arrogance, he described his feelings about the relationship this way: "I had come to regard them with a kindly and personal interest, which any man must feel with regard to the members of any inferior race who had been accustomed to respect and depend on him." He had needed them for their services as dog drivers and hunters and as providers of the skins and ivory tusks he sold for a good profit in America.

They had depended on him for payment in material goods—guns, ammunition, knives, needles, and utensils of various sorts.

"I have used the Eskimos to a greater extent than any other explorer," Peary would boast. In so doing, he had moved them about his northern domain at will, as if they were so many chattels. On each of his last two voyages he had taken between seventy and eighty Inuit, including all the best young men in the tribe, north on the *Roosevelt* to the tip of Ellesmere Island to act as support for his attempts to reach the Pole. Knud Rasmussen, the famous Danish-Greenlandic explorer and anthropologist, would later comment, "Can anyone think of a more serious and extensive contribution to scientific exploration than this wholesale sacrifice of the supremest?"

The glory was Peary's. But there is no denying that the Inuit had benefited, too. When Peary left them, their material standard of living was far higher than when he first came. It was much higher, too, than that of the *qavangangnisat*—the West Greenlanders, many of mixed blood, who lived south of Melville Bay. The first missionary to the region reported, "The Eskimos here have a large number of articles of utility of various kinds, which they have obtained from Peary, so that they, in regard to arms, tools, etc., are better provided than their countrymen in the southern part of the country."

Peary prided himself on this. But it was a selfish and irresponsible pride, for having ensured their almost total dependence on him for material goods, he abandoned them in 1909 with no thought for their future. The Polar Inuit would no longer be Peary's People.

It was fortunate, then, that while Peary's departure marked the end of one era it also marked the beginning of another in the history of the Inuit. Since 1906 the Greenland Church Cause, a private Danish organization whose aim was to extend the influence of the Danish Lutheran Church, had been eager to establish a mission to these Inuit, but it had not proven possible to begin the work until three years later. The establishment of that mission marked the beginning of a long evolution during which the isolated northwestern part of Greenland would gradually become an integral part of Danish Greenland.

On July 23, 1909, a small ship, the *Godthaab*, anchored in North

Star Bay near the Inuit village of Uummannaq. Captain Henning Schoubye and his crew remained for two weeks to help the missionaries with the hasty construction of a mission-station-*cum*-trading-post and a small house for the priest, the catechist, and their families.

The church's choice of priest was fortunate. Usually a Dane was sent as missionary to the outlying areas, but to Uummannaq the church sent Gustav Olsen, a native Greenlander from Jakobshavn in Disko Bay. He was thirty years old and had been ordained into the priesthood only a month earlier. The Inuit called him Guutak. He was accompanied by his wife, Ane Sofia. With them was Sechmann Rosbach, a catechist, also a native of Disko Bay. The thirty-one-year-old—known as Sakki to the Inuit—came with his young wife, Emilie.

It was only a month after the establishment of the North Star Mission that the *Jeanie*, following closely behind the familiar *Roosevelt*, arrived and deposited Minik on the shores of North Star Bay. Minik held back shyly on board the *Jeanie*, afraid to step forward and present himself, but finally he stepped gingerly into a kayak to be taken ashore. He hadn't uttered a word yet, but the sailors introduced him as Minik, son of Qisuk.

Word spread quickly through the village of five tents and thirty-four people. Minik was back! Twelve years is not such a long time for people of an oral culture, whose minds do not need the crutch of the printed word to aid their memories. Of course they remembered him. They had never failed to ask Peary, whenever he returned, about the child who had been taken from their midst so many years before; and if the replies had been evasive or difficult to comprehend, it had been enough to know that he was yet alive. But they had long since given up any idea that he would return.

When Peary's Inuit companions had spread the message that Peary had reached the Pole and was now leaving the region for good, those who still cared had felt certain that now Minik would never return, for there would be no way of traveling from America to Greenland. And now, miraculously, almost at the last minute of the Peary era, here he was!

He had been orphaned in 1898, but he would get no sympathy at Uummannaq on that count, for by Inuit standards he was already an adult. It was unusual, though, in an Inuit society, that he had no siblings to rely on—his only siblings, two sisters, had died in childhood. But he did have relatives, and he would not be alone, for he had cousins: a woman, Inugaarsuk; and three men, Inukittoq, Ivik, and Iggiannguaq. Most importantly, Minik had a step-great-uncle, Soqqaq, a kind, wise, and skilled man, who took Minik in and was to teach him skills critical for his survival.

But—*nallinnaq!*, as the Inuit would say—he was certainly to be pitied. For this young man, this relative of theirs, was something that the Inuit of Uummannaq had never imagined—an Inuk who could not speak a single word of the Inuit tongue!

He came ashore wearing a light sweater and a thin overcoat. He was wearing his only pair of pants. On his feet he wore short socks and everyday shoes, fit for New York but hardly for the Arctic. He carried his medical and dental kits but nothing else.

He was taken to the tent of his relative Soqqaq, who was a respected shaman and hunter. Soqqaq was one of the few who had always resented the migration of the Inuit from Baffin Island to the land of the Polar Inuit half a century earlier. They had brought with them new customs and reintroduced technology long forgotten by the Polar Inuit, but Soqqaq never adopted their ways, and the newcomers usurped some of his influence and a great deal of his glory.

He had once told Knud Rasmussen, "The man who idles about the house when spring is here is wasting his life. See! On the sunny side there is no more snow. Now you can bend down and drink from the ground, and you can lie and rest out on the rocks with the sun for a covering. This is when men start off on their travels."

He was an old man now, lame in one arm, but he still had a reputation as the best dog breeder in northern Greenland, and he was the proud owner of a team of black dogs far superior to those of his tribesmen. He welcomed this pitiful kinsman, Minik, into his home and vowed to teach him the language and the ways of his people and help him to make up, as best he could, for his lost childhood.

The old man had a stepson, Majaq, who had become a sort of step-father, more like a "friendly uncle," to Minik years earlier, when Qisuk and Majaq had exchanged wives permanently, although Minik had remained with his real father. Majaq was a singer, as were most of the Inuit, and a good one. Rasmussen once saw him immersed in song in Soqqaq's tent. "His tightly closed eyes trembled with excitement, and the perspiration poured down from his naked body. His only garment was a pair of bearskin breeches," wrote the explorer. "His face was narrow and clear cut, his nose slightly aquiline. His long hair fell loosely down over his shoulders." He was "buoyant and fiery in his movements."

He was a great hunter and he, too, provided Minik with guidance.

Under the influence of the old shaman and another of his sons, Eri, a man of about thirty-five who was also reputed to be a shaman, Minik learned quickly.

In old age Eri's son Qaaqqutsiaq, who lived to be well past ninety, still remembered the name of a dog that he had given Minik—a black animal with a white patch on its upper back resembling a backpack, and so the dog was named Nangmalik.

In his last few trying years in New York, Minik had found true enjoyment in his camping trips with Chester Beecroft. Now back in the crisp climate of Greenland, he readily took to the life of a young hunter. Most of his fellow Inuit were awed at how quickly he learned the ancient skills.

The theme of the neglected orphan, ignored by his own people and abandoned to find his food among the scraps left by the dogs, is a common one in Inuit mythology. In these myths the orphan invari-ably survives and grows to adulthood to become a mighty hunter who ultimately wreaks his vengeance on those who have most mistreated him. A Polar Inuit man once summed up the merits of this harsh philosophy with the following logic: "An orphan who has a hard time should never be pitied, for he is merely being hardened to a better life. Look, and you will see that the greatest chief hunters living here have all been orphans."

He mentioned an Inuk named Qisunnguaq, who "was left behind by starving foster parents and still made out by seeking out the winter depots of the foxes and at the same time training himself more in hunger than people thought possible. Today, it is impossible for Qisunnguaq to feel cold."

He mentioned another: "Look at Angutilluarsuk, who always manages to cross the tracks of the game animals, and who endures all hardships and can live without sleep more than anybody else. His childhood was spent in constant starvation, and for several winters his only food was stolen from the hunters' meat graves."

The deprivations of Minik's youth, however, had been of a different kind, not physical, but cultural and emotional, and they had hurt him deeply. There was no one at hand to target in revenge, but he did have a goal upon which to focus—within two years of his arrival in Greenland he had become a first-rate hunter, the equal of any of his people and the superior of many. Seal, walrus, polar bear, narwhal—Minik would tackle them all. It was as if he had to prove to his people that he had at last, if belatedly, found his place in the world.

Immediately upon his arrival at Uummannaq, Minik found a friend in the catechist, Sechmann Rosbach. At first the two could barely communicate and relied on an improvised sign language to converse. In fact, Minik, Rosbach, and Olsen all shared one problem—that of how to converse with the Polar Inuit. Although Rosbach and Olsen were native Greenlanders, the Inuit dialect they spoke was radically different from that of the Polar Inuit, but they set about to learn it soon after their arrival. Minik was at even more of a disadvantage; he spoke no Inuit dialect at all, but in the tent of Soqqaq he, too, learned quickly.

On August 25, only two days after his arrival, he went on his first hunting trip, to the head of Uummannaq's fjord, by boat with Sechmann Rosbach and a party of Inuit. Some say that just before the *Roosevelt* had left, Peary, perhaps feeling a twinge of guilt, had given the boy a rifle and a shotgun—although he did not provide him any other articles on the long list he made the young man sign. One way or another, Minik had acquired a weapon. On this hunting excursion, he took to a kayak and, with his rifle, killed his first seal. To the great surprise of Rosbach and the Inuit, he tried to skin it without slitting it down the belly. Rather, he cut it around the head and tried to remove the flesh, bones, and fat through that opening, in effect hollowing it out, leaving a huge skin bag complete with flippers. What on earth was he trying to do? Through signs they asked him. He pointed inland, to where the caribou roamed, and finally, with gestures, he made them understand that he intended to put a caribou skin inside this seal skin and use the two skins together as a sleeping bag. It proved impossible, and he gave up the attempt. His relatives and Rosbach had a hearty laugh and thought him all the more unusual for this innovative approach to skinning a seal.

Despite the kindly help of old Soqqaq and his other relatives, Minik was lonely. Despite his rapidly acquired hunting prowess, he remained in many ways a stranger at home. Although he quickly acquired fluency in his native tongue, he missed the English language, the companionship of Chester Beecroft, and the attention of William Wallace. If his room at Alliance House, one of his last residences in New York, had been small, then Soqqaq's sealskin tent was minuscule—and squalid to boot! Still, he loved the old man for his wisdom and kindness.

One day Minik borrowed Soqqaq's team of powerful dogs and left inland to hunt caribou. He was gone for several days, alone with his thoughts in his homeland, a land almost as foreign to him now as New York City had been to him as a child. Finally he returned. He was dead tired and trudged dejectedly toward the mission house. He stood nervously outside until Emilie noticed him and beckoned him in. Rosbach and his wife, still unable to speak easily with him, nonetheless made him welcome through their smiles and gestures. They made him tea and fed him. After he had eaten his fill, tears were streaming down his face. Embarrassed, he dried his eyes and stood to leave. As he departed, Emilie handed him food to take along.

He turned and spoke to the couple, but they could not understand. Then he left.

Much later, when all three had learned the language of the Polar Inuit, Minik told the Rosbachs about the thoughts that had raced through his mind on that critical day. He told them:

The life I have led has been so embarrassing that I have been unable to tell anyone about it. But I would like to tell you because the two of you care and you have opened up your hearts. Here, among people who are heathens, you have shown me that there is still a God who loves the poor folks and cares for them. In America, when I found out what they had done to my father, I gave up the beliefs that I had had, and I didn't think I would ever want to go back to them. But when I was out caribou hunting, I felt like I was the loneliest person in the world. There, for the first time in a very long time, I cried when I was alone, and I prayed to the God of whom I know so little, and asked that he lead me back to the village while I was yet alive, for I had given up hope, and I was so weak and hungry.

And he led me back to the village. And as I approached your house, I thought, "if they just ignore me, then I will know for sure that I am no more important than a mere animal."

I had already decided that it would be better if I took my own life very quickly. When I was standing outside your house, I saw the priest [Olsen], but I couldn't even talk with him because we couldn't understand each other. I tried to say to him, "I am so miserable and useless that I didn't even see one caribou." He just looked at me and gave a little smile, and I didn't say anything more. Just as I was about to go back to the tent, your wife came out and beckoned me in. That touched my heart, and I was trembling when I came into your house.

When you treated me so kindly and let me eat my fill and had coffee with me, I just couldn't do anything else but cry, because I realized how much God still loved me and wanted to save my life. When I had finished crying, what I said to you was, "I abandoned my heavenly father along life's evil road." Many times after that I often thought that I had led such a terrible life that he would never take me back to him again. But a few days ago, I realized again that he still loves me and has pity on me, and has shown me all this through you. So I want to thank you, man and wife, because you saved my life, and for the rest of my life I will always remember you and always love you.

Sechmann and Emilie Rosbach remained in the area until the early summer of 1915. For all that time, Minik was their close friend, and he never failed to bring them a gift of fresh meat whenever he returned from a hunting trip.

But the loneliness and the feeling of anomie continued. Minik's spirits were raised, briefly, in the summer of 1910 when the American sports hunter Harry Whitney returned to the region on the steamer *Beothic* with Peary's former captain Bob Bartlett. They took eleven families aboard at Cape York, and picked up more Inuit at other camps, including Minik. Whitney went to Anoritooq in Kane Basin in the hope of retrieving records that he thought Cook had cached there, but he found no papers, only instruments, so he continued across to Ellesmere Island to hunt polar bears. Minik was a valuable addition to the ship's complement because of his facility in English. Whitney had first met Minik the previous year on the very day of the young man's return to Greenland, so Whitney knew him and may have actually sought him out as an interpreter. On August 21, before returning to America, the *Beothic* stopped in Uummannaq to drop off Minik, an old man named Meqqusaaq, and a young hunter, Ittukusuk, who was one of the two hunters who had accompanied Cook on his epic journey.

This encounter with Whitney would have given Minik his first opportunity to speak English in almost a year. In addition, it would have provided him with his first awareness of the controversy raging in the United States over whether Peary or Cook had been the first to the North Pole. After a year of immersion in his native Inuktun language, Minik would have had the ability to talk with Ittukusuk and other Inuit about the two expeditions.

In September 1910, after a full year in the Arctic, Minik finally had a chance to send letters to a few friends. He sent one to Vesta Tilley, addressing her as his "Great White Queen." But the longest was the one he wrote to Chester Beecroft. He referred briefly to the controversy between Cook and Peary, and he offered a cutting comment on whether the effort to find the Pole had been worth the price that had been paid. Already his English was becoming rusty:

> I am still alive, how or why I can't tell you. First, let me explain that you would have heard from me long ago only I couldn't get them to take a letter to you. Peary had them land me at North Star Bay a long way south of my home. We had to sign their agreement, you remember, that I would land when Peary said, but they promised in turn for the black-hand papers they made you sign, to take me back to Etah.
>
> But as they had broke faith and human rule with me when I was there [sic] stolen gest [sic] I was not surprised when they dump me off, by Peary's orders, in a strange part of Greenland, with no furs, gun, sleg [sic] dogs, or equipment to battle for life in the desolit [sic] ice.
>
> They refused to carry my letters back to you, though they took my card to Mrs. Cook. . . . In a letter I will tell you a wonderful interesting story of my meeting with the people of my father whome [sic] the Americans murdered in the name of science, how they live, how I efected [sic] them, how the new-old life efected [sic] me, what chanhes [sic] I made in them and them in me; later, because the ship is waiting.
>
> Whitney also refused to take a letter home to you, and mails (sic: malice?) seems to follow me even beyond the North Wind. So to get a letter to you at last I had to make a trip to Cape York. . . . I wanted to prove how I love the only tie that binds me to the land of warmer climate and colder hearts. . . .
>
> I know you will expect something about Cook. Well, Dob, I have gone to the bottom of the matter. No one up here believes that Peary got much farther than when he left his party. His

name up here is hated for his cruelty. Cook made a great trip North. He has nothing in the way of proofs here that I can find. I believe that he went as near as anyone, but the pole has yet to be found. Cook is loved by all, and every Eskimo speaks well of him and hopes that he has the honor over Peary—has he? I will know all soon and will let you know.

I don't think both ends and the middle of the earth are worth the price that has been paid to almost find one pole. See all the white bones. Where is my father? Why am I no longer fit to live where I was born? Not fit to live where I was kidnapped? Why am I an experiment there and here—and tormented since the great white Pirat [*sic*] interfeared [*sic*] with nature and made a failure and left me helpless orfin [*sic*]—young, abandoned 10,000 miles from home?

I do not know if this will reach your hand and be looked at with your eyes, but I wish my hand and eyes were taking the same chance with it. I have no friend here or anywhere. I am lonely, lonely. Come up here and I will show you how to find the pole. I will make you king. Then if you want me I will go back to New York with you or stay here or go to hell for you, my friend when there was none.

The letter ended with a postscript: "I expect a white Xmas, Dob."

18

The Thule Station

On August, 19, 1910, Knud Rasmussen arrived in Uummannaq in North Star Bay to establish a trading post alongside the year-old mission. He called the site Thule, the name the ancient Greeks had given to a mythical archipelago far to the north of Europe. As European knowledge of northern waters had gradually increased, so had Thule moved farther and farther north, always cloaked in mystery, always at the outer edge of European man's geographic knowledge.

A man needs some excuse for putting down roots, and Rasmussen had become a trader as a reason to be in northern Greenland. He was part Inuit himself, and his first language was Greenlandic. Born in Jakobshavn on Disko Bay, he had passed his childhood there, hearing occasional tales of the wild and untamed Inuit of the little-known part of Greenland north of Melville Bay, some five hundred miles distant. He became deeply interested in the folklore and history of his people, and he determined to visit those Inuit who still lived the lifestyle of his ancestors. After an education in Denmark and a spell working as a journalist in Copenhagen, he participated in what was known as the Danish Literary Expedition, led by Ludvig Mylius-Erichsen, to northwestern Greenland in 1903. On that expedition he had met the Polar Inuit for the first time. He was hooked. He knew he must return.

Rasmussen reasoned that Peary would not remain in the area forever. And he knew also that the Inuit had developed far too heavy a dependence on the American and his trade goods. When Peary eventually found the Pole, Rasmussen figured, he would abandon the Inuit who had served him so faithfully. They would be even more isolated, thrown roughly back into the Stone Age from which they had so recently emerged. There would not even be the whalers to fall back on, for the *upernaallit*—those who came in spring—had failed to live up to their name; they had virtually exterminated the bowhead population of Baffin Bay and seldom came to these waters anymore. Only the *Morning* and the *Diana* came now from Scotland, and in a few years they, too, would come no more. Without Peary, the Inuit would have no source of the trade goods on which they relied. Survival may not have depended on them, but these goods certainly made a harsh life more tolerable.

So Rasmussen had nurtured a dream of establishing a trading post in the region. The profits from the trade would support his real ambition of mapping what remained uncharted of northern Greenland, of recording the folklore and history of the Polar Inuit, and ultimately, he hoped, of supporting a mammoth undertaking—a trip through the heartland of the Inuit world, across the central Canadian Arctic and Alaska to the Bering Strait. Along the way he would record ethnological information and folktales, and bring back an immense collection of artifacts for study in Denmark. It was an ambitious and idealistic hope. Ultimately it worked. And it had its humble beginnings at Uummannaq.

Rasmussen, in 1909, had helped the Greenland Church Cause found its North Star Mission. The priest it sent, Olsen, had been Rasmussen's childhood friend in Disko Bay. Rasmussen built his trading post the following year, near the mission, in the shadow of Mount Dundas, afterward known as Thule Mountain.

With Rasmussen was a giant of a man from Denmark, Peter Freuchen, who at twenty-four years of age had already been on one Greenland expedition. He, too, had become hooked on the Arctic. He met Knud Rasmussen in Denmark after Freuchen's return from his earlier expedition, and the two became fast friends. When Rasmussen outlined to Freuchen his plans for the station, Freuchen expressed his willingness—indeed his eagerness—to go. He would manage the Thule Station for the next ten years and go on to earn a reputation as one of the Arctic's most entertaining and prolific writers.

Minik had been in the area for a year when Rasmussen and Freuchen arrived. He lived first with Soqqaq, and then with Uutaaq, the man who had led the group of four Inuit who accompanied Peary on his

final dash for the North Pole. In that year Minik had proven himself
a capable hunter. In August he killed his first polar bear, harpooning
it from his kayak.

In 1910 Minik was living at Uummannaq with his cousin Inukittoq,
a young man, an orphan whose parents had died in the epidemic of
1895–96, whom Rasmussen had quickly taken under his wing almost
as a foster son. Rasmussen had met him previously and knew him to
be competent. Inukittoq had been on Peary's last expedition, serving
as a member of one of the advance parties, which cached supplies
far out on the ice of the Arctic Ocean to support Peary's final dash.
He had been popular among the crew, who gave him the nickname
"Harrigan," a character from a popular song written for a 1907 Broadway musical, *Fifty Miles from Boston*. He was married to Malaviaq,
a servant from southern Greenland who worked in the home of the
priest, Gustav Olsen.

Rasmussen liked both Minik and Inukittoq, and employed them
on a part-time basis as assistants at the post. In a letter to a member
of the committee responsible for the station, he pointed out that both
were excellent hunters and that a condition of them living at the post
was that the traders had first call on purchasing their catch, and that
much of the meat resulting from their hunt would be part of the
post's store of dog food. Minik had his own supply of tea and tobacco,
enough for an entire year.

Rasmussen went on to say that although Minik was still learning
to speak the local language, he was fluent in English, speaking "like
a native-born American." Rasmussen described him as "an extraordinarily interesting phenomenon," and thought that he would eventually be a positive influence on his countrymen. He was impressed
by the way Minik, despite his upbringing among wealthy Americans,
had adjusted to the pace of life in Greenland and adopted the life of
a hunter.

Peter Freuchen got to know Minik very well because the two traveled together extensively. In company with other Inuit, they hunted
together first in mid-September 1910, when Freuchen had been in the
area for only a month. It's possible that Peter found encouragement in

knowing that Minik had become such a good hunter in a short time. Minik was perhaps someone to emulate. For another trip, in which Minik did not participate, Freuchen borrowed a dog from him. In December, at the height of the dark season, they were both on a long sled trip south to Melville Bay. More trips followed throughout the following year. In July, near Agpat, known to mapmakers as Saunders Island, they visited the whaling ship *Morning*, from Dundee, on its last ever voyage to the far north. They boarded the vessel at the invitation of its captain, William Adams. Freuchen wrote that Minik impressed the captain with his English and that he and Minik joined the captain in his cabin, where they enjoyed hot food, soft bread, and chocolate with sugar. Minik asked Adams to take him back to Scotland, but the captain refused.

Knud Rasmussen loved a party. During the Christmas season of 1910 or 1911, he hosted one at his post while Freuchen was away traveling. Both Gustav Olsen and Sechmann Rosbach attended with their wives. They and Rasmussen penned a letter of greeting to Rasmussen's mother in Denmark, in which Rasmussen mentions, "I have gathered all the people together and am celebrating with them." The document is signed by Rasmussen, the missionaries, their wives, and twenty-one Inuit. One signature is "Mene Wallace," the American spelling of his name. He was "one of the boys."

But there was a dark side to Minik's new life. In September 1909, about a month after his return from America, someone reported to Gustav Olsen that Minik was lying unconscious in his tent. Olsen went to look into the matter, and later wrote in his diary that he thought Minik may have had a fit.

In October 1910 Freuchen returned from a hunting trip feeling ill, but he told no one. Rasmussen left the next day on a trip to an Inuit camp at Natsilivik. Within a day Freuchen's condition worsened and he fell unconscious for five days. Minik thought the world of Freuchen, and sledded north with Ittukusuk to bring Rasmussen back. They drove quickly because they believed that Freuchen was dying. During a night that the two Inuit spent in a tent together, Minik fell into a trance and began to sing something his partner could not understand. Then Minik burst from the tent, crying out, "My father shall make Peter well. The great Peter must be cured. Hear me, my great grandfather." The next day they continued northward, where Minik again had a sort of seizure and began to chant. Ittukusuk later described the incident to Freuchen, who eventually mentioned the unusual event in his diary. Minik had said in his chant that Peter was dead, but when he was back at Uummannaq and saw that Freuchen was alive, he said nothing about the episode. He expressed only happiness that Freuchen, though still ill, had survived.

Shortly thereafter Freuchen witnessed Minik's aberrant behavior firsthand, when he saw Minik lying on his bunk with his eyes closed, singing, "Aja-ja-jah-ha. The spirit is upon me. I see misfortune happening in Uummannaq. He is coming to me. I see it all, but no one will believe me. Aja-ja-jah. I have pity for Agpalersuarsuk [a hunter] and now I have agreed to heal him. I can and I will do it. He must be strong. The great Peter was on his way to death, but he has returned to us, the living. I see it all. The spirit is with me and I follow it."

One day when Freuchen was beginning to recover, he sat on the bunk beside Minik, who held him by the wrist and began to sing: "Great Peter had departed from the living but is now on his way back. The spirit is with me and gives me strength. Big Peter is good to me, and that is the reason I have done this." Then he lay back on the bunk, mute and motionless. Freuchen put a skin over him, and Minik woke and thanked him. Minik told Freuchen that his grandfather was with him and had talked with him; other people were unable to see his grandfather, though he could.

After securing a promise from Freuchen that he would not tell the other Inuit, Minik told him that illness and death would come to the people of Uummannaq during the coming winter. Freuchen asked specifically who would die, and Minik named his cousins Ittukusuk and Iggiannguaq, two of the youngest and most skilled hunters. Fortunately, he was wrong in his predictions.

There were other occasions of bizarre behavior:

On a Sunday afternoon in mid-November, Minik was sitting inside a dwelling, telling stories about America to several Inuit, when he began to spit blood and lost consciousness for several minutes, recovered, then began to sing softly but breathlessly, again predicting bad luck for the people of the village.

During one spell, someone became so alarmed he called for a missionary to help, but Minik chastised the man—probably Gustav Olsen—while pointing out the inequities of the Christian religion. The priest promptly left.

Freuchen recorded no further episodes of Minik's unusual behavior, even though the two traveled together often in 1911.

Had these episodes simply been attempts to gain attention? Was he trying to duplicate the shamanic behavior of other Inuit? Had he watched, and perhaps misunderstood, the actions of his aging relative Soqqaq, the well-known shaman? The earliest occasion, recorded by Olsen in 1909, might be attributed to depression over his changed circumstances, a realization that he was, unlike the other young men of his age in northern Greenland, unmarried and unskilled. But a year later, by the time he met Freuchen and Rasmussen, he had at least become a skilled and respected hunter. Perhaps he was regretting his decision to return to Greenland.

Minik eventually decided that he would change one thing that made him different from the other young men. He would find a wife. Freuchen wrote that "he travelled about, sometimes north, sometimes south, in search of women, and he never travelled in vain."

Finally, in October 1911, he found a marriage prospect, a young woman named Arnannguaq. She was not new to relationships.

Arnannguaq had been offered to Freuchen the previous year by Majaq, the man who had become Minik's mother's husband many years before. Majaq had been Freuchen's host at a small camp where the Dane had stopped for the night. He pitied Freuchen, a healthy young man, for everyone knew, he said, that it was not good for a man to be without a woman. He immediately brought Arnannguaq forth, and Freuchen described the rest:

> In a whisk Arnannguaq was completely undressed, and her
> master stood her before me and pointed out, like a slave trader,

her especial qualifications, leaving nothing to my imagination. It was a great recommendation, of course, that she was cross-eyed, which would make her the more valuable to me—I would not have to waste my time fighting over her. Her body was not without its virtues, and her manager would have us marry immediately.

I was both young and bashful, and was more embarrassed for the girl than for myself. Without giving too much offense, I tried to explain my reasons for not wanting to marry her, and finally lay down to sleep. . . . She went away, and I did not go to her.

When Minik took an interest in her, Arnannguaq was living as the joint mistress of four young men in one of the houses set aside for the youth of Uummannaq. Gustav Olsen was concerned about this seemingly immoral arrangement. But that didn't faze Freuchen, who had an abiding dislike of missionaries, and who was sorry that there were any in Uummannaq at all. He wrote,

> We must realize that missionaries are going to violate all manner of racial rules and traditions, and even trample upon what the pagans have already believed to be decent.
>
> Usually they set to work on the question of sex. It is strange how sex has always interested the Church. . . . I have always been a little embarrassed for preachers, who seem to wield such small influence over their own flocks at home, daring to interfere with the ways of an alien race.

At one time, when he was traveling with a Polar Inuit man on an extended trip through southern Greenland, Freuchen heartily concurred when the Inuk, Ajaku, explained to a local minister, "Up in our country, we consider it wedding enough when one gets the pants off the girl."

Sex had been much on the mind of one of the missionaries. Sechmann Rosbach had run afoul of his employers because of his interest in the Inuit women of Uummannaq. Freuchen observed that the catechist had "spread the seed" but not in the way the church had intended. As a result, the pastor in far-off Upernavik, who had responsibility for the North Star Mission, barred Rosbach from the mission and his quarters in the mission building. That left Rosbach with no place to go, until Rasmussen invited him and his wife, Emilie, to live at the trading station. On August 1, 1911, Rosbach officially became an assistant at the post and Emilie became the station's housekeeper.

Support for the church and its moral codes was among the few subjects on which Freuchen and Rasmussen differed. Rasmussen one day asked Freuchen what they should do about Arnannguaq's involvement with the four men. Freuchen told Rasmussen that he thought the matter was none of their business, but Rasmussen went to talk with the girl about the situation anyway. Her reply was one of charming innocence. "Don't you think," she asked, "that I would rather marry one single man? This is the only way I have of getting in touch with them."

That same evening, however, Minik came to Rasmussen's house and told the two Danes that he wanted to marry Arnannguaq. The problem was that he had no house of his own to offer her. He wondered if the Danes would allow him and Arnannguaq to move in with them for the winter, and in the spring he would build his own place.

Freuchen and Rasmussen agreed. They decided, in Freuchen's words, that Minik was "probably a good enough fellow and only needed a break." The next day Minik and Arnannguaq left for the north on a honeymoon trip. There was no marriage ceremony.

Upon their return, as planned, Minik and his bride moved into Freuchen's and Rasmussen's home. Freuchen for a while had been concerned about Minik's state of mind, especially his preoccupation with America and his recounting of a number of improbable adventures there. After the marriage, however, Freuchen thought he saw a change for the better in the young man. "I saw Minik . . . adjusting to conditions and trying to make a living for himself and his wife," Freuchen wrote. "He had exaggerated his own importance, he said . . . and he promised to begin over again and forget the outside world."

Minik and Freuchen built another house, a smaller one, beside the larger trading post where they had all lived with Rasmussen. The old house would serve as office, dining room, and trading post, and Rasmussen would sleep in the attic. Freuchen would live with Minik and Arnannguaq in the newer and smaller building.

But despite the improved accommodations, Minik's marriage to Arnannguaq began unraveling. She liked nothing better than to spend the whole day sleeping. In describing her laziness, Freuchen also claimed that she was the most resourceless girl he had ever met. As a result, Minik began to remain away longer and longer on his hunting trips, and in so doing he inadvertently played a role in Freuchen's own famous marriage to Mequpaluk, who took the name Navarana on her marriage.

One day Minik, tired of Arnannguaq's indolence, announced that he was going north on an extended trip. He left Freuchen alone in the house with his young wife. Even so, he let Freuchen know that "he did not want to make appointments for exchange of women" with anyone, contrary to the general wife exchanging that occurred throughout the region, which the missionaries were trying to end. Freuchen described the events that ensued:

> To circumvent any whisper of scandal Arnannguaq invited Mequpaluk to spend the night with her. Each evening after the girl had done her chores at home she came running down to the house. . . . She was always in the best of humor and our room became a cheerier place when she entered it. . . . Each night we awaited her arrival with impatience.
>
> Finally one evening when she came Arnannguaq was absent, and I told Mequpaluk that she had better stay with me. She looked at me a moment and then remarked simply:
>
> "I am unable to make any decisions, being merely a weak little girl. It is for you to decide that."
>
> But her eyes were eloquent, and spoke the language every girl knows regardless of race or clime.
>
> I only asked her to move from the opposite side of the ledge over to mine—that was all the wedding necessary in this land of the innocents.

Shortly afterward Freuchen and the newly named Navarana set off north on a honeymoon of their own. They wanted to find her aging grandfather, one-eyed Meqqusaaq, and bring him back to live with them. On their way north, they encountered Minik, finally returning from his long hunt. They told him that his wife was expecting him. He appeared, said Freuchen, "none too enthusiastic."

Shortly after, he left her. He was an alert and active young hunter, and he told his friend Rosbach, the catechist, "Some of the women are very clever, but others are just lazy. Arnannguaq is nothing but sleep in disguise, and I don't want to be married to her."

At some point, the friendship between Freuchen and Minik ended. Freuchen offers no explanation for it, but in later years he mentions Minik occasionally in his autobiographical writings, and almost always disparagingly. Nor does Rasmussen offer insight into what transpired between the two former friends. Freuchen thought Minik was "an extraordinary fellow" becuase of his unusual upbringing, who nonetheless had a litany of problems. He considered him to be listless and sullen. In *Arctic Adventure: My Life in the Frozen North*, the Dane said: "Minik was a great nuisance to all of us. He was an unhappy lad with a bad disposition. . . . He was absolutely destitute when I first saw him." He called him "the boy who had given us so much trouble."

In contrast with what Rasmussen had written about Minik, Freuchen claimed, "We had taken him into our house, and soon found that he did not remember a thing he had learned in America, and could barely read or write." Contrary to all the evidence, Freuchen claimed that "even in Greenland, Minik was regarded as unintelligent and irresponsible."

Freuchen's comments also contradict what the Inuit themselves remembered about Minik over half a century later. Inuutersuaq, recognized as the historian of the Polar Inuit, found Minik to be open and likable, a good hunter with well-trained dogs, who learned from others how to read the weather and the currents.

An old hunter recalled that Minik was cheerful and that he showed great ability hunting polar bears and walrus from a kayak. One elderly woman thought that he had had a difficult time settling into Inuit life. Another woman remembered him being funny, good-natured, and popular.

The hunter and guide Imiina offered a dissenting opinion: He said that Minik drank too much and didn't want to work. He also said Minik on at least one occasion spoke of returning to America. But Imiina's reminiscences may have been colored by having read Rosbach's account of Minik's life, published in Greenlandic in 1935. On a long trip to Melville Bay, Imiina said, Minik asked if he would like to accompany him to the United States some day, but Imiina wanted no part of such an idea. He said he would rather live the life of a hunter in Greenland.

Significantly, none of the Inuit mentioned Minik's experimentation with shamanism or any of the unusual behavior he had exhibited in his first year of learning to be an Inuk. If they remembered it, they didn't consider it worthy of mention.

Freuchen had not written disparagingly of Minik in his diaries for his early years in Uummannaq. His critical comments appeared only in material written decades later. In *Vagrant Viking*, his autobiography published in 1953, he wrote, "For a while we tried to help him, sure that he had been mistreated in the United States, but we soon found he was utterly unreliable. In a short time he nearly exhausted our liquor supply, which we did not lock up until too late. He was impossible to handle, hysterical and lazy. Finally we had to throw him out."

Freuchen wrote also that when Minik was thrown out, he cried and promised to improve. When that didn't work, he pretended to stab himself. Freuchen wrote that Rasmussen once found Minik lying on his back with a knife through one of the buttonholes on his coat, the hilt projecting upward. It was dark, and Rasmussen feared at first that he had committed suicide. He and Freuchen carried Minik into a room in the house and pulled out the knife. As it turned out, nothing was damaged, not even his clothes. He was a laughingstock among the Inuit, said Freuchen, and the two traders refused him access to their house. Later, he claimed, they tried repeatedly to help him, but to no avail.

What had happened between these two men to cause such vitriol to flow from the pen of Peter Freuchen?

On June 16, 1916, Navarana Freuchen gave birth to a boy. She named him Meqqusaaq after her father. Indeed, there was no doubt in anyone's mind that he was the rebirth of the old man, for the baby was slightly cross-eyed and old Meqqusaaq had only one eye. He had lost the other when he was stabbed in a fight on Ellesmere Island by a crazed Inuk intent on cannibalism, a man whose name, ironically, was Minik.

Meqqusaaq, who had been immensely pleased at his daughter's marriage to Freuchen, eventually became ill and tired of life. "It is not impossible that someone is going to sleep and keep on sleeping," he one day informed Navarana and Peter. The next morning he lay dead in his tent. And so to honor him, Navarana's firstborn was named Meqqusaaq.

An American expedition doctor happened to be present at Uummannaq when Meqqusaaq was born. He didn't deliver the baby, but he saw the infant soon after birth and noted that he was healthy and dark-skinned. The boy appeared to be "wholly Eskimo," and by that he meant Peter Freuchen was probably not the boy's father.

Many Inuit also thought that an Inuk was the father, and they surmised it was Minik. Other suspicions have been voiced, one being from Freuchen's own daughter, Pipaluk, who told a researcher years later that she did not believe that she and her brother had the same father.

In 1930 Peter Freuchen published a novel, *Ivalu*, in which he told a bizarre tale about a young Inuit woman, Ivalu, and her romances. It is a tale of flirtations, drunkenness, abuse, sex, and love, and is modeled on real-life characters.

Even as a child on Peary's ships, Ivalu has the desire to someday marry a white man. The arrival of a white trader rekindles her early dreams and "brings her to the drama of her wooing and the epic of her winning." Ivalu is, of course, Navarana. The trader, Bozi, is an approximation of Freuchen himself. And the villain of the piece, the malevolent Inuk who grew up in New York and returned to Greenland where he ended up in a relationship with Ivalu, is unapologetically named Minik.

Freuchen drew on negative experiences from the life of the real Minik—his work at the trading station, his invocation to the spirit of his grandfather, the staged suicide farce—to portray an irredeemably evil Minik.

Minik wins Ivalu's heart, then violently mistreats her. The white trader rescues Ivalu, beats Minik, and throws him out into the cold, presumably to die.

"Sad things have happened to you," Bozi tells Ivalu. "I, too, am unhappy. A woman of my own land has proven herself full of lies to me. . . . Therefore my mind, too, is dark and I have heavy thoughts." This, too, was true to the facts of the novelist's own life.

And that was enough. Two pained souls. Their marriage was consummated that night as they snuggled together for warmth in an icy cave. The next morning Bozi tells Ivalu, "We must never speak again of Minik." Minik is absent from the rest of the novel.

This is indeed a strange way to write about one's wife. Navarana never knew about the book, for she died in 1921, almost a decade before it appeared. Writing the story may have been cathartic for Freuchen. It gave him a chance to write about his wife, to express the different sexual mores of the Inuit, and to present a fictionalized account of an Inuit marriage. But more than anything, it gave him a chance to vilify Minik, the man who may have fathered Freuchen's first child.

60. Missionaries at Uummannaq, 1910. On the left are Emilie and Sechmann Rosbach. In the center is Ane Sofia, wife of Gustav Olsen, who is on the extreme right. The others are a Polar Inuit man, Uusaqqaq, and a woman, Antonethe.

61. Gustav Olsen and his family and a group of Polar Inuit children.

62. Three Inuit in the house of the Thule Trading Station, about 1910.

63. Knud Rasmussen, who established a trading post in 1910 in northern Greenland, where Minik worked occasionally.

64. Minik's signature (Mene Wallace) appears with those of other Inuit on a letter of greeting to Knud Rasmussen's mother.

65. Peter Fruechen and a group of Inuit at the Thule Trading Station, Uummannaq, about 1915.

66. Navarana, wife of Peter Freuchen, with daughter, Pipaluk, and son, Meqqusaaq.

67. Arnannguaq, who was Minik's wife for a time at Uummannaq, photographed in 1916. The child is Peter Freuchen's son, Meqqusaaq, who may have been fathered by Minik.

68. Minik hitching his dogs.

69. Minik in a kayak, at Uummannaq.

70. Minik and some of the men of the Crocker Land Expedition in MacMillan's house at Etah. *From left to right*, Minik, Small, Allen, and Tanqueray.

71. Minik sitting with his gun and binoculars in the doorway of the Crocker Land Expedition quarters at Etah.

72. Minik and Sigluk, with two women, on the ice in Parker Snow Bay in front of the *George B. Cluett*, winter, 1915–16.

73. Donald B. MacMillan, leader of the
Crocker Land Expedition.

74. A group of Inuit at Etah during the Crocker Land Expedition.

75. Minik after his
return to the United
States in 1916.

REGISTRATION CERTIFICATE.

To whom it may concern, Greetings:

THESE PRESENTS ATTEST,
That in accordance with the
proclamation of the President of the United States, and in compliance with law,

No. _115_

(This number must correspond with
that on the Registration Card.)

Mene Peary Wallace Coengh
(name)   (City or P. O.)

Precinct _Franklin Bor_ County of *Cambria* State of *Pena*

has submitted himself to registration and has by me been duly registered this _3_

day of _June_ , 1917.

C L Lambert
Registrant

3—4227

76. Copy of Minik's military registration certificate. June 1917.

16th Sept., 1916.

Permit Mene Wallace, a native of Greenland
to embark on the S.S. Stephano for New
York.

_____
Deputy Minister of Customs.

77. Permit from the customs
department, St John's,
Newfoundland, allowing Minik
to embark for New York, 1916.

Assembly Dist. No. ___25___ Borough of ___Man___ New York City
STATE OF NEW YORK
Military Census and Inventory of 1917
BY COMMAND OF THE GOVERNOR
This Certifies that the bearer whose signature appears
on the line following

Name ___Mene Wallace___

Residence ___550 W-36 St___

has been enrolled in the Census and Inventory of Military Resources
of the State.

NOT TRANSFERABLE

E. P. Goodrich
New York City Director of Census

by ___Wm H. Blackie___

Agent

78. Minik's military census card, State of New York, 1917.

Form 2203
U. S. DEPARTMENT OF LABOR
NATURALIZATION SERVICE

No. 14031?
JRC-286-77

UNITED STATES OF AMERICA

DECLARATION OF INTENTION

Invalid for all purposes seven years after the date hereof

State of New York, } ss:
County of New York, }

In the Supreme Court of New York County.

I, _____Mene Peary Wallace_____, aged ___27___ years,

occupation _____Clerk_____, do declare on oath that my personal description is: Color ___white___, complexion ___dark___, height _5_ feet _8_ inches, weight __155__ pounds, color of hair ___black___, color of eyes ___brown___ other visible distinctive marks ___none___

I was born in _____Etah, Greenland_____

on the ___5th___ day of ___August___, anno Domini 1_889_; I now reside at _____550 Third Avenue_____, New York City, N. Y.
(Give number and street.)

I emigrated to the United States of America from ___Parker Snow Bay, Greenland___

on the vessel ___George B. Cleutt___; my last
(If the alien arrived otherwise than by vessel, the character of conveyance or name of transportation company should be given.)

foreign residence was _____Etah, Greenland_____

I am unmarried

It is my bona fide intention to renounce forever all allegiance and fidelity to any foreign prince, potentate, state, or sovereignty, and particularly to ___Christian X,___ ___King of Denmark___, of whom I am now a subject; I arrived at the port of _____New York_____, in the State of _____New York_____, on or about the ___21st___ day of ___September___, anno Domini 1_916_; I am not an anarchist; I am not a polygamist nor a believer in the practice of polygamy; and it is my intention in good faith to become a citizen of the United States of America and to permanently reside therein:

SO HELP ME GOD.

Mene Peary Wallace
(Original signature of declarant.)

Subscribed and sworn to before me in the office of the Clerk of said Court at New York City, N. Y., this ___30th___ day of ___January___ anno Domini 191 7

[SEAL]

WILLIAM F. SCHNEIDER

Clerk of the Supreme Court.

By *Thomas J. Shalvey* Special Clerk.

79. Minik's copy of his declaration of intent to become a citizen of the United States, January 1917.

80. Avoortungiaq and Amaunnalik, two elderly women in Qaanaaq, who told the author of their memories of Minik.

81. Inuutersuaq Ulloriaq, the historian of the Polar Inuit, playing a traditional game at his home in Siorapaluk in 1984.

82. Amaunnalik, who was with the author in New Hampshire when they found Minik's grave.

83. Jared van Wagenen III of Lawyersville, New York, who remembered Minik from his youth, 1982.

84. The burial place of the four Inuit whose bodies were interred in Qaanaaq in 1993, covered in snow.

85. A plaque marks the grave of Minik's father and three other Inuit whose bodies were returned to Greenland for burial in 1993.

86. Minik's grave in the Indian Stream Cemetery, Pittsburg, New Hampshire. His date of birth is incorrect.

19

Uisaakassak: The Big Liar

In 1909 Uisaakassak, the only other Inuk to have survived the year in
New York, was living in Inglefield Bay, the next major fjord north of
Uummannaq. Minik would have reconnected with him, perhaps on a
hunting trip. He had not seen him for twelve years.

In 1898 the *Windward* had taken Uisaakassak back to Greenland,
leaving Minik behind in America. Uisaakassak was twenty-three years
old when he returned to his people, the first adult Polar Inuk ever to
visit the land of the white men and return to tell about it. That telling
was to color his fellows' perceptions of him for the rest of his life.

Uisaakassak had been away for only one year, so language was not a
problem for him on his return. Once back among the Inuit he assem-
bled an audience of his campmates and began to describe to them his
experiences among the "man-made mountains" of New York:

> The ships sailed in and out there, like eiders on the brooding
> cliffs when their young begin to swim. There weren't many free
> drops of water in the harbor itself; it was filled with ships. You'd
> risk your life if you tried to go out there in a kayak, you'd simply
> not be noticed, and you'd be run down unmercifully. People
> lived up in the air like auks on a bird cliff. The houses are as big
> as icebergs on a glacial bank, and they stretch inland as far as
> you can see, like a steep chain of mountains with innumerable
> canyons that serve as roads.
>
> And the people. Yes, there are so many of them that when
> smoke rises from the chimneys and the women are about to
> make breakfast, clouds fill the sky, and the sun is eclipsed.

Encouraged by his listeners' incredulous expressions, he went on. He told about "the streetcars, big as houses, with masses of glass windows as transparent as freshwater ice. They raced on without dogs to haul them, without smoke, and full of smiling people who had no fear of their fate. And all this just because a man pulled on a cord."

The amazement turned to amusement and finally to disbelief. The final straw was his description of the "distance shrinker." Uisaakassak had stood and talked to Peary, who was visiting another village. Without shouting to each other, they had talked together "through a funnel, along a cord."

This was too much. Old Soqqaq rose and told him, "Uisaakassak, go tell your big lies to the women!" He got the message. A few years later an Inuk commented to a white explorer that Uisaakassak "can tell a lot from over there (America), but he really doesn't want to, for nobody believes him. To begin with, when he came home, he told us so much about Peary's land that it can't possibly be true. Now he's fortunately stopped trying to make us believe more of his tales."

From that point on Uisaakassak was known by the unfortunate nickname "the Big Liar." He was an excellent hunter, but he was relegated to a position of low prestige within the community because of his tales.

The winter following his return, he worked for Peary as a dog driver and hunter. That winter he almost lost his life far north in Kennedy Channel. Peary recorded that "a biting wind swept down the channel and numbed the Eskimo who had spent the previous winter in the States to such an extent that to save him we were obliged to halt . . . and dig a burrow in a snowdrift. When the storm ceased, I left him with another Eskimo and one of the poorest dogs and pushed on."

When Knud Rasmussen visited the area on the Literary Expedition in 1903, Uisaakassak was living in the rich hunting grounds of Inglefield Bay with his wife, Aleqasinnguaq. With her, he participated in the area's general wife exchange; that winter he and Piugaattoq, whose wife had the confusingly similar name Aleqasina (and was also known sometimes as Aleqasinnguaq), often exchanged wives, sometimes for a night, but often for longer periods.

Wife exchange was the only part of Inuit society in which women did not have a say. It was a mutual decision on the part of two men, always friends and often hunting partners. It could be done for a night or a longer period. It occurred without jealousy and sometimes became a permanent arrangement. When the Danish Literary Expedition was at Saunders Island in 1903, expedition members observed that eight Inuit men exchanged wives, offering as a reason, if any were required, that the practice would result in an improvement in the weather, which had been bad. The next morning, the weather was better. Piugaattoq's wife, Aleqasina, was later questioned about the wife swapping by an expedition member. "'What shall one do?' she asked, resigned to the reality. 'We women are not the ones who make the rules. We find a strange man sent in to the bunk to us, where we live with our children. And so we must go ahead and be his wife.'"

This wife exchange with Piugaattoq may have been responsible for Uisaakassak's eventual falling-out with Peary, for although Uisaakassak worked for Peary in 1898 and 1899, there is no evidence that he ever worked for him again. And on March 31, 1900, while at Fort Conger in the far north of Ellesmere Island, Peary, in written instructions on which natives were to board his ship as assistants, included the statement, "The following natives are not to be allowed on board ship under any circumstances. . . . Should they get on board by 'mistake,' you will see that they are put off at once." The list included the name "Uisaakassak, the young man who was in the States."

Peary had been enamored of Piugaattoq's wife Aleqasina since at least 1896, when he had described her as "the belle of the tribe," and he had long been sharing her with her husband. Peary was known to be extremely jealous whenever any other man showed an interest in her.

Puigaattoq's wife, however, was not the only object of Uisaakassak's attention, for the Inuit described him to Mylius-Erichsen, the leader of the Danish Literary Expedition, as a man "who has a bad habit of borrowing other men's wives in an irregular way—that is, without the permission of the man in question."

Uisaakassak wanted to go to America to visit his former haunts again and, despite the falling-out he had had with Peary in 1900, he held out hope that Peary would take him. Aleqasina, who was living with Uisaakassak for part of 1903, told a member of the Literary Expedition that he wanted to go south and that she wanted very much to go with him. Peary's response to this idea is not known but can be imagined. The couple did not travel south.

Uisaakassak was an intelligent man but temperamental. While he could be good-humored and entertaining, he was also greedy and acquisitive and "not the kind of person who would offer to help people who could not be expected to do something for him in return—he had, unfortunately not for nothing, spent a year in a civilized people's land!"

In 1905 Uisaakassak, with a few of his kinsmen, moved farther south than the Polar Inuit had ever lived, to Tuttulissuaq, the great caribou land. On the shore of Melville Bay, it was a haven for caribou, polar bear, narwhal, and seal. Uisaakassak was the unquestioned leader of the small camp he established there. A fearless man, he did not hesitate to challenge a bear with only a harpoon and a flensing knife. He was, moreover, a man of imagination and a bit of a dreamer. He had always felt himself superior to others, and his stay in America only confirmed that notion. He had been humiliated by the sharp tongue of Soqqaq shortly after his return from America, but at Tuttulissuaq he had found a place where he might restore his reputation, so unjustly ruined thanks to the ignorance of his countrymen.

Rasmussen visited Uisaakassak at Tuttulissuaq in 1907. His host regaled him with hunting stories, recounted over generous feasts of the bounty of land and sea. Uisaakassak was a man whose meat racks were full, and he was proud to display this evidence of his prowess to his infrequent guests.

Rasmussen continued on northward and tried to restore the reputation of Uisaakassak, for whom he felt great sympathy, by assuring the Inuit that he was, after all, not such a fabricator of tales as they had thought. But he was cautioned, "Yes, Uisaakassak was a great hunter, he had the best dogs, and was awfully good company; but you could never believe what he told you, for he was incorrigible and full of lies."

For some reason, Uisaakassak and his band moved back to Inglefield Bay sometime after Rasmussen visited them. He was there in

1909, and it is possible that Minik may have met him. Uisaakassak and his real wife, Aleqasinnguaq, had separated before the move to Tuttulissuaq, and Uisaakassak had taken another wife, Aatitaq. When another man, Maasannguaq, died in April 1910, Uisaakassak also took his widow Mequ as a second wife. Then he stole Aleqasinnguaq back from her new husband, Sigluk, giving him three women. Worse, he arrogantly taunted Sigluk, deriding him for his loneliness while reminding him publicly of his wife's erotic abilities. But he had picked a formidable enemy. Sigluk had recently been with Peary to his farthest north and had received rich rewards from the explorer for his services. Such a man could not lose a wife to an incorrigible liar like Uisaakassak! So Sigluk bided his time.

On a summer day in 1910, the great Uutaaq, Peary's chief guide, arrived at the village by kayak. He, too, had a problem. His wife had died the previous year, and he was having difficulty finding a new one, for men in that region considerably outnumbered women.

One day narwhal were seen in Inglefield Bay, and the men of the village took to their kayaks. But it was not narwhal that occupied the thoughts of Sigluk and Uutaaq. They now had the chance for a simple solution to both of their problems. Sigluk shot Uisaakassak, but hit him only in the shoulder. Uutaaq finished the job with a bullet through the head. Uisaakassak rose momentarily as if to speak, then slid from his kayak into the frigid waters of Inglefield Bay. He was thirty-five years old and left three wives and no children.

20

Wanted: Dead or Alive

Minik wanted to be somebody, too, like Uisaakassak. But unlike Uisaakassak he was unable to talk with his kinsmen upon arrival at Uummannaq. True, a few Inuit men could speak and understand a bit of English, but it was expedition and trade jargon they grasped and not the sort of vocabulary that would help one comprehend tales of life in America. Until Minik relearned his native tongue well enough to communicate easily with his own people, he had to keep the memories of his troubled life bottled up, festering in his mind. And there, like an insidious cancer, they fed on the trauma he had experienced in America and the loneliness he was enduring in Greenland; the memories grew into an extravagant melding of fact and fantasy. But the emphasis was on the fantasy. His countrymen, inured to the tales of Uisaakassak a decade earlier, and reassured by Rasmussen that many of the stories had in fact been true, listened and believed. By the time Minik was able to recount the adventure he had concocted to his fellow Inuit and to his friend Sechmann Rosbach, Minik may have believed his embellished or imagined stories himself.

The beginning of his tale was credible enough. He had boarded Peary's big ship with his father and the rest of the Inuit party to make the trip to America. On their way south they stopped at Godhavn on Disko Island; he had not forgotten it, for it was in the land of the Kalaallit, the West Greenlanders of whom he had heard. But to a small boy the only thing worth remembering about the place was that the houses were beautiful and the people friendly. From Godhavn they crossed Davis Strait and made a brief stop at Cape Haven, a whaling and trading station on southern Baffin Island, and from there they made for America and the wonders of New York.

He told Rosbach of his first impressions of the city. "There are many large ships and huge buildings there," he said, "and between the tall buildings the streets are crowded with people. Vehicles with many people inside them go every which way, and at first I didn't realize that we were going to get inside one of them and travel a great distance." The people of the big city had never seen an Inuk before and came in throngs to gawk and stare. "If I hadn't had a white person looking after me, I'd have been stepped on just like a mosquito," Minik remembered.

Finally they reached a large building where they were to stay. They were pleased at first, for they had never been inside such a structure. But soon the pleasure turned to discomfort, and they were all down with colds. "It was so hot that we could hardly breathe," said Minik, "but I got used to it quickly and got over my cold."

The others were not so fortunate. Soon Qisuk was dead—some of the survivors said he had been murdered in the hospital—and Minik had gone with the white people to see his father buried. With the deaths of the others, save Uisaakassak, he was alone in a world of strangers.

That part of the story his kinsmen already knew, for they had heard as much from Uisaakassak. In fact, Minik's account was far more down-to-earth than Uisaakassak's description had been. Perhaps that is why they unquestioningly believed the rest of the story.

A rich man named Jesup had taken him in first, he told them, but shortly after had decided, for unknown reasons, not to keep the boy. Another wealthy man, by the name of Wallace, had then taken him in as a son. Minik told them about his early life with the Wallaces. "Unlike Jesup, my new father was a good man, kind and helpful," he said. "When I lived at his place, he taught me everything; he took me to the movies and to the zoo to see the animals. And I also started to learn how to read and write—I found it hard at first, and sometimes I cried. It was difficult for me sometimes because I didn't know the language very well."

Wallace had hired a tutor for him, a friend who also happened to be a minister. One day, when Minik had been in America for almost two years, Wallace decided to teach Minik a peculiar lesson about the importance of learning English well. He taught him a new phrase that he should use to greet his tutor the next time he came to the house. Minik practiced the phrase until he could repeat it well. When the priest visited again, Minik ran to him, took his hand, and uttered the greeting. The priest drew back in surprise, and the smile vanished from his face. He hurried into an adjoining room to fetch Wallace, leaving Minik standing alone wondering what he had done wrong. The priest and Wallace came into the room laughing, and Minik learned the meaning of what he had said, which was: "What are you doing here, you silly old fool?" Minik was crushed. He didn't realize the purpose of this cruel joke. But it seemed to work nonetheless. Minik threw himself into his studies, and soon he was able to speak English just like an American boy.

Finally Minik had learned enough of America's language and customs that Wallace felt him ready for baptism. He suggested that Minik take a new Christian name at his baptism, but Minik replied, "I have never met another person anywhere as kind as you are. I want to keep the name, Minik, that my parents gave me as a baby; but if you agree, I would like to take your surname to go with it." Wallace did agree, and the following Sunday the boy was baptized Minik Peary Wallace. At a quiet reception at the Wallace home that afternoon, Minik claimed, William Wallace made him a gift of twenty thousand dollars, but Minik was not to receive it until he reached the age of twenty-five years. In explaining to his countrymen Wallace's generosity, he conveniently forgot about Willie, his Cobleskill playmate, and told them that Wallace was a wealthy man who had no children of his own.

The figure of twenty thousand dollars could not have meant anything to the Inuit who heard this story. Fox and bearskins and ivory tusks were their currency. But Sechmann Rosbach knew that it represented a very large sum of money indeed. He was impressed.

But was this sum real or another figment of Minik's freewheeling imagination?

There is no doubt that Minik was given a Christian upbringing in the Wallace home, at least until the death of Rhetta Wallace. The

Wallaces were churchgoers. In Schoharie County, the family attended the Reformed Church of Lawyersville, and in New York they attended Park Presbyterian Church. Minik attended Sunday school regularly and sang solos in the Lawyersville church, but neither church has any record of him having been baptized.

Baptism or not, it's possible that Wallace at some point did promise Minik a large gift in the future. If Wallace made such a promise, however, it would have been while he was still living his flamboyant lifestyle. With the disappearance of the Wallace financial empire, the promise of any substantial gift likely disappeared, too, from all but Minik's fertile mind.

Minik's story continued. It was now time for him to choose a career and embark seriously on a course of studies. He decided that he would become a dentist. His Inuit listeners found this easy to believe, for other than the clothes on his back, his medical and dental kits—gifts given to him just before he left New York—were all he carried on his return. He enrolled in a university, he said, where the students at first thought he was Japanese. When they discovered that he was an Inuk, they began to tease and ridicule him and suggest that it would be impossible for a person of such a primitive race to succeed. Minik took that only as a challenge and excelled even more in his studies.

One day he went to the museum to study the teeth of the various animals whose skeletons were on display. He recounted:

> There were many human skeletons on exhibit. Above each one was a little sign identifying the person and where he was from. I went from case to case, looking at the teeth of the exhibits. And in the corner of that room I came across a box containing a skeleton and bearing a label that read "The Skeleton of Qisuk, a Polar Eskimo." I thought that perhaps it was the skeleton of another man who had had the same name as my father and had gone to America before us and died there. But from all the books I had read, I couldn't recall any such thing having happened. My heart began to pound, and I was trembling. I think I already understood the truth. But I went to the curator's office anyway

and asked him when that particular skeleton had arrived at the museum. The curator didn't suspect that I was an Inuk—he too thought I was Japanese—and he gave me the information. I fell into a chair and began to cry. With my own eyes, I had seen my father's body buried in the ground, so I certainly never expected to find his skeleton displayed in a museum!

Minik talked to the curator for some time and poured out his grief. He asked if it would be difficult to have his father's grave opened to confirm what he had just discovered. The curator could only suggest that he contact the museum's director to discuss the matter.

Minik then described his visit to the director, and it is obvious, although he gave no name, that he was describing the bumbling, confused Hermon Bumpus:

> He lived in a large, fine house. His servant showed me in. The director was a fat man and very friendly. When I told him I wanted to speak with him, he put his arm around my shoulder and ushered me into his sitting-room. We sat down, and he turned to me and asked, "Now, what can I do to help you?" I replied that I wanted to ask him how the museum had acquired the skeleton it had on display of a "Polar Eskimo" named Qisuk. He asked me to wait a few minutes while he went to fetch some books. When he came back in with his books, he asked me, "What was the number of the exhibit?" I answered him, "Exhibit No. 5 in Room 3." He thumbed through the book and finally found the information he was looking for. He read aloud, "Jesup sold it to the museum. It is the skeleton of a Polar Eskimo, Qisuk." Then he turned to me and asked, "Why do you want to know about that?" And I told him, "Because he was my father. He died when I was just a child, and I cried at his graveside as he was buried. I wasn't expecting to see him in the museum!"

The museum director was taken aback. He had also taken Minik for a Japanese. Minik asked him if he thought it would be possible to have his father's grave opened to see what had been buried there. Yes, the director told him, it would probably be possible, but it might be expensive. Did Minik have any money to pay for it? Minik did not, but after some discussion they decided that if the grave proved to be empty then Jesup could be forced to pay all the costs incurred.

When Minik left the director's house, he claimed, he went home to tell William Wallace of his heartbreaking discovery and what he had decided to do. Wallace advised him, however, to do nothing; he thought the effort would be emotionally disturbing and ultimately unsuccessful.

But Minik persisted. He remembered where the burial had occurred, and he went to the spot and had the coffin dug up. Inside were his father's guts and a bit of flesh!

With that discovery, Minik reported to Rosbach, his life in America changed drastically. He left school and the Wallace home and gave up the beliefs he had held. "If Christian people can be such hypocrites," he said, "then I don't need Christianity anymore." He had only one goal in life now—to take revenge on Jesup.

He became a drifter and a ne'er-do-well. One night he and fifteen accomplices dug up all the plants from Jesup's huge garden, put them in cases, and drove them away from Jesup's country estate. He drew up a time sheet purporting to be for the removal of weeds, then plied Jesup's foreman with alcohol and got him so drunk that he signed the sheet. The next day, with his face made up so he would not be recognized, Minik went to Jesup's financial office and had the cashier honor the time sheet. With the money in his pocket he began to leave. Just outside the door he met Jesup himself, but the old man failed to recognize him. Jesup continued in and asked the cashier who the man in the doorway was. He was someone who came in with a time sheet for work the foreman had ordered in the gardens, the cashier told him. Jesup just nodded in Minik's direction. Minik returned his nod—and left.

The next day Minik and his accomplices took all the boxes of plants to a rail freight depot with instructions that Jesup was sending them to a dealer in another city. He even managed to get paid for the delivery job, and Jesup would foot that bill, too.

Soon the newspapers began to mention the swindle that had been perpetrated on Jesup. A reward was promised for the apprehension of the thieves. Minik was even audacious enough to participate in the search himself and would have turned in some of his partners for the reward. Later he met Jesup on two occasions. The last time he met him, he beat him unconscious and stole his wallet and watch.

The fantasy continued. He used Jesup's money to buy alcohol. At that time there was a strong movement in New York against alcohol use—ironically, Jesup was one of the leaders of the movement—and bars had to close at nine o'clock. Naturally, illicit drinking establishments flourished. Minik, by his account, became a regular customer of these grog shops and made many unsavory acquaintances there. One day he and three friends were surprised in a bar after closing hours when police burst in. Minik and his gang tried to escape, but the policemen overpowered them and hauled them off to jail. They could sleep off their drunkenness and appear in court the next morning. But by the next morning they were gone, for during the night they had broken out of jail.

Minik stuck with his three fellow escapees. The others were bigger and stronger, but Minik was the smartest. He became the leader of this small but dangerous band of thieves. They roamed freely, beating up people at will and stealing their property. Minik planned the crimes, and his henchmen carried them out. They stayed in hotels, or in the summer in the open air. And they spent considerable time after hours in the illicit bars of New York City.

Minik and his gang devised a clever scheme whereby they could visit a certain bar after hours without fear of being seen entering the building. At some distance from the bar stood an old hollow tree. Working only at night, under cover of darkness, and with a policeman they had plied with liquor to stand guard, Minik and his band dug a secret tunnel from the tree to the cellar of the bar. Now he and his comrades, with whatever friends they chose to share their secret, could visit the establishment whenever they wished.

One night in 1909, he and his three companions sat drinking in the cellar waiting for the bar upstairs to close. It was only eight o'clock in the evening. Suddenly they heard the sound of scuffling and shouting above them. Minik and his partners rushed up to see two knife-wielding men fighting violently. Minik was carrying a club with him and jumped drunkenly into the fray. He knocked the stronger of the two over the head. The man fell to the floor. The other man pounced on his fallen foe and killed him with a thrust of his knife through the breast. The bar owner had called the police, and suddenly three uniformed officers rushed in, locking the door behind them. But Minik was quick; he broke a window, jumped out to the street, and escaped through the confusion of the crowd that had gathered at the scene.

A few days later Minik's Inuit features graced the front pages of the city's newspapers. He was being sought as a dangerous criminal. A reward had been offered for his capture—dead or alive!

He was alone. His henchmen had been caught and were in jail, along with the shop owner. WANTED posters bearing Minik's likeness were being distributed throughout North America. Minik was an outlaw! He fled the city, traveling only at night and sleeping in the forests during the daytime.

One day he was roused from his sleep by a sharp kick to his foot. He woke to see two strong men standing over him. They asked if he was Minik. He tried to escape, but they seized him and began to tie him. He fought back desperately and managed to grab his club. He struck one of them a fierce blow across the side of the head, knocking him unconscious. He told the other one to stand aside or he would receive the same treatment. The man fled, but he shouted back to Minik that, now that he had found him, Minik would not get away. He would be back for him the following day, and Minik would not be so lucky the next time.

To avoid being followed, Minik changed direction. Avoiding the roads and public places, he traveled for three days and nights without meeting a single person. Finally he approached a small town. That night, when it was dark, he went into the town and found a hotel. Starving, he entered the restaurant. He recalled:

> I was the only one in the dining room. I ordered a cheap meal, and when it came I gulped it down like a hungry wolf. While I

was eating I heard someone walking up to me from behind. I turned and saw a fat, kind-faced lady standing there. I turned away from her. She came closer, tapped me on the shoulder and asked, in a low voice, "Are you Minik?" I said that I was not. But she insisted, "I think you are Minik." Just then we heard footsteps, and she left me quickly. She went to a table in the corner and sat down and ordered coffee. When her coffee was served, she brought it to my table and sat down with me. She started to talk about her husband. He had been traveling for a few years in the Arctic, she said. In fact, he was still away in the north at that time, on an expedition. If I had not already met Peary's wife, I would have thought it was she. As it was, I didn't know who this woman was with whom I was speaking.

She asked, "Weren't you living in New York earlier?" I said that I had not been. But she answered me, "This picture I have is a picture of you. But I am not here to capture you. I have come here to help you. You will understand why later." . . . She gave me money so I could stay overnight in the hotel, and left. When I had finished eating, I took a room and fell into a deep sleep.

Suddenly I was woken from my sleep. Two men were in my room, and they bound me up. They warned me not to make a sound or they would kill me.

They hustled him outside to a waiting car and traveled in silence for some time. Finally they stopped at a train station. Minik thought for certain that they were about to take him back to New York City and to jail; he looked about frantically for a means of escape. But there was none. They took him into a railway car, unbound him, and went out, locking the door securely behind them. After a seemingly endless fifteen minutes, the train began to move.

Minik sat there, alone and helpless, staring blankly out the window as the train sped through the darkness. Suddenly he heard the sound of a key in the door to his compartment. He looked around, hardly knowing what to expect. To his utter surprise, he saw the lady who had befriended him in the hotel. He described what followed:

She was smiling and asked me if I was frightened. I was terrified, but I am a man, and so I replied, "No, I'm not afraid." She closed the door and sat down beside me. She took my hand and began to talk. "At the hotel you didn't recognize me," she said, "but now I have time to tell you. I am the wife of Dr. Cook who is in the Arctic, in your country, on an expedition. Everyone knows how much my husband has been helped up there by the Eskimos. When I read about your escapades in the newspapers, I decided to help you, to show my thanks for what your people have done for my husband. I clipped a picture of you from one of the papers and set out in search of you, and I was lucky to find you."

The train took them to Quebec City, where, Minik claimed, Mrs. Cook lived in a fine house. Is it just a coincidence that, when Minik ran away from New York in the spring of 1909, Chester Beecroft had finally found him in Quebec City? Minik was weaving into this fantasy odd details from real life. But Marie Cook, a tall, thin lady, lived comfortably in Brooklyn while her husband was trying to reach the North Pole. Minik probably had met her at some time during his stay in America. It is also probable that she had played a part in the decision of the Arctic Club of America in early 1909 to take him back to Greenland if the club sent a ship for the relief of Dr. Cook that year.

The incredible story continued. Mrs. Cook had a plan to send Minik back to his people. There was a small ship leaving for the Arctic from Newfoundland, she said, and she had already contacted the captain to arrange discreetly for passage for Minik. The captain had agreed. The only problem would be in getting Minik from Quebec to Newfoundland, for as a fugitive whose face was on WANTED posters throughout the continent, he could not simply go to the dock and board a ship. But Mrs. Cook had solved that problem, too.

He was smuggled aboard the ship in a large wooden box. It was padded on the inside to make it comfortable, and holes had been bored in one side to allow him to breathe. There was even food enough for three days in the box.

The trip to Newfoundland took two days and one night. When the ship docked in St. John's, Minik could feel the box being carried ashore. It was put into a vehicle and driven away from the harbor. Finally it was opened, and Minik stepped out to greet the captain of the vessel that would take him home. The next day he wrote a note of thanks to Mrs. Cook and boarded the little ship that had brought him to Uummannaq.

Here the fantasies had ended, and he was thrown roughly back into a real world he had never known. Physically, he had taken to it well. But emotionally and intellectually, he had turned his thoughts inward during that painful period when he was unable to communicate with his own kin or with Rosbach, his friend. He had blended fact and fancy until he ceased to be Minik, the Inuit boy so misunderstood and hard-done-by in America, ultimately seen aboard ship and exiled back to his native land by the publicity agent of the despised Peary. Instead, he had become Minik, the tough and reckless outlaw, smuggled out of North America with a price on his head.

The Inuit and Rosbach never tired of hearing the stories. Minik told and retold them, embellishing them with each retelling. This gave him some of the attention he had been accustomed to in New York. And with each telling of his imaginary adventures, he longed more and more for America. He had become the true marginal man, condemned to exist in two extremely different cultures and to feel at home in neither.

Peter Freuchen, a master raconteur himself, apparently believed many of Minik's wild fantasies. "In America he had been adopted by very decent people and been given every opportunity," he wrote, "but he was a born good-for-nothing. He felt that rules did not concern him, and laws were made for him to disobey. After countless attempts to get him interested in something—anything—he was given the opportunity to choose a profession. His choice was to steal money and run away. He was apprehended at the Canadian border, sent back to New York, and finally brought home to Greenland. . . . He returned to the north with no property or money—he had been given plenty in America but had spent it all during the trip for liquor and such."

Freuchen carped about Minik's obsession with America: "He believed that the world had been bad for him and blamed others for his lack of character. In America he had longed for Greenland, and now that he was in Greenland he wanted to be back in America."

Freuchen may have had good reason for his disdain for Minik. But he should have known better than to trivialize his longing for America. He should have known that many of Minik's stories were fabrications and that he was emotionally troubled by being torn from his homeland, and then from his adopted homeland, each time to be thrust into a culture so different from that to which he was accustomed. Freuchen should have acknowledged this because he and his wife knew well one other Inuk who had been to America and returned to her people while still a child. This was Eqariusaq, who had accompanied Mrs. Peary south in 1894 and returned the following year. The Americans had dubbed her "Miss Bill." Unlike Uisaakassak and Minik, when Eqariusaq returned to Greenland, she had refused to tell anyone about her trip. When asked, she said only that she could not remember, or did not feel like talking about it.

Once, while on a sled trip bound for one of the distant Danish colonies in a more southerly part of Greenland, Freuchen and Navarana had passed a few days at Cape Seddon with Eqariusaq and her husband, Miteq. Navarana had never been south of Melville Bay and was looking forward eagerly to the trip. One afternoon she and Eqariusaq took a stroll on the ice. Suddenly Eqariusaq turned to Navarana and said, "When you go to the white man's country, be careful not to absorb too much of their spirit. If you do, it will cause you many tears, for you can never rid yourself of it."

When Navarana told Freuchen this, he felt that he finally understood the young woman's reticence to speak of her year in America. "Poor woman!" he wrote. "I understood then that it was a desperate, hopeless longing that stilled her voice."

Freuchen should have known that Minik shared that same hopeless longing, but expressed it in a very different way.

21

The Crocker Land Expedition

In the summer of 1913, Americans returned to northern Greenland. Donald Baxter MacMillan, who had been a young assistant on Peary's last expedition, had felt the magnetism of the Arctic draw him back, as it was to do repeatedly for the rest of his life. An ardent Peary supporter, MacMillan's primary purpose on this expedition he commanded was to "reach, map the coast-line, and explore Crocker Land," a land Peary claimed to have seen far to the northwest of Axel Heiberg Island in the Arctic Ocean. The expedition, poorly organized and even more poorly supported by its sponsor, the American Museum of Natural History, would spend four years in the Arctic and, much to MacMillan's chagrin, disprove the existence of his mentor's fantasy island.

Ice conditions prevented the supply vessel *Erik* from reaching Flagler Bay on the Ellesmere Island coast—where MacMillan had hoped to establish his headquarters—so the supplies, scientists, and support staff of the expedition were dumped at Etah on the Greenland coast, in the protected bay that had been the home of previous Arctic expeditions. They built a large wooden headquarters there and named it Borup Lodge, after George Borup, a young man who, like MacMillan, had been on Peary's final expedition. He would have been on this one, too, but for his accidental drowning before the expedition left America.

MacMillan had first put in at Cape York on the northward voyage to pick up three families of Inuit—Peary's People—and they joined the nineteen men, women, and children who were already camped at Etah when the ship arrived.

Inuit from the surrounding region soon heard of the arrival of the Americans, and many of them headed for Etah as well to offer their services to the expedition. Borup Lodge was thirty-five feet square, and soon after it was completed MacMillan wrote in his journal: "Our home was overcrowded with the bodies of sixty Eskimos, sleeping in our attic, in the carpenter's shop, in the dark-room, under our beds, and under the floor."

Minik was living at Uutaaq's camp in Kangerlussuaq when he heard of the arrival of Naalagapaluk—the little boss—and both men decided to make the trip to Etah. Uutaaq had been one of Peary's most trusted native assistants. He was a natural leader. At five feet eight inches, he was tall for an Inuk. An aquiline nose dominated a round face presenting a stern countenance. "Uutaaq was related to everyone," Peter Freuchen once wrote. Minik, for his part, was overjoyed at the possibility of meeting Americans with whom he could speak English, for he was tiring of the broken English of Freuchen at the post at Uummannaq.

The Americans, aroused by a shout from the Inuit who had seen two sleds approaching, were outside watching the arrival of the two men. Uutaaq began to speak and MacMillan, using his appalling Inuktun, translated for the others. Perhaps MacMillan had not immediately recognized the young man who stood beside Uutaaq. They had met only briefly in 1909. But something triggered recognition, for he finally turned to Minik and asked, "Have you forgotten your English?"

"I guess not," was Minik's answer.

The expedition's members had heard of Minik, of course. They were fascinated by him, an Inuk, but so unlike the Inuit they had been among for the last few months. The expedition doctor, Harrison Hunt, known to all as Hal, thought him "a fine fellow." The Americans thought Minik's fine command of English would be a unique asset for them; he was a strong young man who could double as an interpreter. But MacMillan was not so sure; after all, this was the young man who had had so many unkind things to say in the American press about the great Peary. But he did not hesitate for long. That same day Fitzhugh Green, a handsome twenty-six-year-old naval ensign with a background in geology, meteorology, and navigation, wrote in

his journal, "Mac feels that he will be of great assistance as an interpreter and has told him to stay." Jerome Lee Allen, wireless operator
and electrician, also wrote, "He is invaluable as an interpreter, and in
the preparation for the Crocker Land Trip he will be a great help in
choosing the men to go on the ice, the dogs, etc."

Minik wasted no time in finding some men of the expedition with
whom to speak English. That same day Allen wrote a more lengthy
journal entry:

> Minik Wallace, the English-speaking Eskimo, and Uutaaq,
> arrived today. Minik is an interesting character to us—he has
> talked a great deal and we have learned a great many new things
> about the Eskimos from him. He had mastered the Eskimo
> language and is now as much of an Eskimo as any of them. He
> says he would like to get back to New York, but says also that his
> health was never good there and he doesn't want to stay there
> always. It seems very funny to us to suddenly have this man,
> in appearance no different from the ordinary Eskimo, suddenly
> come to us and talk to us in our own language and with us about
> our own land—for Coney Island is as familiar to him as Etah.

Hal Hunt remarked, "He seems to be in good health and prosper-
ous. He is to stay with us. He talks the Eskimo and English well and
will be a help to us in learning the language."

Minik reported a sick child at Uummannaq, and MacMillan gave
Dr. Hunt permission to go attend it. On December 6 Minik, Uutaaq,
and Hunt left on the three-day trip to North Star Bay. It would be the
first of many trips Hunt would make with Minik. On their arrival,
Dr. Hunt attended to routine medical tasks for the native population;
the following day, by the light from a native lamp, he amputated two
fingers from a hunter who had been injured by an exploding rifle
cartridge. Hunt reported that Minik ably assisted him in this operation by administering ether to the patient. Minik also hunted for
the party. On the fifteenth they were off again for Etah, this time
traveling via Kangerlussuaq, where they spent two days in Uutaaq's

house. It was three times as large as any native home Hunt had yet seen, testimony to Uutaaq's prestige and the prosperity he had gained through the rewards given him by Peary. The party returned to Etah on December 21, the darkest day of the year.

Hunt was impressed with Minik and pleased with his service. Early the following month, he wrote in a letter to his wife, "Last month I took a trip to North Star Bay with Minik Wallace, of whom you have heard, and who proves to be a nice fellow in his native environment. . . . From there we went to Kangerlussuaq. . . . There I stayed with Uutaaq and Iggiannguaq, two north pole men. They are fine fellows and it is with them that Minik lives."

In February, MacMillan left on his futile search for Crocker Land. The advance parties, comprising nineteen men, fifteen sleds, and 165 dogs, had already proceeded to the Canadian coast when MacMillan, with Piugaattoq, an experienced guide and expert hunter, and Minik, left Etah on Friday, February 13. MacMillan professed not to be superstitious, but it was an inauspicious day to begin an expedition, and, as it turned out, it was a false start. Before they had reached Sunrise Point, MacMillan discovered that Minik had forgotten the tobacco and sent him back for it, commenting drily, "Can't discover new land without tobacco."

The weather was bitterly cold. At their first camp, the thermometer registered forty-eight degrees below zero Fahrenheit. As they traveled through Rice Strait behind Pim Island, the wind was so cutting that the men were forced to lie down on their sleds with their faces buried in their furs. Alexandra Fjord was so windswept that there was insufficient snow for a snowhouse, so the three built a fire of their biscuit boxes and slept in their sleeping bags beside it. When they finally reached the advance party in Hayes Fjord, many of the men were sick and the Inuit did not want to go on. Minik spoke with them and reported to MacMillan that they all wanted to return to Etah, feed up the dogs on walrus meat, and try again. Reluctantly, the entire group turned back for Etah.

With a smaller group, the expedition departed Borup Lodge again on March 11. They planned to cross Ellesmere Island via Beitstad Fjord and the awesome glacier that forms its head. When they reached it, MacMillan described it as "an almost vertical wall of ice" and wondered how they were ever to get up it. They slept in a shelter carved in a snowbank at the foot of the glacier; Piugaattoq and another man named Qajuuttaq spent the entire next day cutting steps and handholds in the face of the glacier. The following day the laborious task of hauling the supplies fifty feet up the glacier face began. Ittukusuk, "who simply loved hard work," set the pace when he put a tumpline on his 125-pound sled and started the ascent. He was "our best man . . . clean grit," and "the best Eskimo I ever employed," in MacMillan's words. Elmer Ekblaw, expedition botanist and geologist, described him as "loyal, capable, and energetic." He was about twenty-six years old, only five feet two inches tall, with shoulder-length hair and a ready smile. A crack shot with rifle or slingshot, he was also a top-notch dog driver. Only one other man was able to duplicate Ittukusuk's feat at Beitstad Glacier. Nevertheless, by nightfall four thousand pounds of supplies had been ferried to the top.

That night the Inuit gathered around Piugaattoq, the only man of the party who had ever crossed the glacier, to learn the conditions that faced them on the other side. Minik slept on what he heard. The next morning, instead of climbing the glacier to head west with the rest of the party, he told MacMillan that he was going back to Etah. MacMillan did not try to dissuade him, but in his diary he poured out scorn on him. "I feel that we are well rid of a worthless and useless thing," he wrote, adding that Minik "decided that hard work didn't agree with him so [he] left."

But as Minik rounded a headland almost an hour later, Elmer Ekblaw noticed from the top of the glacier another sled also heading eastward. He called to MacMillan, asking him if he knew that Tautsiannguaq had left for Etah as well. MacMillan did not know it, nor at first would he believe it. He thought Tautsiannguaq was on the glacier, but when a hasty search failed to find him, he had to concede that the man had deserted.

Minik's departure and Tautsiannguaq's desertion put the success, perhaps even the survival, of the expedition in jeopardy, for the two took with them sixteen strong dogs and a large amount of food. The amount of food that could now be drawn by the remaining members of the party was substantially reduced. Their survival would depend on finding game on the west coast of Ellesmere or beyond. That night after supper, "when gossip and tobacco smoke were equally thick," MacMillan learned the reason for Tautsiannguaq's desertion:

> Tautsiannguaq had a pretty wife. Minik certainly thought so; therefore he decided to return to Etah, where he might enjoy her company. Tautsiannguaq, unsuspecting, would go on with me and be absent for several weeks. After Minik had gone, one of the boys whispered into Tautsiannguaq's ear; as a consequence, I lost Tautsiannguaq. He didn't bother to climb the glacier and state his reasons for going. His wife was at stake and off he went.

MacMillan commented in his report that hard work at fifty below zero did not agree with Minik. Perhaps it was the drudgery of expedition work that did not agree. To Minik and to most of the other Inuit, this pushing to the limit of both man and beast to find distant geographic points made no sense. For Minik it had a more personal meaning as well. He had nothing against MacMillan, but the whole exercise reminded him too much of Peary. And MacMillan was wrong in thinking him lazy. The Inuit who knew him are unanimous in their recollection that Minik was, on the contrary, a very active young man who had learned well the skills he needed to survive in his northern home. In fact, he fit well MacMillan's description of the ideal type of sled driver to take along on a lengthy trip. "Young Eskimos for a long and dangerous trip are much to be preferred," MacMillan wrote, "as they are fond of adventure and willing to take a chance."

Minik may have been very lucky that he did turn back. Once the descent to the ice of Bay Fjord had been made safely, MacMillan sent most of the men back to Etah while he and Fitzhugh Green, along with Piugaattoq and Ittukusuk, continued their search for Crocker Land. Had Minik remained with the party, it's likely he would have been asked to go along because of his fluency in English. And he could well have become part of the tragedy that was about to unfold.

Having explored far out on the sea ice for a number of days in the direction where Crocker Land was supposed to be, the party of four men returned to Axel Heiberg Island. MacMillan reluctantly had to admit that Crocker Land did not exist; it had been a mirage. Indeed, a recent history asserts that the expedition's "greatest achievement was subtracting land from the world map."

MacMillan sent Green and Piugaattoq south to explore a portion of the Axel Heiberg coastline that was as yet uncharted. Six days later Green returned—alone. He and Piugaattoq had taken refuge from a storm in a snowhouse. A snowslide had buried Green's sled and killed his dogs. The following day, when the storm worsened, Piugaattoq had insisted on turning back. He forced Green to walk, knowing that the activity was necessary to keep his toes from freezing, as his feet were very wet. Green was on the verge of giving up, but Piugaattoq kept his dogs going at a steady pace. Green complained that he could not keep up, but Piugaattoq, knowing that the pace was imperative for survival, insisted that he follow his trail. Green was inexperienced in dealing with natives and in his nervous despair he misunderstood Piugaattoq's speed and his exhortations to continue the journey back to MacMillan's camp as an attempt to abandon him. Green snatched the rifle from the sled and warned Piugaattoq to keep behind him. When he turned a few minutes later he saw a frightened Piugaattoq whipping the dogs frantically off in another direction. Green reports the rest in a matter-of-fact manner in his journal: "I shot once in the air. He did not stop. I then killed him with a shot through the shoulder and another through the head."

Piugaattoq, a man in his mid-thirties, had been a trusted travel companion of Peary and the man whose wife Peary shared. Knud Rasmussen described him as "a calm and extra-ordinarily sober-minded man, who could not cause dispute or quarrel of any sort." He was "not only a man whom one could trust, but he was a comrade who in difficult or dangerous circumstances was ready to make personal sacrifices in order to help and support his companions." Piugaattoq had tried to save Green's life. Green had taken his.

MacMillan and Green determined to keep the truth from the Inuit. They concocted a story that was half true: There had been a snowslide and Piugaattoq had suffocated under it. But Ittukusuk knew enough English that he understood the truth from the beginning, for he had overheard the distraught Green telling his dismal tale to MacMillan. Ittukusuk told the others on their return to Etah; they should know that these were men easy to anger who must be treated cautiously.

MacMillan and Green never realized that the Inuit knew the truth. And Minik, who could have told them, never did. To him it was just one more example of the cheapness of Inuit life to a white explorer. He wasn't surprised. But it hurt him deeply to reflect on it.

22

On Thin Ice

Although Minik had left the employ of the Americans, he did not stop enjoying their company. Indeed, he relished it because it gave him more opportunity to speak English. And so he traveled and hunted with his fellow Inuit but spent as much time as possible with those members of the expedition who did not confine themselves to Borup Lodge.

In early April he returned to Etah in the company of Peter Freuchen, who was paying his first visit to the Americans. Relations had been strained between the Danes and the Americans, who were both competing for the natives' furs. Minik heard frequent grumblings from some Inuit who thought the Americans miserly, and he often had to defuse potentially volatile situations. Allen, the wireless operator, wrote in his journal about Freuchen's visit: "We cooked up some beans for Minik and Mr. Freuchen, and gave the eskimoes [*sic*] only tea and dog-biscuit. Mr. Freuchen told us that he had overheard Minik sticking up for Mac and the expedition several times . . . and he thinks that Minik wishes the eskimoes [*sic*] to help us and does not think he would try to influence them the other way."

Minik spent the summer of 1914 at Uummannaq, with Elmer Ekblaw and Maurice Tanquary of the expedition. Ekblaw, still recovering from toes badly frozen during the winter, hunted seals with Minik occasionally. Minik proved to be of great assistance to Ekblaw. Freuchen, in whose house the two scientists were staying, had gone bear hunting in Melville Bay, and as Ekblaw said, "Our supplies were gone, the Eskimos were short of meat, and we had no dogs to go out hunting. Had not Minik helped us out by killing occasional seal for us

at this time, we should repeatedly have been hard pressed for food."
Finally Sechmann Rosbach invited Ekblaw and Tanquary to share his
house with him and his family. For the rest of their stay at Uummannaq, the scientists were comfortable.

Ekblaw and Rosbach had a hair-raising experience traveling with
Minik on a spring hunting excursion near Cape Parry. A storm was
approaching from the southwest, and the men were on the ice about
fifteen miles from shore. A telltale pennant of cloud rising above
North Star Bay foretold the storm in a way that no experienced hunter
could mistake. The moment Minik saw it, he yelled to the other two
men to waste no time in leaving.

"We untied our dogs and hitched them to the sledges," wrote
Ekblaw. "We left our tent, our sleeping-bags, our heap of walrus
meat . . . and raced away as fast as our well-fed dogs could carry us."

They raced for North Star Bay for an hour before the crisis arose.
Ekblaw recounted the sudden danger they faced: "Spread black and
threatening before us, a dark lead of new, thin ice stretched across the
whole sound. How wide it was, we could not see in the haze of wind-
driven snow. How thin it was, we could readily see, as our killing-irons
broke through it of their own weight. How far it extended, we could
only guess."

"Our chances were slim in any direction," Ekblaw wrote.

"No use. The ice is too young and thin. We can't make it," said Minik.

Sechmann Rosbach disagreed. "But it's our only chance," he protested.
"The storm is coming fast. . . . We have to try it; we have no other way.
We can only hope that the lead isn't wide and the ice will hold."

Minik acquiesced to the opinion of the older Rosbach. They must
race their dogs and sleds as fast as possible across the thin ice of the
lead, hoping to make the solid ice on the other side without any loss of
dogs, sleds, or men. They must stagger their departures so as not to all
be on the ice at the same time, and they must be spread out to lessen
pressure on the ice and to avoid crossing where the previous team's
crossing may have weakened the ice.

Ekblaw tells the rest of the adventure:

As Sechmann drew his dogs back from the lead for a good
running start, Minik moved along the lead a half hundred yards
and I drew back a little further than Sechmann had done . . . for,
as Sechmann explained, we must not strike the ice at the same
time or near together.

As Sechmann's dogs struck out across the thin ice, they
spread wide apart in the line. Low and swift, with feet wide-
spread, they ran. . . . Beneath the runners of his sledge, the
yielding ice bent down. It rose in a wave-like fold before and
behind.

As Minik's sledge struck the dark band, I saw that, while the
rounded front part of the runners was holding up on the ice
as the dogs sped along, the sharp square corners at the back
were cutting through and little jets of water were spraying up on
either side of the runner.

Ekblaw, the last to make the dash, hoped his sled would hold him,
for he outweighed both Minik and Sechmann by a good fifty pounds.
He wrote:

But my runners were shod a quarter-inch wider, and, though
the ice bent deep under the sledge, this extra width carried my
greater weight.

With my heart in my mouth, scarcely daring to breathe, I sat
rigid, watching the water spraying out from the sides of both
runners. If a dog had stumbled, or bumped into another, to
slow the sledge a moment, we would have dropped through.
But not a dog faltered. Never did my team make such speed.
The first moments were the most perilous. The young ice was
thin, but it was also smooth as glass and we gathered momen-
tum as we raced on. The lead proved to be over half a mile
wide.

As he struck the solid ice, Sechmann gave a wild yell of relief.
Minik gave another as he achieved it a moment later. But, until I
had taken a breath or two, I could not even whisper. To them, it

was an old, oft-repeated adventure. To me—well, I vowed it was my last hazard over such thin ice!

In February 1915 Dr. Hunt traveled to Pitoraarfik to attend to some sick Inuit. Pitoraarfik is a famous gathering point for the Polar Inuit in the late winter of each year as the first light is returning. Open water is not far away, and walrus and bearded seal are plentiful. People from far away traveled there to renew old acquaintances and fill their bellies after the hardships of the winter's dark. Hunt met Minik there, and then accompanied him back to Etah. Minik wanted his job back. He told MacMillan he was "very repentant over his failure of the year before. He urgently requested that he be given another trial." MacMillan took him back.

On April 10 MacMillan accompanied Minik and two others, Torngi and Taliilannguaq, on a hunting trip. The explorer described Minik's part in a walrus hunt over thin ice in a way that indicated that Minik had learned well the tricks of the trade and had become a tough and resourceful hunter, but that even an experienced hunter could make embarrassing mistakes:

> At length a large walrus was discovered asleep on the rapidly moving drift ice some 300 yards away. I thought it was positive suicide to approach him over such a treacherous surface. Yet Minik and Taliilannguaq, without the slightest bit of hesitation made their way from cake to cake, now and then carefully gliding across dark, bending ice, up to within twenty yards of the ponderous, sleeping bulk, and here they were blocked by an impassable stretch of water. We saw them now flat on their breasts with sighted rifles. Two sharp reports were followed by a tremendous splash as the 2,000 pounds of meat disappeared, to be lost beneath the surface.

Not only had they lost the walrus, but the ice they were on had drifted slowly away. There was no way back. MacMillan and Torngi ran along the edge of the fast ice and indicated with frantic gestures a spot through where they thought the two men could make it back to firmer ice. They made it, dripping with perspiration, and breaking through the ice and filling their boots on the very last step.

Yet they did not give up. Within a few minutes a herd of ten walrus appeared on the surface nearby. The Inuit men seized their harpoons; MacMillan grabbed his camera.

"The action began with a swirl," he wrote, "followed by a mass of grim, ugly faces at the very feet of the hunters—so near, in fact, that the men, astounded, were caught unawares, delayed action for a few seconds, and then excitedly hurled their harpoons. The harpoon of Torngi plunged over their heads and backs; that of Minik stopped suddenly in mid-air and fell harmlessly flat down. Torngi, disgusted and ashamed, expressed himself as befitted the occasion. Minik grinned sheepishly upon discovering that he was standing upon a flake of his coil."

The party returned to Pitoraarfik empty-handed after a trip of thirty-six hours.

Undaunted, Minik left shortly afterward with Qajuuttaq and another hunter, Aserpannguaq, in search of musk ox on Ellesmere Island on the opposite side of Smith Sound.

How strange it must have been for him on these trips, when the men whiled away the hours of storm-bound days recounting the tales of their heritage, stories that they had learned from parents and grandparents as they grew to adulthood. Minik had missed out on those carefree years and had nothing to contribute to these smoke-filled hours save fantastic tales of his life in America. But the details of his stories were incomprehensible to his hunting companions, most of whom had never been south of Melville Bay. He was doing his best to learn the traditions of his ancestors now as an adult. Yet one cannot hope to learn in a few years everything that a child takes all his forma-tive years to learn, and these long days, pleasurable though they were, can only have strengthened his sense of rootlessness.

Fitzhugh Green, who fancied himself an artistic soul, had earlier written of Minik, "He wants the south and at the same time admits that he could not live without the ice and snow that gives him life today." He was a "savage boy snatched from his home in the Arctic desert, planted in the blaze of New York life." Green thought that "happiness would always elude him," adding, "It is always so with the wanderer."

Minik was often MacMillan's personal guide. MacMillan liked him, and there was the added advantage that Minik could interpret accurately for him and provide him with information on various subjects that the explorer would otherwise understand imperfectly or not at all.

On a trip between Etah and Neqi in late March 1916, the two became separated from their traveling companions, Ulloriaq and Nukappiannguaq, and were in considerable danger. Neither Minik nor MacMillan knew exactly where they themselves were. MacMillan wrote:

> We hardly knew what to do in our dilemma. To await the men and have them pass unseen would result in our sleeping on the icecap with no sleeping bags—not a warm outlook. There were ominous discomforts and no small amount of danger in going on. A descent by the wrong glacier might result in a drop into one of the numerous intersecting cracks, or we might bring up against a vertical face blocking our course completely.
>
> We went on. The *sastrugi* [wind-carved ridges] cut our path at right angles, and the intervening hollows gave to our sledges the motion of a ship in a heavy sea. I was too much occupied with the antics of my own sledge, and I soon lost Minik as he disappeared in the darkness, stern first, after running over his dogs and capsizing his sledge. He was waiting for me at the bottom of the Clements Markham Glacier, having made record time.
>
> Even here, where sea ice generally exists, there was open water, which forced us to take to the ice-foot along the shore until we were blocked by a projecting buttress. We could plainly see phosphorescence on the surface of the ice, indicative of only a few hours' freezing.

We made tea and ate a piece of chocolate—all we had—under
a shelf of rock. Within an hour the other two men overtook us,
exclaiming that they thought we were back on the glacier.

As we were about to prepare for the night, to my astonishment we saw a light out on the ice. Nukappiannguaq was looking it over with a candle, and he declared it to be perfectly safe.
We drove on at once to Neqi and remained three nights.

In the summer of 1915, a three-masted auxiliary schooner, the *George
B. Cluett*, arrived at Uummannaq. Under charter to the American
Museum of Natural History, she had come to the relief of the Crocker
Land Expedition. The vessel was a floating wreck. Captain Pickles
refused to take her north of Uummannaq, and those who were
due to leave the Arctic that year had to travel from Etah in Peter
Freuchen's motor launch to join the vessel there. But ninety miles out
from Uummannaq, the ship drifted, disabled, into Parker Snow Bay
and was frozen in for the winter. MacMillan described the vessel as
"absolutely unfit for Arctic work."

Equally unfit for Arctic work was one of her passengers. Dr. Otis
Hovey was curator of the museum's Department of Geology and
Invertebrate Paleontology, but he was also chairman of the Crocker
Land Expedition. He had come north for the summer cruise to check
on the expedition and, incidentally, to secure material for a book of
his own on the Arctic. Relations between him and MacMillan had
been severely strained even before the expedition left New York in
1913, and he was generally disliked by everyone he met in the Arctic.
He was aghast at the prospect of overwintering.

He unintentionally insulted Peter Freuchen on first meeting him.
As Freuchen recounted, with his characteristic good humor, "He
asked me what crime I had committed that had banished me to the
Arctic. I was, he said, a fine fellow and ought to be able to find a decent
job somewhere in the outside world, even if I were guilty of a misde-
meanor." Freuchen was even more unflattering, suggesting Hovey
probably was "a mild little man at home," but in the Arctic he was "a

tactless, impolite person" who "whined and expostulated" over every adjustment he was compelled to make because of the misfortune of being stranded so far from home.

Hovey had little regard for the natives. Hunt said he "called the Eskimo savages and treated them with contempt."

Freuchen, as usual, provided more detail:

> He showed me the gifts and trinkets he had brought along to please the natives and to pay them for their favors—empty rifle shells of two different makes, one a little larger than the other so that they would fit together.
>
> "These can be polished and used for needle cases," he said. "Eskimos like to sit about during the winter and polish things to make them shine. They will be delighted with these."
>
> Evidently he had believed, and still did believe, that the natives were anxious to be permitted to give everything away to white men. A needle, he said, was more precious to an Eskimo than a dog. They need only be told what to do, not paid for it.

But even more chilling is another piece of information about this petulant and foolish man, for, if Hovey was at all indicative of the caliber of men employed in responsible positions by the museum at the time, it shows that the museum had learned nothing at all from the tragedy of 1898, when four Polar Inuit had died in New York as a result of Peary's foolishness, with the complicity of the museum, in bringing them there in the first place. Nor had it learned from the sad follow-up to those events, the trauma experienced by a lonely Inuit boy as he grew to manhood in involuntary exile from the homeland from which he had been taken. For Hovey, it seems, made a startling suggestion to another young Polar Inuk, Imiina, with whom he traveled that winter.

The story was recounted to the French anthropologist Jean Malaurie by his friend Kuuttiikittoq in 1950. Kuuttiikittoq had casually remarked to Malaurie in their tent one evening that he could have been very rich if he had wanted to be. "I would have sat on a little chair," he said, "dressed in bearskin pants—my most beautiful *qulittaq*. As Uve [Hovey] used to tell Imiina every time they stopped . . . I would have held a large harpoon in my hand, and all day long well-dressed, perfumed *qallunaat* would have filed by in front of me. I'd have been well paid. *Tollar amerlaqqaat*—bundles of dollars!"

Malaurie thought drily, "Not just a mannequin but a real live display: what a godsend for a natural history museum!"

Kuuttiikittoq continued, "We could all be rich, you see. . . . For the Inuit, *sapinngilaq*, nothing is too hard. But not one of us agreed. That's not fit work for Inuit. . . . And yet, and yet, Piulersuaq certainly managed to drag us down there. How could you say no to such a great leader? Six Eskimos left with him on his big boat. Only two of them ever came back."

But one Inuk did want to go to America. Minik was still longing for New York. The companionship of English-speaking explorers over the past few years had only heightened his desire to return.

One day in 1915, he sat talking for a long time with a few of the Americans who were visiting Uummannaq. When the conversation ended, Minik, obviously pleased, came out and told his friend Rosbach, "Now I am only waiting for passage. Those men in there have already written a letter about me and have received a reply that I can go to America. They have agreed to take me with them when they go." But he had not counted on the *Cluett* being iced in for a winter; his plans were delayed by a year.

Rosbach was happy for him. He felt sure that his young friend would be able to claim his twenty-thousand-dollar baptismal gift immediately upon reaching New York.

When the *Cluett* broke free of the ice in Parker Snow Bay on July 29, 1916, she had few passengers to take south. Hovey had sent a letter out by dog team via Upernavik in the winter, requesting the museum to send up another relief ship. Anticipating that this ship would arrive, he and Ekblaw had refused to sail on the *Cluett*. Even George Comer, the veteran whaling captain who had come north as the *Cluett*'s ice pilot, found her so unsafe that he, too, remained behind. But Minik Wallace was aboard, bound once again for America, this time voluntarily. Hovey was displeased. "I do not approve of the matter at all," he had written earlier.

Peter Freuchen was happy to see Minik go. He wrote in an unpublished note that Minik left "to the sorrow of no-one and with no loss to the Thule Station because he had never delivered anything to our store." Two decades later, he wrote, "The captain made the mistake of taking Minik . . . back with him. We were glad to be rid of him." In the manuscript introduction to a book that he published in 1955, Freuchen described the young man as "our troubled soul, whose mind had been poisoned by living in America for many years, so that he could no longer be happy anywhere." But that description never made it into the book as published. Perhaps, on second thought, Freuchen found it too charitable.

Navarana Freuchen gave birth to her first son a month before Minik left northern Greenland for good. It is not known if Minik saw the boy, who may have been his son, before his departure.

23

Back on Broadway

In March 1911 the US Congress passed an act placing Robert Peary on the retired list of the Corps of Civil Engineers of the Navy with the highest retired pay of the rank of rear admiral. The act also tendered Peary the thanks of Congress for "various alleged Arctic explorations, which he claimed resulted in his reaching the North Pole." With this curious wording Peary, who had been in the navy for twenty-nine years, was simultaneously promoted and retired. He had been on active duty for only twelve years and nine days, and on leave or awaiting orders for the balance of that time, yet he had been on the payroll for all except six months in 1896!

In 1915 Congressman Henry T. Helgesen of North Dakota launched an exhaustive analysis of the evidence that Peary had presented to justify his claim of having reached the Pole. The following year Helgesen spoke extensively in the House of Representatives on the subject, and on July 21, 1916, asserting that "Robert E. Peary's claims to discoveries in the Arctic regions have been proven to rest on fiction and not on geographical facts," he introduced a resolution that the 1911 act be repealed. The resolution further demanded that Peary's name be stricken from the retired list in order to save the taxpayers his stipend of six thousand dollars per year "for services which he never performed" and to ensure that "historic and geographic truth may prevail."

Many who were accustomed to the virulent partisanship that characterized the polar controversy in 1909 assumed that this belated attack on Peary automatically made Helgesen a Cook supporter, but the representative denied it, claiming that he was "not a defender of Cook's claims, but . . . a champion of fair play" who believed simply that Cook was "entitled to a hearing."

Nonetheless, the work of debunking the Peary mystique led Helgesen to become interested in Cook's claim to prior discovery of the Pole, and in August of that year he began to investigate those claims. It was a brief investigation. On September 4 he reported on the subject and concluded with a question rather than a statement: "Is it possible for anyone who gives this matter any thought or study at all to believe that Dr. Cook ever attained or remotely approached the Pole?" Helgesen had, in effect, debunked both explorers' claims.

This was not his final word on the subject, however, for he continued his investigation and delivered another speech in the House, denouncing Cook as a fraud, in December of that year.

On September 21, 1916, in the midst of Helgesen's renewed interest in the polar controversy, Minik Wallace arrived in New York aboard the Red Cross Line steamer *Stephano*, on which he had embarked a few days earlier at St. John's, Newfoundland.

One of the first persons he looked up was an old childhood playmate, John Clark. They had dinner together at Clark's home in Brooklyn, then went for a walk. Clark, five years older than Minik, asked him why he had returned. Minik told him that he realized that the bright lights of Broadway were more appealing than the northern lights.

Minik took a room at the McAlpin Hotel and immediately called a press conference.

He knew that the polar controversy had been big news in 1909. That story had broken shortly after he had arrived back in Greenland, but he had not known about it for almost a year, until the arrival of the sports hunter Harry Whitney in 1910. In subsequent years he had heard much about it. He had heard some of the details from the two Danes at North Star Bay, Peter Freuchen and Knud Rasmussen. Rasmussen had vacillated between pledging support for Cook or for Peary, while Freuchen had been a staunch Peary man from the beginning. But it was Donald MacMillan and the members of the Crocker Land Expedition from whom Minik heard the most detail about the controversy. This had been strongly partisan information, for MacMillan had been with Peary in 1909, and the purpose of his Crocker Land Expedition had been to vindicate Peary's reputation by proving the existence of the land he claimed to have discovered in the polar sea. From the talk he had heard at Etah during his time with the expedition, Minik knew something of the intensity of the controversy that had ensued when Cook and Peary had each claimed the Pole. He assumed, as did many in America, that both explorers had made big money selling the stories of their adventures. Minik thought it was now time that he found a piece of that action.

He told the reporters,

> I've got a big story about Peary and Cook. After I get a lawyer for a manager, you know, the same way as you would open up any show, I'll tell you the price. . . .
>
> One fellow on a Brooklyn paper asked me what I would take for my big story. Just to put him off, I told him a million dollars. He said that he would have to call up his office before he could talk business.

"My information will startle the world," Minik claimed. "I have absolute proof of who discovered the pole."

Of course, Minik had to provide a bit more information than that to entice the newspapers to compete for his story, but he did so with conflicting details:

> No, I don't know who discovered the North Pole. I don't know that it was ever discovered by anybody. What I know is what the Eskimos who accompanied Cook and Peary tell me. They may not be scientists, but they made their observations just the same. For instance, you remember that Peary had four Eskimos with him on the last 180-mile dash to the place where he said, "Here we are—we go no further." I've been living with Uutaaq, Iggiannguaq, Sigluk and Ukkujaaq, who were with Peary. They know just how many days passed during the journey. Wouldn't it be interesting to compare their records with Admiral Peary's proofs of his discovery? I've also talked with Ittukusuk and Aapilak, the men who accompanied Dr. Cook on his expedition in 1908.

"All this information is locked up in here," concluded Minik, tapping his forehead. "Tomorrow, after I see a lawyer, I will be ready to receive offers."

But the game was over. The public's interest in the North Pole controversy had in fact been short-lived. It had peaked in late 1909, while newspapers were still touting the merits of the rival claims, but had waned steadily since. Occasionally there was renewed interest, with hints of new information to be disclosed, but these spates of interest were quickly forgotten. Respectable sums had been paid in 1909 for polar stories, but now, seven years later, there was no interest. Minik waited in vain for the offers that never came.

Minik didn't hear from any newspaper, but he did hear from Ernst C. Rost, a paid lobbyist of Dr. Cook who was promoting the doctor's claims in Washington. Rost misrepresented himself as the secretary to Representative Helgesen and invited Minik to Washington to meet with the congressman to "impart the information he says he obtained from the natives of Greenland regarding the relative merits of the claims of Admiral Peary and Dr. Cook." Rost intimated that Minik should be in Washington the first week in October. But the trip never took place.

On October 24, by which time he had still not received an official invitation, Minik wrote the congressman. He received a reply from Helgesen's real secretary, who informed him that the congressman was in his home state and would not be in the capital until early December. The letter was not encouraging:

> I have no doubt whatever but what the Congressman would be interested to a certain extent in meeting you and hearing your story or any statement you might care to make, but at the same time, there is nothing in the circumstances in the case to warrant you in predicating your future conduct on any interest that Mr. Helgesen might have in your particular version of the Peary-Cook controversy, and I want to assure you that so far as this office is concerned you are perfectly free to make any disposition of any information you have as you deem best for your own interests.

The simple fact was that in 1916 the United States was less interested in Arctic exploration than it was in the war being fought in
Europe. In fact, in that year, the United States formally renounced any
claim it may have had to any part of Greenland at the same time as it
paid Denmark twenty-five million dollars to acquire the Danish West
Indies, since known as the Virgin Islands.

The game was over in another sense. The New York newspapers did
not take the same interest in Minik that they had a decade earlier—for
he was no longer a wronged child but a grown adult. The trauma he
had undergone a decade earlier when he had discovered his father's
skeleton in the American Museum of Natural History had been
largely forgotten by the public.

The newspapers treated him briefly as a minor curiosity. The
Tribune reported that he was "back on Broadway, after spending seven
dark years in the igloos of his tribe," and, in fact, he did appear briefly
in a vaudeville routine, dressed up in Inuit garb. The *Times* reported
the nonsense that, after checking into the McAlpin Hotel, he "took
a bath with a lump of ice in it, donned cool clothing, and inspected
Broadway." Minik told the reporter that the memory of "the igloos
[buildings] of Broadway" had made his evenings somewhat dull in
the snowhouses of northern Greenland.

Down with the flu at the end of October, he nonetheless rallied
and soon agreed to appear in a new show, *Hip-Hip-Hooray*, that had
him on stage offering stereotypical descriptions of northern life that
he thought the audience expected. In late December he appeared
at Carnegie Hall alongside Norwegian explorer Christian Leden,
who had traveled with Inuit through the barren lands of northern
Canada, in a benefit show for the "B.F.B. Permanent Blind Relief
War Fund."

On stage, Minik described his seven years in Greenland:

> I had to learn the language again. . . . I lived as they lived; I
> studied their needs; I tried to find what civilization could do
> for them. My food consisted of walrus, seal and narwal [*sic*]

fat, always boiled over an oil lamp. When I go down to dinner
tonight I may ask for cold blubber just by habit.

Was I satisfied with the crude life there? Yes and no. The
climate suited me, and my health was better than when here.
But the hard, dreary life of the people and the conditions under
which they live are very monotonous to one who knows of the
high state of civilization here.

For my own part, I could have been happy there—but for this.
In fact there were times, and I still have the impression, that it
would have been better for me had I never been brought to civilization and educated. It leaves me between two extremes, where
it would seem that I can get nowhere.

It would have been better if I had never been educated. . . . It's
like rotting in a cellar to go back there after living in a civilized
country.

Minik announced that this trip to New York was only a visit and
that he would eventually go back north. He mused about trying
marriage again. "Of course, I made a hit with the ladies when I first
went back," he claimed, "but I found I couldn't settle down and marry.
You see, I'd been educated."

In thinking that he might try again, he noted that, "You can support
a family cheaply there, and at night there is no place to go but home."

For now, there was no place to go at all. He was in touch with Beecroft
from time to time, and periodically visited William Wallace, who had
never managed to win again the lifestyle he had once enjoyed. Minik
found his foster brother, William Jr., living in Manasquan, New Jersey,
with his wife, Matilda, and two young sons. His friend Harry Radford
had come to a tragic end.

In 1911 Radford had gone again to northern Canada to collect musk
ox and wood bison specimens for American museums. He and a man
named Thomas George Street had pushed far into the central Arctic.
Early in 1912 they were in Bathurst Inlet, and it was there that Inuit
killed both men. When the Royal Canadian Mounted Police finally

investigated the events, they laid no charges, concluding that the killings had been done under severe provocation from Radford, who had viciously whipped an Inuk who had refused to travel because his wife was ill. Radford was well known to the Mounties and surprisingly, in light of his kindly interest in Minik a few years earlier, they noted that it was well known that "he did not get on with natives."

Minik hung about the McAlpin Hotel for much of the fall, awaiting offers that never came for his story of Cook's and Peary's attempts on the Pole. He received a letter from a gentleman who proposed that he and Minik start a trading post in the Thule District in the interest of "assisting the tribe and protecting them from dishonest traders." Nothing came of the scheme except that for a time the pursuit of the idea provided Minik with free lodging at the home of the proponent. During the winter he considered a publishing company's idea for a book about his life, but that project, too, came to naught.

He was in touch with the museum's president, Henry Fairfield Osborn, not to renew efforts to secure the release of his father's body, but rather to request payment of fifty dollars for work he had done for Elmer Ekblaw at North Star Bay. Museum officials noted that he was entirely friendly to the institution. They sent him the requested payment, and Osborn, who felt considerable sympathy for him, wrote a brief memo to a colleague asking, "Can we not find some employment for Minik?"

Minik applied for American citizenship early in 1917 and registered with the military census in June. For a time he used his father's name as a surname, calling himself Minik Qisuk, but on these applications he used his old name of Minik [Mene] Peary Wallace.

He thought that perhaps his citizenship application might not even be necessary, remarking, "I don't know whether I'm on the road to being an American citizen or whether I've been an American citizen right along," noting that Etah is north of where Denmark had jurisdiction in Greenland and "American expeditions 'put Etah on the map' as you would say here." Presumably Minik did not know that the United States had renounced any claim to Greenland only five days before he signed his application.

He took work for a time in a machine shop, but he once again felt the urge to return north, although, again, there was no way to get there. He expressed an interest in going to Alaska, where he knew there were Inuit like himself. In May 1917 he secured an introduction to the manager of the Alaska Mines Corporation in Nome, but he never made the trip.

On his peripatetic travels, he visited Hal Hunt, his old friend from the Crocker Land Expedition, in Bangor, Maine. Minik had gotten along well with the doctor on the expedition, and traveled often with him. No doubt they had many memories to share.

Minik received a letter from a woman who had been his first nurse in America, in the Wallace home so many years before. This was Lizzie, who had taught him to say his prayers each night. In June 1917 he went to Pennsylvania to pay her a short visit. She saw a handsome man in his late twenties. At five feet six inches, he was average in height, and at 155 pounds a sturdy and employable individual. But he was restless and rootless. Most of the time he drifted, from one odd job to another, from one city to another.

The fears that had been expressed by a reporter, more perceptive than most, just before he had returned to the Arctic, had been realized, and now, "neither fish nor fowl, no longer a simple Eskimo and yet not a complicated Yankee, he was more than ever alone."

His wanderlust took him to Boston in late 1917, and there he sought work through a local employment agency.

24

The North Country

The northwestern corner of the state of New Hampshire has had a turbulent and somewhat ridiculous history. Its troubles began with the Treaty of Paris in 1783, an agreement that drew the border between the new United States and Canada along the Connecticut River. The only problem was that, in the absence of surveys, nobody was quite sure where the head of that river was. In 1789 New Hampshire sent a Colonel Jeremiah Eames to survey the boundary.

Unfortunately, Eames was a scoundrel—he drew the border along a more westerly waterway, Halls Stream, and then bought all the land between it and the Connecticut River for himself from an Abenaki Indian chief, in return for the promise that the chief and his two wives would be fed and clothed for the rest of their lives. Three years later the governor of Lower Canada refused to recognize Halls Stream as the border and began to survey Eames's stolen territory, naming it Drayton Township. The Canadian authorities invited settlers in and gave land grants to homesteaders.

Settlers drifted in, along with renegades and fugitives of every stripe. The area was as remote from the governing authorities in Sherbrooke, Canada, as it was from those in Lancaster, New Hampshire, and for a time it mattered little to the pioneers who were carving homesteads out of the wilderness that two countries claimed the territory. In 1819 Canada offered to settle the dispute by agreeing on a boundary along the Indian Stream, which wanders right through the middle of the territory. The United States refused, however, and the dispute was submitted to the king of the Netherlands for arbitration. In 1831 the Dutch king upheld the Treaty of Paris and decreed that the boundary should follow the Connecticut River, but the US Senate refused, by a vote of twenty-three to twenty-two, to abide by his decision. In the meantime, the efforts of both countries to tax the disputed area's few inhabitants were becoming intolerable.

There were few enough inhabitants in the territory—the total population was about a hundred. In 1832 they made a dramatic move to settle the dispute themselves—by a vote of fifty-six to three they declared themselves an independent republic under the name of United Inhabitants of Indian Stream. They adopted a constitution and drew up a bill of rights, which established freedom of religion and the right to life, liberty, and property. Every male inhabitant over the age of twenty-one was to be a member of the General Assembly. Taxes were levied and a forty-man reserve army created. Three judges were appointed, as well as a sheriff. Since he had no jail, the sheriff kept his prisoners one at a time in a seven-hundred-pound potash kettle turned upside down over a flat rock.

Of course neither Canada nor the United States recognized this upstart republic, but it took three years for either of them to do anything about it. A series of arrests and attempted arrests by both Canadian and American authorities finally resulted in an armed invasion of the Indian Stream Republic by the New Hampshire militia in November 1835. One key individual was jailed, and others fled to Canada. The president, Luther Parker, quietly packed his wagon and emigrated with his family to Wisconsin. The Indian Stream Republic had been conquered. Or so it seemed. But then the General Assembly of the republic met for one final session. It realized that the New Hampshire militia was firmly in control; the militia force, however small, was half the size of the republic's entire population! The proud members of the assembly passed a series of resolutions that legislated an end to their four-year-old republic, surely the only country in the world ever to legislate itself out of existence.

The area became Pittsburg Township in the state of New Hampshire. The old-time families there call it and its surroundings simply the North Country.

By the turn of the century, the Connecticut Valley Lumber Company had become the dominant industry in northern New Hampshire. The company, too, had an unusual beginning: A New York banker had gained the timberland of the Connecticut Lakes region as payment for a debt. From that unexpected start, he built an empire that came to dominate commerce there.

Pittsburg, the largest town in this sparsely populated area, was a farming community. But this was a rugged and mountainous part of the state in which to eke out a living from the soil. Lumbering was a godsend to the local farmers, for lumbering meant winter work. There was not much to do on the farms in winter anyway; with the crops in and the winter hay stored, the farmers took to the woods, leaving the women at home to attend to the milking and routine chores.

The lumber industry's need for manpower in the harsh winter months was such that local labor could not meet the entire demand. Workers had to be imported from out of state. Many were inexperienced men who had never held an ax before. Connecticut Valley Lumber recruited them through a Boston employment agency.

In the fall of 1917 Minik Wallace stepped off a train in North Stratford, New Hampshire, bound for Pittsburg. The Boston employment agency had paid for his ticket; its cost would be deducted over the course of the winter from his salary of fifty cents per day. Bill Buck's livery stable in nearby Canaan, Vermont, provided the only transportation to Pittsburg, in an open wagon. Many of the workers arrived so ill clad and poorly prepared for winter in the mountains that they had to run behind the team much of the distance into Pittsburg just to keep warm. The lumber company maintained a large bunkhouse that was home to these out-of-state recruits. For a time this was Minik's new home.

Life here was different from anything Minik had ever known. The lumbering crews were a mixed bag of French Canadians, Poles, Finns, Swedes, and local Yankees, and among them were a fair sampling of misfits, rejects, and the plain unfortunate. Minik was not a freak here, unless they were all freaks together. No one was going to pander to him. These were tough men, hard workers earning a living here in a hard industry. Those from out of state had all had their share of life's ups and downs, or they wouldn't have ended up here in the first place.

Here in Pittsburg, Minik determined to make a new start. Here there would be none of the bravado of his earlier days in New York. His fellow lumberjacks were, like him, mostly young, single, and self-reliant. Ironically, he spoke English much better than many of them. He did his best to fit in, and for the first time in his life he succeeded. The people of Pittsburg thought him a good worker and a genuinely "nice fellow to have around."

The work was hard. In this mountain environment the winters were long and harsh. It wasn't as dark as the sunless winter months of northern Greenland, but it could be just as cold. While the ground was frozen the workers felled trees and carved slick roads out of the forests to skid the trees to the riverbanks to await the spring runoff and the log drives downriver to the mills.

The novice in the lumber camps started as a swamper, clearing brush from the swamps in preparation for the construction of the slick roads. The next position in the hierarchy of jobs was that of chopper, followed by scaler, a man who had to be expert at estimating the board feet or cords in a log. Minik learned quickly during his winter in Pittsburg, for he reached the position of scaler.

He soon tired of living in the company bunkhouse. It was not that he disliked any of his colleagues; quite the contrary—he liked them and the feeling was mutual. But they were a noisy and rowdy bunch, and Minik had put noisiness and rowdiness behind him in New York before embarking for this new world. He would rather spend his evenings reading and working sporadically on the autobiography he had promised a New York publisher. So he built himself a tiny shack up across from the little cemetery where the bodies of unclaimed river drivers were buried. Here he could be alone and keep his books. Nobody minded. As long as he was at the work site when work was to be done, a man could be excused for his eccentricities.

To the taciturn natives of northern New Hampshire, early spring is "mud season." The lumber camps closed down then. Those who were not needed for the river drives were let go, to find whatever work they might back in the cities. But Minik didn't board the train in

North Stratford in the spring of 1918 for the long journey back to the prison of an American city; during the winter he had made a strong friendship with a local farmer.

His name was Afton Hall and he was just a few years older than Minik. Quiet and reserved, like Minik he was a logger. He was single and lived with his father and mother in a tidy frame house in rural Clarksville, high on a hill overlooking the Connecticut River and Pittsburg. Afton Hall, like his father, Fred, his brother, Barney, and all the other farmers in the area, worked for Connecticut Valley Lumber in the winter. Minik had met Afton in the lumber camp. When mud season brought the winter's work to an inglorious end, Afton had invited the Inuk to come and live with the Hall family. Minik spent the rest of the spring, the summer, and the early fall with them. He helped about the farm, taking his part in the planting and the harvest, as well as the milking and the routine chores. The Halls were poor folk and had nothing to offer him except their hospitality. That was enough for Minik. He was content to work for his room and board.

He loved it there. It was the happiest period of his adulthood and the most peaceful time he had experienced since leaving Lawyersville in 1904. Physically, the area reminded him of Lawyersville. Both were mountainous, and both were farming country. But here in Pittsburg, he was no one special. He was not the adopted Inuit son of a seemingly wealthy local businessman and philanthropist, shown off as a curiosity at the agricultural fair and made to sing his native songs in the local Sunday school. Nor was he the wronged Inuit boy that he had been a few years later in New York City, suffering the trauma of finding that his father's skeleton was on display in the American Museum of Natural History and being pandered to by the press in search of sensational copy. Here he was virtually anonymous, and he was content to have it that way. He seldom even went into town. He preferred to remain on the farm and spend his free time wandering the hills, valleys, and riverbanks of the surrounding countryside.

He felt a part of the Hall family, and they were content to have him. The independent, old-time families of the North Country are a reserved lot, and it is difficult—some say impossible—for an outsider to penetrate their shell of reticence. But with the Halls, Minik succeeded. As one longtime resident put it, "It's hard for them to take a stranger into their hearts. If he hadn't been a good worker, he wouldn't have kept a job here long." He told Afton that he never wanted to leave. That was fine with Afton and his parents. Minik was welcome to stay.

But like the youthful idyll of life in Lawyersville, this experience was too good to last. In the fall of 1918, just as the men had returned to lumbering, the Spanish flu swept the camps, as it swept the world. In the close confines of the company bunkhouse, it wrought havoc. The sick from the camps were brought in and laid out on the bunkhouse floor, each with his own blanket. A doctor came once a day, earning a dollar per visit, to remove the dead and do what he could for the living. The dead were buried immediately; those with no identification were interred in a common grave. But Minik Wallace was not among those.

The flu hit him hard. But Afton Hall would not hear of him suffering his illness in the common bunkhouse. Afton took him to the Hall home, where both his own parents were already down with the flu. There Afton nursed him, but to no avail. On October 29, after a short illness, Minik died of bronchial pneumonia.

In December, James Beecroft of New York City received a letter from Afton Hall:

> I am asking a favor of you which I feel sure you will grant. I would like to get into communication with Mr. William Wallace that I might inform him of the death of Minik at my home October 29 of pneumonia following influenza. Although everything possible [was done] that the best physicians could do, the fight seemed against him from the start, and he only lived seven days. The doctors said he must be buried at once, so I had him interned [sic] in the cemetery here. He often spoke of you and your brother, and of all the people I heard him speak of, yours was the only address I found among his papers.

Our home was a regular hospital for six weeks; my father and Minik had pneumonia and my mother and myself were down with the influenza. We had a hospital nurse and a doctor in daily attendance most of the time. My father is just up around the house, and I wish poor Minik was also. Any information you can give me or, better still, if you could have Mr. Wallace communicate with me, I will try and supply any information he will wish to know.

Minik was buried in the little cemetery on the banks of the Indian Stream on October 30, 1918. His grave, covered with a small stone placed there by the Hall family, is on a knoll overlooking a bend in the slow-moving, meandering stream. In a remote corner of the state that boasts the motto "Live Free or Die," the man without a country found his final resting place, here in the no-man's-land of the Indian Stream Republic, the country that could never be.

They still remember Minik in Pittsburg, not for the sadness or excitement with which his short and tragic life was filled, but simply because, in the words of a local historian, "he was a nice guy and everybody liked him."

25

"They Have Come Home"

The American Museum of Natural History was embarrassed. It had succeeded in covering up the story of Minik and its treatment of the remains of Qisuk and his fellow Inuit for the better part of a century. Then, with the first publication of this story in 1986, under the title *Give Me My Father's Body: The Life of Minik, the New York Eskimo*, the story had come back to haunt the institution. But public attention wanes, and Qisuk's bones continued to lie in a box in the museum under accession number 99/3610, alongside those of Nuktaq, Atangana, and Aviaq. Minik's desire to have his father's remains released from the museum and properly buried went unrealized. From time to time, representations were made to the museum to have the bones released, but to no avail. And the museum continued to lie, when necessary, to deny its part in the whole sordid affair. At one point following publication, a politician from Greenland, Aqqaluk Lynge, while visiting in New York, contacted the museum about the matter. "I asked about Qisuk," he said. "The museum told me they didn't know anything about that story. I didn't know what to do. I wasn't really sure they [the bones] were there."

I had long felt that, if the museum were ever to release the remains, the proper place for Qisuk to rest would be beside his son in the peaceful Indian Stream Cemetery. This was the area where Minik had found true happiness with his friend Afton Hall, and Hall's relatives, in the northern mountains of New Hampshire. Elderly members of the Hall family still remembered Minik and tended his grave. They remembered Afton's stories of Minik with fondness. Were Qisuk to be buried beside Minik, father and son could pass together into eternity, as they had passed together into legend. As for the other Inuit, they should be returned to northern Greenland for burial if that were the wish of the community there. But the museum would not hear of my suggestion. I was not a relative of the deceased or an official of a government responsible for the deceased. I was merely the author who had embarrassed them. The museum's position was that the bones should remain in the museum.

Then, in 1992, two reporters rediscovered *Give Me My Father's Body*. They were Miro Cernetig of Toronto's *The Globe and Mail* and William Claiborne of *The Washington Post*. Both interviewed me and wrote articles that were prominently featured in their newspapers. Once again, ninety-five years after six Inuit had first been brought to New York, the museum was embarrassed. And once again came the demands for the bones of Qisuk and his countrymen to be released from the museum and properly buried. A request came from as far away as Saudi Arabia, where William Wallace's great-granddaughter Wendy Wallace was working. Stating that she was a relative, through adoption, of Minik, she felt she had a legitimate interest in seeing his father buried, and she, too, requested that he be buried in the Indian Stream Cemetery in Pittsburg, New Hampshire, beside his son. But we both agreed that if the museum refused to consider that location, it would be appropriate for the remains of all four Inuit to be transported to Greenland for burial. Better that than that they should continue to languish in the museum.

This time the interest in having the bones removed from the museum remained high. Since 1986, things had changed in the conservative world of American museums. Native Americans had made progress in forcing museums to deal appropriately with the remains of their ancestors.

In 1990 the Native American Grave and Burial Protection Act was passed. Under that legislation, American museums are required to return skeletal remains to native groups that request them and have a valid claim on them. Qisuk and the other Polar Inuit, however, were not covered by this legislation. They were Greenlanders, not Americans, and the American Museum of Natural History was under no obligation to send their bones to Greenland or anywhere else for burial.

But the museum authorities had had enough. In the summer of 1992, they decided to lay the story to rest once and for all and quietly dispatched their agents to Qaanaaq, the main community of the Polar Inuit today and the administrative center of Avanersuup Kommunia (the regional municipality), to meet with the local council. Jørgen Melgaard, an esteemed archaeologist with the National Museum of Denmark, and Edmund Carpenter, a retired American anthropologist, brought a simple message to the community: Ask the American Museum of Natural History for the remains to be returned for burial, and the museum will comply with your request. Bureaucracy works no faster in Greenland than it does elsewhere, and it was not until well into 1993 that the request was officially made. It was a request for the remains of all four Inuit to be returned to Qaanaaq for interment.

I contacted Wendy Wallace to advise her. She was delighted, as I was, that the episode begun so long ago, one in which her great-grandfather had played such a major role, would at last come to an appropriate end.

On July 28, 1993, the bones of the four Polar Inuit were loaded aboard an American military transport aircraft at McGuire Air Force Base in New Jersey and transported to Thule Air Base in northern Greenland. The journey that had taken over a month in 1897 was accomplished in a few short hours. At Thule the cargo was transferred to a Greenlandair helicopter for the trip to Qaanaaq, less than an hour away.

Officialdom almost had one last surprise for the souls of the four returning Inuit. The Lutheran Church, the state church of Greenland and Denmark, had initially decided that, because the Inuit were pagans and unbaptized, they could not be buried in a Christian ceremony. That decision, however, was quickly reconsidered, and the bodies were received at the small church in Qaanaaq. Torben Diklev, curator of the community's museum, looked after the logistics of the ceremony.

Perhaps a Christian burial is not what the Inuit would have wanted after all. One should remember that Atangana, before her death in New York, had stated that she did not want to be buried under the sand and wanted no coffin. Nor did she want the stones to be placed too closely together, for fear that she might not breathe. Nonetheless, the burial of all four was carried out in the modern Christian manner.

On August 1 the bodies, each in its own small casket, were placed in a common grave in hallowed ground on a hillside with a splendid view of the sea to the west. Rocks were piled on top of the grave in the traditional manner. In the presence of about one hundred local residents, a brief service was held at the graveside. Three people spoke: the priest, Hans Johan Lennert; the mayor of the community, August Eipe; and Edmund Carpenter, representing the American Museum of Natural History. A number of Polar Inuit were in attendance, along with Emil Rosing, director of the National Museum of Greenland, and Jørgen Melgaard, from Denmark.

The service, and the printed remarks and press release that resulted from it, were carefully orchestrated by Edmund Carpenter and the American Museum of Natural History to secure maximum credit for themselves. The press release noted: "In recent years, Avanersuup Kommunia and the American Museum of Natural History have been working to repatriate the skeletons to the location from which they set out while still alive. The initiative was taken by the Americans themselves. Prime movers and couriers were Mr. and Mrs. Carpenter."

Mayor August Eipe referred to "the long-sought final resting place of our ancestors Qisuk, Nuktaq, Atangana and Aviaq." He noted that they had "against their will, helped to write our history."

The vicar, Hans Johan Lennert, observing that "life was not kind to these people," explained, "When it became known that the dead had not been laid to rest, many questions came up. Today the answer is that they shall be allowed to rest in the spirit of God." He also remarked,

"Through their life stories . . . we have gained great knowledge and understanding of many things."

His words presaged the peculiar remarks of Edmund Carpenter, who described the four dead Inuit as volunteers in a noble quest for knowledge:

> Museums of natural history were founded on the belief that all life belongs to a common order subject to common principles. There is the further belief that science can contribute to human betterment. To this end, scientists gather information from many lands.
>
> It was in this spirit that citizens from this area visited New York nearly a century ago. There they contributed details of their customs and beliefs to this grand pursuit of knowledge. They did not live to know the importance of their contribution, but we do, and it should not be forgotten.

"Visited"? "Contributed"? These were not the sentiments that the mayor had just expressed on behalf of the community of Qaanaaq.

Carpenter, a wealthy patron of the museum, was a pushy man, and accustomed to using his wife's considerable fortune to buy his way into situations that fed his enormous ego. So it was completely in character that he would publish an article four years later that denigrated *Give Me My Father's Body*, the book that had embarrassed the museum into finally ridding itself of the skeletal remains. Perhaps he had forgotten the personal note he had sent me in 1987 congratulating me on its publication. In 1997 he restated the contribution that Qisuk and his fellow deceased had made to science. Describing them as "ethnographic and linguistic informants"—again implying that they had traveled to New York voluntarily—he noted, "Their bodies were measured and cast. When four died, their skeletons were measured. An autopsy was performed on one. . . . These findings helped Boas challenge racism."

He continued, "The one good thing that came out of this sad tale went unmentioned in any press account I read. Boas and Hrdlička rejected the theory, beloved by racists, that various tribal peoples were arrested at different evolutionary stages. Knowledge gained from these six Polar Eskimos challenged that belief."

For Carpenter, then, it was all right. The ends justified the means. Four Inuit died agonizing, unnecessary deaths, but science—perhaps all of mankind—benefited, and to him that justified the unwilling sacrifice they made.

A plaque was provided for eventual erection at the grave site. It began with the terse statement, NUNAMINGNUT UTEQIHUT, which translates simply as "They have come home." This statement is followed by the names of the four Inuit, with details of their births and deaths and the statement 1897 NEW YORK-IMUT, 1993 QAANAAMUT.

On August 4, 1997, one hundred years after Qisuk, Nuktaq, Atangana, and Aviaq left the Thule District for New York aboard the *Hope*, and four years after the return of their remains to Greenland and their burial in the graveyard at Qaanaq, the memorial plaque was finally placed over their common grave. Queen Margrethe of Denmark and her husband, Prince Henrik, attended its unveiling in a touching ceremony presided over by the mayor, Lars Jeremiassen, who spoke of the community's wish to honor their forefathers who loved their living and grieved their dead.

Among the Polar Inuit there was a profound sense of relief that the events that began over one hundred years ago had finally reached a conclusion. As my research into the story of Minik and his fellow "New York Eskimos" proceeded, many Inuit followed the narrative with fascination. In Qaanaaq people would question me about the story, about the fate of Minik, and about the four unfortunate souls who had succumbed to disease so soon after their arrival in Peary's land.

To the elders of the community, Minik's adventurous life had taken on the character of legend. When he left the district, World War I was raging. He had told some of the Inuit that he intended to become a fighter pilot and fight in that war. They didn't doubt he would try—he had had so many fascinating adventures already. And so, some said, he had gone back to America, become a skilled pilot, and died a hero's death in a spectacular crash after being shot down by the enemy. For others he had returned to America, collected his baptismal gift—the amount had fluctuated wildly in their recollections and their imaginations—and lived a long and respectable life. He spoke the language of the Americans so well and he had proved, by the way he had become such a skilled hunter in his seven years back home in the Arctic, that he could adapt to almost any circumstances. But to most of the Inuit, he had simply disappeared. They talked about him from time to time, recalling his adventures and the ultimate sadness of his life, but no one was sure until 1979 what had been his final fate.

In 1977 I married Navarana, a Polar Inuk who had been named for Peter Freuchen's wife. Two years later, with my mother-in-law, Amaunnalik, named for Minik's maternal aunt, we visited New Hampshire. I had become fascinated by the fragmented and contradictory details of Minik's life that I had heard recounted in Greenland, and we were in search of Minik. On a warm spring afternoon, we found him in the quietness of the Indian Stream Cemetery.

Amaunnalik had been born in 1907. As a little girl, she had known Minik and seen him often on his travels about the district. Uutaaq, with whom Minik lived and traveled, was her uncle. She had heard Minik's stories, and after he left the district she listened to the tales her elders told as Minik passed slowly into myth. She had tears in her eyes, as did we all, as we stood beside the inconspicuous grave. What had finally become of Minik would be a mystery no more to the Polar Inuit.

In Qaanaaq there was tremendous interest when Amaunnalik, Navarana, and I reported our finding of Minik's simple grave marker; and a feeling grew that Minik's fondest wish should be realized and that Qisuk, along with the other Inuit, should be properly buried. The American Museum of Natural History finally complied with the people's request, and with common sense, and the Inuit were given the burial they so long deserved.

I am often asked: Should Minik's body be disinterred and taken also to Qaanaaq for reburial? The answer must be an unequivocal no.

Minik lived a tortured and lonely life. Out of place in New York, he felt no more at home when he returned to northern Greenland. In the fall of 1917 he arrived in northern New Hampshire, where he died one year later. The Hall family were perhaps the truest friends he ever had. Minik died among friends. Let him remain there.

EPILOGUE

Robert Peary died in 1920 at the age of sixty-three, embittered over the vicious controversy surrounding the discovery of the North Pole, a dispute that he felt had robbed him of deserved glory. The rival claimant to the Pole, Frederick Cook, died in 1940, at the age of seventy-five. The controversy has never been resolved. Herbert L. Bridgman died in 1924, at age eighty. Active to the very end, he died of a heart attack aboard the New York State School ship, *Newport*, in the mid-Atlantic while returning from a European cruise.

Franz Boas, Alfred Kroeber, and Aleš Hrdlička went on to distinguished careers in anthropology. Boas was the most influential anthropologist of his time.

Knud Rasmussen succeeded in his long-held dream of a sled trip through the Canadian Arctic and Alaska to the Bering Strait. The trip, known as the Fifth Thule Expedition, was the triumph of his distinguished career. He died in Denmark in 1933. His lifelong friend Peter Freuchen ran the Thule Station until 1920. He participated in the Fifth Thule Expedition and went on to become a prolific writer and well-known lecturer, usually on Arctic subjects. He died in Alaska in 1957. His body was cremated and his ashes scattered over his beloved Thule Mountain.

Arnannguaq continued to live with Peter Freuchen and Navarana for some time after her separation from Minik. Eventually she married a hunter, Ittullak, with whom she had two children. Her love of sleep made her a poor wife for a hunter, and she and Ittullak eventually separated. She then married Aaqqioq, and they both accompanied Rasmussen on the Fifth Thule Expedition. Aaqqioq subsequently accompanied a German explorer, Hans Krueger, on an expedition into the Canadian Arctic, from which neither man returned. Aaqqioq was presumed dead. Later Arnannguaq married another man, Qaerngaaq; she died at Uummannaq in the mid 1940s.

Navarana Freuchen, like so many Inuit, died an early death from influenza in 1921 at Upernavik, Greenland. Her husband buried her himself—the local priest would not consent to her burial in the churchyard, for she was unbaptized. Her son, Meqqusaaq, whose father may well have been Minik, was handicapped and unable to live the life of a hunter. He lived with relatives in Greenland until 1939, when he moved to Denmark, where he died in 1962. To Peter Freuchen, he was always his son.

William Wallace never recovered from his financial setbacks. He drifted from job to job and from one address to another in New York City and East Orange. His disgrace at the American Museum of Natural History dogged him for the rest of his life; in 1940 he was described as being "in bad shape physically and financially" and as having "comingled the funds of the Museum with his personal funds." He died penniless in November 1941 in Greystone Park, a home for the mentally ill in Parsippany, New Jersey. He was eighty-six years of age and senile. He and his son had not gotten along well for many years, and although William Jr. was living at the time near New York City, as were his own two sons, then married and with families of their own, no one claimed the body, and William Wallace was given a pauper's funeral at the expense of the state. In the spring of the following year, a longtime friend of the family, Florence Padula, had the body disinterred and moved to the family plot in the Cobleskill Rural Cemetery in Cobleskill, New York. Pamela Wallace died in East Orange, New Jersey, in March 1937, and is also buried in the Wallace plot in Cobleskill.

William Wallace Jr. had left home while still in his teens. As a young man, he was a race-car driver. Later he became a chauffeur for the Kohler family, of piano manufacturing fame; he and his wife lived in a house on the Kohler estate in Mahwah, New Jersey. He died in 1955 in Suffern, New York.

Chester Beecroft lived a varied life. The former child actor went on to be a screenwriter and film producer. His dream was to turn Tampa, Florida, into a movie location to rival Hollywood, but he was unsuccessful. For a time he was a war correspondent; he also worked as quartermaster on round-the-world cruise ships. He and his wife were childless. He died in 1959.

Afton Hall was married briefly. He died in 1969 at the age of eighty-three and is buried a few yards from Minik in the Indian Stream Cemetery. After his death, his nephew, Howard Young, purchased a small stone marker bearing Minik's name and had it placed over the grave of Hall's Inuit friend. Young felt that, with Afton gone, Minik's grave would eventually be forgotten if were not marked.

Sechmann Rosbach left Thule in September 1915, about a year before Minik's departure. He moved to Godhavn in Disko Bay where, a few years later, he met Peter Pedersen, captain of Knud Rasmussen's ship, and learned from him that Minik had returned to America. He later heard, erroneously, that Minik had collected his twenty thousand dollars and had been doing quite well for himself when suddenly he had taken ill and died.

In 1934 Rosbach published a short account of Minik's life in *Avangnaamioq*, a small Greenlandic regional newspaper. Most of the account told of Minik's fictitious adventures in America, which Rosbach had taken as fact. Rosbach's story was accepted as true for many years after its publication. In 1982 it was reprinted in its entirety in Greenland's national newspaper, *Atuagagdliutit*, to fool a whole new generation of Greenlandic readers. The editor of that paper, Jørgen Fleischer, then used the article as his sole source for a chapter on Minik in a book published in 1983 in Danish and Greenlandic, and that chapter was translated into English and published in *Arctic Policy Review*, the organ of the Inuit Circumpolar Conference.

At the end of the account Rosbach speculated on what might have become of Minik's money after his death. It had been a large sum and, he suggested, most of it must still be there, somewhere, in America. He ventured a simple and touching suggestion. In those years, he wrote, there was never enough money to build proper houses for the people of the far north, the Inuit he remembered with such fondness. Perhaps, if Minik's money could be found, it could be used to build houses for his people. In that way, could not this unimportant Inuk, about whom no one had cared very much in his life, be of real assistance to his people in the end?

It was a naive hope. There was no money. There never had been. There was only a humble grave forgotten in a quiet rural cemetery to remind anyone that there had ever been a Minik.

The American Museum of Natural History bore a continuing shame and sense of guilt over its role in the tragic events that surrounded Minik's life in New York. In 1950 a high-school student, Ruth Sturm, wrote the museum from Cobleskill; she was preparing an essay on the Inuit who had once lived in the area, and she requested information from the museum's files to help her in the project. The museum's vice director wrote her a kind letter, advising her that the institution's files on the subject were sketchy but suggesting that she might contact George Pindar, retired registrar of the museum, who, by coincidence, lived in Sharon Springs, a town neighboring Cobleskill, and whose recollection of the events would be clear and helpful. On the same day the vice director wrote to Mr. Pindar as well, suggesting that, if the student approached him, he should not give her any details of the incident but should instead try to dissuade her from pressing the inquiry further.

Another inquirer was given similar treatment in 1963 after museum staff concluded that the incidents had placed the museum in a bad light and no good could come from bringing them all before the public again.

In the interim, however, a member of the museum's own staff, Dr. Robert Cushman Murphy, had published an article on Minik and his father. Called "Skeleton in the Museum Closet," it is by far the most tasteless and offensive article to appear on Minik. The article made light of the problems that had been created through the museum's acquisition of Qisuk's skeleton. Wrong in most of its details, it ends with the ludicrous statement that, after a lifetime of attempts to get the release of his father's bones, Minik's own skeleton ended up in the box next to his father's. That the article did not create embarrassment for the museum is probably due only to the fact that it appeared in the *Peruvian Times*.

In the early 1980s, while researching this story, I made an appointment to use the archives of the Explorers Club in New York City. I arrived at the appointed time and was met by the archivist-librarian, Janet Baldwin, who informed me that, before I could proceed with my research, the chairman of the Archives Committee had some questions for me. And so I had the dubious pleasure of meeting "Commander" George Michanowsky, who lived in a small apartment on the premises. We got off to a bad start when he questioned the motives behind my research. Who would waste their time, he wanted to know, in writing the biography of an "Eskimo." This was, to him, a poorly devised ruse to get into the archives and dig up some dirt on Peary. He suggested that I was probably working for the producers of a forthcoming movie on Peary and Cook. My protestations failed to convince him otherwise, and I was sent away.

I returned to Canada and wrote a letter to the club's president, appealing Michanowsky's decision. I also learned that Michanowsky's title of "Commander" was self-bestowed. He claimed to be a self-taught archaeologist, linguist, Egyptologist, epigrapher, and expert in Mesopotamian astronomy. He was, moreover, the author of a book that linked a supernova explosion in the constellation Vela with the development of civilization and the mystery of the lost continent of Atlantis.

In due course I received a telephone call from the Explorers Club, from the polymath himself. He explained that he had had a change of heart and invited me back to the club to pursue my research. For good measure he added that he had made this decision entirely on his own and that it had nothing to do with the totally unnecessary letter I had written to the president. I returned to New York. Janet Baldwin provided me the files I requested and I passed a few days in the archives. It was quite unnerving that the commander sat at the end of my table watching me for the entirety of my time there, and inspected my notebooks before I left each day.

Some years later, while pursuing more research at the Explorers
Club, I inquired of Miss Baldwin about the commander. Was he
still there, I asked. Yes and no, she replied. I was perplexed by her
response. She explained that the commander had died, but now the
club had his ashes.

A few years ago a film clip from the Crocker Land Expedition,
containing footage of a young Inuit man who appears to be Minik,
was found in the Library of Congress. Donald MacMillan shot film
on the expedition, but it was on flammable nitrate and most was
eventually destroyed for safety reasons. It is therefore exciting that a
researcher from the Peary-MacMillan Arctic Museum in Brunswick,
Maine, working under the direction of the museum's curator, Genny
LeMoine, found some MacMillan film in Washington.

It was shot near Borup Lodge at Etah—the lodge can be seen in
some of the shots. In one sequence a young man is seen sitting on a
sled, where MacMillan joins him. The young man, obviously Inuk, is
wearing Polar Inuit clothing except for his footwear. Although he is
on the sea ice he is wearing leather shoes. Scholars knowledgeable on
the Crocker Land Expedition consider this short sequence to be of
Minik, the only film footage of him known to exist.

The Canadian Canoe Museum in Peterborough, Ontario, has a
kayak that has been cataloged as Minik's. I doubt that it is, but I think it
may be his father's. The museum acquired it through a circuitous route
years ago. Apparently it came originally from a William C. Orchard.
They had assumed that Orchard bought it from Minik between 1916
and 1918. But there is no indication that Orchard met Minik then, and
there are no references to Minik bringing his kayak with him on his
return to the United States. Orchard was a photographer who photographed the Polar Inuit in New York in 1897–98. It is much more likely
that he acquired the kayak then, and that it belonged to Qisuk.

In 2012 an inspiring young artist, Tanya Linn Albrigtsen-Frable, a
member of a nonprofit artists' group, Groundswell, organized a group
of students to include Minik on a mural to be painted on a wall at the
Brooklyn Navy Yard. Groundswell is dedicated to beautifying neigh-

borhoods through the involvement of low-income and working-class families, and to bringing out the hidden histories of communities. They help "stories hidden behind walls to be expressed on the walls." The first half of the mural, dedicated to Minik and two other individuals, was done by fourth- and fifth-grade students from Brooklyn Public School 307, across the street from the navy yard where the Inuit began the sad American chapter of their lives. The students were told the story of Minik, and engaged in a dialogue on his life, centering on the questions "How do you think he felt?" and "Why do you think stories like this aren't told often?"

The result is a striking mural, done in a graffiti style, in which Minik is prominently displayed, in the same location where he began his life in America. It is a tribute both to the resilience of inner-city youth and to Minik's own triumph over tragedy.

Minik has taken a prominent place in Greenlandic popular culture.

The precursor to this book, *Give Me My Father's Body*, was published in 1986 and again in 2000. It was published in Danish in 1987 so that Greenlanders, many of whom are bilingual in Greenlandic and Danish, would have access to this story that forms part of the heritage of the Polar Inuit. It was finally published in Greenlandic in 2001

In 2014 the students of Greenland's National School of Theatre wrote and produced a play titled simply *Minik*. It has been performed in Greenland and Europe. In 2016 the production, which features only four actors, was presented for the first time in North America, at the Alianait Arts Festival in Iqaluit, Nunavut, Canada. Susanne Andreasen, tour manager and director, said, "[The play] is about having your identity stolen, having the responsibility for your own life taken away from you. It's about not knowing who you are and where you come from. . . . Being alone, being scared, we have all the spectrum of feelings in the play."

In 2011 Atlantic Music Studio in Greenland produced a CD for the local Amarok Theatre. It, too, was titled simply *Minik*. The cover art features the iconic picture of Minik with his bicycle. Described as experimental pop, the CD depicts the life of Minik in eleven songs.

Greenland keeps detailed records of personal names. The name Minik was rarely used prior to the publication of *Give Me My Father's Body* in 1986. One hunter in Thule, Minik Daorana, bore the name, as did a Greenlandic geologist, Minik Rosing. But there were almost no other people named Minik in the 1950s, '60s, or '70s. That changed starting in the mid-1980s. In a book, *Greenlandic Personal Names*, the scholar Nuka Møller documents that by 2015, 152 people in Greenland and 72 in Denmark bore the name Minik. One is Prince Vincent Frederik Minik Alexander, son of Crown Prince Frederik and Crown Princess Mary and fourth in line to the throne of Denmark.

The name Minik is not used only as a personal name. The Royal Arctic Line, a Greenland shipping company, took delivery of a new freight-hauling ship in September 2016. Its name? *Minik Arctica.*

In New Hampshire, Howard Young was the custodian of the few personal papers that Minik left on his death. They included his declaration of intention to become a US citizen, his military census card, his military registration certificate, and a few letters and other documents. It had always been Howard's desire to visit Greenland and present the documents to the archives there. Unfortunately he died without achieving this goal. In 2001, with the permission of his sister, Lou Young, I took the documents to Nuuk, Greenland, and presented them to Niels Frandsen, head archivist of the Greenland National Museum and Archives, in memory of Howard Young and Afton Hall. The meager tangible remains of Minik's life in America had also come home to Greenland.

—Kenn Harper, April 2017

APPENDIX

Names

There are a number of different spellings used in the original sources for most of the Inuit names of both places and people in this story. Both Peary and MacMillan butchered the spellings of Inuit names to such an extent that it has sometimes been almost impossible to decipher what is meant by their renditions. Danish and Greenlandic sources generally follow the old Greenlandic orthography (the so-called Kleinschmidt orthography), although there are occasional deviations from this.

In the text, all Inuit words have been spelled consistently following the current official Greenlandic orthography (a revision of the Kleinschmidt orthography). This has required changing the spellings of the names of many people who were written about in the past. In many instances it has also necessitated changing the spellings used in direct quotations. While this had been done throughout the text, the original spellings have of course been retained if they appear in the bibliography. I have allowed one exception to the above guideline. The well-known home of so many polar expeditions, Etah (really Iita), had been spelled consistently as Etah for over a hundred years by English, Danish, and many Greenlandic writers. It remains Etah in this book.

Most American references to Minik spell his name "Mene." In fact, the only Americans who have ever spelled his name correctly were the scientists Boas and Kroeber. Official references to him in the United States, such as his declaration of intention to become an American citizen, use the name Mene Peary Wallace or Mene Wallace, the name he used himself when in America. All references to him from Danish and Greenlandic sources spell his name correctly as Minik. I have spelled it consistently as Minik throughout the book. When I considered all the injustices of his short and unhappy life, I thought the least I could do was to spell his name correctly.

A list follows of Inuit words (people and place-names as well as other words) found in the text. Beside some of them are given some of the more common variant spellings one will find in the original source material. This will help those who may want to refer to sources in which Inuit names have been used so inconsistently. For words other than names, English glosses have been given.

People

Standard Spelling	Variant Spellings
Aapilak	Apilyah
Aaqqioq	
Aatitaq	
Agpalersuarsuk	
Ajaku	Ajago
Akitteq	Akitseq
Aleqaherruaq	
Aleqasina	
Aleqasinnguaq	Allakasingwah
Aleqatsiaq	Tallakoteah
Amaunnalik	
Angutilluarsuk	Angutidluarssuak, Angutiluajuk
Arnaaluk	
Arnakittoq	Arnakitsoq
Arnannguaq	Arnanguaq
Arrutarsuaq	Arrotoksuah
Aserpannguaq	Iopungya, I-o-oung-wa
Atangana	Atana, Artona, Ahtungahnak(soah), Ahtungnah
Aviaq	Hawia, Ahweah, Ahweelah
Avoortungiaq	
Eqariusaq	Eqariussaq, Ek-kai-a-sha
Equ	Ikwa, Ikwah, Ik-qua
Eri	Ere
Iggiannguaq	Egingwa, Egingwah, Inginwa
Ilaittoq	
Imiina	Ee-meen-ya
Inugaarsuk	
Inukittoq	Inighito, Inukitsoq
Inuutersuaq	

Ittukusuk	Etookashoo, Itookuechuk
Ittullak	
Ivalu	Ivalo
Ivik	
Kuuttiikittoq	Kutsikitsoq, Kuutsiikitsoq
Maasannguaq	
Majaq	Myah, Mayark
Malaviaq	
Mannik	Mane
Meqqusaaq	Merkoshak, Merktoshar
Mequ	Meqo
Mequpaluk	
Salloq	
Mikissuk	
Minik	Mene, Menie, Meenie, Minnie
Miteq	
Navarana	
Nukappiannguaq	Nookapingwa
Nuktaq	Nooktaq, Nuktan, Natooka, Nooktak, Nooktan
Panippak	Panikpak, Panikpa, Panikpah
Piugaattog	
Piugaatoq	Piuvaitsuq, Pee-a-wah-to
Piuli	Peary
Piulerriaq	Pearyaksoah
Piulersuaq	Pearyaksoah
Porsimat	
Qaaqqutsiaq	
Qaerngaaq	
Qajuuttaq	Kaiota, Kai-oto, Kyutah
Qisuk	Kishu, Kissuk, Kessuh, Kissuh, Kubliknik, Qissuk, Kusshan
Qisunnguaq	Qisunguaq, Ka-shung-wa
Qujaukittoq	Kyogwito, Qujaukitsoq
Qulutana	Koolootoonah, Koolatoonah
Serminnguaq	
Sigluk	Sigdluk, Seegloo, Siglook
Siuleqatuk	
Soqqaq	Sorqaq
Taliilannguaq	Teddy-ling-wa
Tautsiannguaq	Tau-ching-wa, Tawchingwah
Torngi	Tornge, Tung-we
Uisaakassak	Uisaakaavsak, Ujaragapsuck, Wee-shak-up-si, Yaragapsuk, Weakupshi, Ujaragapssuq, Wesharkoupsi
Ukkujaaq	Ookeyah, Ooklya
Ulloriaq	Ooblooya, Ooblooyah
Uutaaq	Odaq, Ootah, Wootah

Places

Standard Spelling	Variant Spellings
Anoritooq	
Etah	
Itilleq	Ittibloo
Kangerlussuaq	Kangerdluksuaq, Kangalookswa
Natsilivik	Netiulume
Neqi	
Pitoraarfik	Peteravik
Qaanaaq	Qanaq, Kanak
Quinisut	Koinisuni
Savissivik	
Siorapaluk	
Tuttulissuaq	Tugtuligssuaq, Took-too-lik-suah
Upernavik	
Uummannaq	Umanak

Words

Standard Spelling	Variant Spelling	Meaning
amerlaqqaat		many
angakkoq	angakoq	shaman
Avangnaamioq		resident of a northern district (also the name of a newspaper published in Godhavn, Greenland)
kiiha	kissa, kiisa	finally
Naalagapaluk		the little boss (Polar Inuit name for Donald MacMillan)
nallinnaq		pitiable, to be pitied
nangmalik		that which carries a backpack
qallunaaq	koblunah	white man
qallunaat		white men
qavangangnisat		residents of a southern district
qulittaq	qulitsaq	parka
sapinngilaq		not incapable
sermeq	sermik	glacier, ice cap
sermersuaq	sermik-soak	great glacier, ice cap
tikeqihunga	tikeri-unga	I've arrived, I'm arriving
toorngat	toornat	helping spirit
tupiq	tupik	tent
upernaallit		whalers
uppissuaq	opiksoak	snowy owl

NOTES

In the chapter notes that follow, all archival references are summarized as follows:

AMNH refers to the American Museum of Natural History. All file references are to that institution's General Files (that is, administrative files), unless specified as being from the Department of Anthropology or the Rare Book and Manuscript Collection.

PFC refers to the Peary Family collection in the US National Archives, Record Group 401 (1).

PAC refers to the records of the Peary Arctic Club in the archives of the Explorers Club.

NYHS refers to the New-York Historical Society.

Rigsarkivet refers to the Royal Archives, Copenhagen, Denmark, Records of the Danish Ministry of Foreign Affairs, File A.S.95/08 of the Royal Danish Consulate, New York.

Other references are abbreviated as follows: Books, manuscripts, magazines, and journals are referred to by author's name; the year is included if more than one source is used from one author; the title is given if more than one item was published in one year. Newspaper references name the paper and date. Complete references are given in the bibliography.

All references are to the page on which each quotation appears.

Epigraphs
"To many a good person": Peary 1898 (vol. 1), 507–08.
"Our tales are narratives": Rasmussen, n.d., 27.
"This Minik seems gradually": Holtved, 11.

1. Arrival in America
"curious, long-haired": Burnes, 323.
"The crowd afterward boarded": *The New York Times*, 3 October 1897.
"The children are sick": ibid.
"Gentle, pious Mary": Marie Peary Stafford, "Discoverer of the North Pole," quoted in Herbert, 37.

"I cannot bear": Letter, Robert Peary to his mother, quoted in Weems, 1967, 52–53.

"Remember, Mother": letter, Robert Peary to his mother, 27 February 1887, in PFC, quoted in Bryce, 22.

"The ship's men brought off the cask": PFC, Journal of 1896 Expedition, 134. On the purchase of skeletons from Peary, the records of the AMNH, Department of Anthropology (Accession file 99/105-111), show that in 1896 the museum purchased from Robert Peary three skeletons (a man, a woman, and a child), three crania, and one calvarium. These were the remains of Qujaukittoq, his wife, Amaunnalik, and their infant daughter, Ilaittoq. Amaunnalik was Minik's maternal aunt.

"I understand Peary brought this party": AMNH, File 517; handwritten note by Morris Jesup on bottom of memo from William Wallace to Jesup, 31 March 1898.

"I beg to suggest": AMNH, Department of Anthropology, File 1896–38; letter of Franz Boas to Robert Peary, 24 May 1897.

"It was believed": *New-York Tribune* [illustrated supplement], 27 March 1898.

"it was his idea": Green, 158.

"We have on board six Eskimos": *The New York Times*, 27 September 1897.

"When I leave again": *The New York Times*, 25 September 1897.

"A collection of the implements": *The New York Times*, 1 October 1897.

"All of the Eskimos": *The New York Times*, 3 October 1897.

"It was felt": AMNH, File 517; memo by Dr. Bumpus, April 1909.

"Oh, I can remember": *New York World*, 6 January 1907.

"When they took us ashore": ibid.

"the several scores of visitors": *The New York Times*, 11 October 1897.

"The unusual crowd": ibid.

"For the first time": ibid.

"insisted upon their rights": ibid.

"when . . . some ten or fifteen": ibid.

"Qisuk's little son": ibid.

"the little fellow": ibid.

"One of the most amusing forms": ibid.

"in the United States": Kroeber, "The Eskimo of Smith Sound," 1899, 306.

"had begun to pick up": *New-York Tribune* [illustrated supplement], 27 March 1898.

2. Peary's People

"a big boat" and "a whole island of wood": Rasmussen, n.d., 1–2.

"turned towards the sea": ibid.

"If you point to the east": Gilberg, 1974–75, 160.

"Then it really grew winter": Hendrik, 24.

"They had no wood": Kane (vol. 1), 206.

"incorrigible scamps": ibid., 211.

"When they were first allowed": ibid., 207.

"He learned to drive": Green, 76–78.

"I have often been asked": ibid., 68.

"did not produce": Malaurie, 235.

"a great leader": Uutaaq quoted in Malaurie, 233.

"their respect for the man": Rasmussen, n.d., 8.

"by threats": Malaurie, 235.

"my faithful, trusty Eskimo allies": Peary, 1898 (vol. 2), 207–08.

"effective instruments": Peary, 1910, 47.
"these people are much like children": ibid., 50.
"their feeling for me": ibid., 48.
"it would be misleading": ibid., 51–52.
"the great tormentor" and "People were afraid of him": Malaurie, 234.

3. The Iron Mountain

"I scratched a rough 'P'": Peary, 1898 (vol. 2), 147.
"This means that if the ship comes": Green, 125.
"I have failed": ibid., 140.
"I shall never see the North Pole": Freeman, 45, quoting *New-York Tribune*, 2 October 1895.
"the man who": Fitzhugh Green's biography of Peary was *Peary: The Man Who Refused to Fail*.
"The summer's voyage": Peary, 1898 (vol. 1), xlix.
"the knowledge an explorer has acquired": Weems, 1967, 229, quoting a typescript fragment, undated, in PFC.
"Never was a man more fortunate": Peary, 1898 (vol. 1), lv.
"a man of fine instincts": Kane (vol. 2), 109.
The story of Atangana burning the lodge is from personal communication with Balika Jensen, Qaanaaq, Greenland.
"His face was broad" and "a thoroughly splendid man": Astrup, 296–97.
"the old man is aging": Peary, 1898 (vol. 2), 416.
The story of Arrutarsuaq's prowess as a shaman is from personal communication with Inuutersuaq Ulloriaq, Siorapaluk, Greenland.
Minik's birthdate is unknown, there being no explorers or others in northwestern Greenland at the time of his birth to record it. In *Mennesket Minik*, Rolf Gilberg summarizes some of the statements of Minik's presumed birthdate from various sources. He notes that Peary in *Northward Over the Great Ice* (vol. 1), page 187, gives it as "before 1891"; Hrdlička as 1889; Rosbach as 1888; *The New York Times* in 1897 as 1888, in 1899 as 1890, and in 1909 as 1891; and my *Give Me My Father's Body* as 1890 or 1891. The inscription on Minik's grave marker says 1887, but that was only a guess by the Hall family. His declaration of intention to become an American citizen gives August 5, 1889, but such a degree of precision was impossible at the time. There are others. I have considered all of them and reconsidered my own previous conclusion. A reconstructed birth date is needed because, of course, Minik's age, referred to many times in the text, derives from his birth date. I have settled on a birth date of the beginning of the year 1890. Accordingly, on his arrival in America in 1897, Minik was seven years old.
"Panippak . . . tells me": ibid., 403.
"little Minik had heard": Peary, 1904, 35–36.
"I sent my faithful Eskimos": Peary, 1898 (vol. 2), 591.
"I can remember very well": *New York World*, 6 January 1907.
"he coaxed my father": *San Francisco Examiner* [magazine supplement], 9 May 1909.
"They promised us": *New York World*, 6 January 1907.
"He asked with so strong a will": Rasmussen, n.d., 6.
"Our people were afraid": *San Francisco Examiner* [magazine supplement], 9 May 1909.
"Uisaakassak wants to go": PFC, Journal of 1897 Expedition, entry for 26 August 1897.

4. An Inuit Orphan in New York

"the life of the party" and "as lively as a cricket": *The New York Sun* [supplement], 24 April 1898.

"What do the Eskimos do all day?" and "Oh, we try": *New-York Tribune* [illustrated supplement], 27 March 1898.

"They just sit there": *The New York Sun* [supplement], 24 April 1898.

"He was dearer to me": *San Francisco Examiner* [magazine supplement], 9 May 1909.

"an attendant (speaking Eskimo)": Kroeber, "The Eskimo of Smith Sound," 1899, 313.

"When informed": Boas report, quoted in ibid., 314–16.

"When you found they were sick": *New-York Tribune* [illustrated supplement], 27 March 1898.

"Deeply regret Eskimo's death": AMNH, Department of Anthropology, file 1900-6; telegram from Robert Peary to Secretary John Winser, 25 February 1898.

"I would like very much" and "This matter is left with Wallace": AMNH, File 517; letter of William Wallace to Morris Jesup, 31 March 1898.

"very ill of consumption": *The Cobleskill (NY) Index*, 19 May 1898.

"He had refused to return": ibid.

"Only one of the Eskimos": AMNH, File 517; letter of William Wallace to Morris Jesup, 25 May 1898.

"jumped about the deck": *The New York Times*, 3 July 1898, 11.

"the sun was burning": ibid.

"he would always keep it": ibid.

"As I sit here writing" and "Fortunately for them": Peary, 1898 (vol. 1), 508–09.

"Among the tribe": Peary, 1904, 31.

5. Minik, the American

"lived in mortal fear": *San Francisco Examiner* [magazine supplement], 9 May 1909.

"Minik's father is gone": ibid.

"give Minik a name": AMNH, File 517; letter of Wallace to Jesup, 21 January 1907.

"Taming a Little Savage" and "dreary region" and "barren Arctic habitat": *New York World*, 27 January 1899.

"If there is one small boy": *New-York Tribune* [illustrated supplement], 8 January 1899.

"Born in a land": *New York World*, 27 January 1899.

"he is an American now": ibid.

"We hope that this little ward": Sheldon, 527.

"an experiment, and a promising one": *New-York Tribune* [illustrated supplement], 8 January 1899.

"one of the ordinary duties of life": *New-York Tribune* [illustrated supplement], 18 November 1900.

"rather guarded": *New York World*, 27 January 1899.

"Once my father had": Sheldon, 526–27.

"never better pleased": *New-York Tribune* [illustrated supplement], 8 January 1898.

"I learned to read": *New York World*, 6 January 1907.

"a faithful pupil": *The New York Times*, 27 June 1899.

"uncommonly sturdy": *New-York Tribune* [illustrated supplement], 18 November 1900.

"He doesn't like to be too warm": Sheldon, 527.

"handshakes, smiles and familiar pats": *New-York Tribune* [illustrated supplement], 18 November 1900.

"can impart": *New York World*, 17 January 1899.

"in the quiet of his own home": *New-York Tribune* [illustrated supplement], 18 November 1900.

"I am going back north": Von Linden, 20.

"if Minik still retains his native tongue": AMNH, File 517; letter of Herbert Bridgman, Peary Arctic Club, to John Winser, 15 June 1899.

"with a view to preparing him": *San Francisco Examiner* [magazine supplement], 9 May 1909.

"being educated by Mr. and Mrs. Wallace": *The Cobleskill Index*, 7 July 1898.

"with such foster parents": *New York World*, 27 January 1899.

"I want to stay here": ibid., 6 January 1907.

"Mr. Wallace has more orders": *The Cobleskill Index*, 4 November 1897.

"Mr. Wallace is the children's friend": ibid., 7 July 1898.

"Mr. Wallace believes": ibid., 8 June 1899.

"Resolved. That it is contrary": ibid., 22 June 1899.

"when he started for bed": *New-York Tribune* [illustrated supplement], 8 January 1899.

"See Lizzie, pray said": ibid.

"the Eskimo who lives": *The Cobleskill Index*, 22 September 1898: p. 1.

6. The Wallace Affair

"somewhat anxious": AMNH, File 517; Statement of Albert S. Bickmore, 8 December 1900.

"there was usually a long delay": ibid.

"our friend Mr. Wallace": ibid.

"engaged extensively in the milk business": AMNH, File 517; letter of J. C. Cady to Jesup, 26 November 1900.

"I have just seen your report": AMNH, File 517; letter of Jesup to William Wallace, undated.

"on the pretext": *New-York Tribune*, 20 March 1901.

"I can say nothing": ibid.

"spent all of the time": AMNH, File 517; letter of assistant to the president to Robert M. Fox, 16 April 1901.

"macerating" and "bone-bleaching": AMNH, File 517; both terms are used in official letters of the museum.

"merely superintendent of the Museum": AMNH, File 682; Form for Insertion in Minutes of Meeting of Executive Committee held on 18 April 1901.

"a great institution": AMNH, File 517; letter of Jesup to Henry F. Osborn and H. C. Bumpus, 24 July 1901.

"Wallace, a trusted servant": ibid.

"The only mistake I have made": ibid.

7. Scam

"most of the time": Osbon, 210.

"I send the president": PAC, File 1.2.11; letter of Peary to Peary Arctic Club, Cape York, 25 July 1898.

"two or three bundles": PAC, File 1.2.11.

"unruffled patience and coolness in an emergency": www.frederickcooksociety.org/about .htm, accessed 11 November 2016.

"a consignment of goods": Freeman, 115, quoting *Brooklyn Daily Eagle*, 16 November 1908.

"We shall be very glad": PAC, File 1.2.22; letter of Hermon C. Bumpus, American Museum of Natural History, to Herbert Bridgman, Peary Arctic Club, 26 October 1908.

"Among the material sent up": PFC, File 1907, Letters Sent; letter of Peary to Bumpus, 1 April 1907.

"He [Jesup] feels that in everything received": PAC, File 1.2.21; letter of Morris Jesup's secretary to Herbert Bridgman, 5 June 1907.

"From the dazzling May morning": Peary, 1898 (vol. 2), 614.

"peerless and unique": ibid., 618.

"I have offered the three meteorites": PFC, File 1907, Letters Received; letter of Jesup to Peary, 29 April 1907.

"the Museum of Natural History": ibid.

"I think it only fair": AMNH, File 124; letter of Josephine Peary to Henry F. Osborn, 15 March 1908.

"at present Wallace seems": AMNH, File 682; letter of Edward M. Shepard to Jesup, 14 February 1901.

"I shall have to say": NYHS, Osborn Papers, Box XX, File: Bumpus Affair, Item III—The Recent Administration of the Museum. Statement of Edward M. Shepard, 7 October 1910.

8. "Destined to a Life of Tears"

"bills paid by the museum": AMNH, File 517.

"give Minik a name": AMNH, File 517; letter of Wallace to Jesup, 21 January 1907.

"You probably know something": AMNH, File 517; letter of Jesup to Winser, 3 April 1902.

"never heard you speak": AMNH, File 517; letter of Winser to Jesup, 8 April 1902.

"you had requested him": ibid.

"Hush, Minik," "poor little fellow," and "Aunt Rhetta's last kiss": *San Francisco Examiner* [magazine supplement], 9 May 1909.

"a woman of kind heart": *The Cobleskill Index*, 31 March 1904.

"is survived by one son": ibid.

"made a reputation for grit": "Esquimau Mimi [*sic*] Now Selling Lots," unidentified newspaper article, 9 October 1904, in AMNH, File 517.

"thrash the first one": ibid.

"given up his idea": ibid.

"like a prison": *San Francisco Examiner* [magazine supplement], 9 May 1909,

"We had planned much for him": *New York Evening Mail*, 21 April 1909.

9. "Give Me My Father's Body"

"Minik, the Esquimau boy": *New York World*, 6 January 1907.

"I hardly believe": AMNH, Department of Anthropology, File 1900-6; Memo, Robert W. Daley, Bellevue Hospital, to Franz Boas, 17 February 1898.

"The disposition of the body": *New-York Daily Tribune*, 19 February 1898.

"visit the [supposed] grave": Boas in Kroeber, "The Eskimo of Smith Sound," 1899, 316.

"It is an Eskimo custom": *New York Evening Mail*, 21 April 1909.

"when a woman dies": Kroeber, "The Eskimo of Smith Sound," 1899, 301.

"when Qisuk died": Boas in ibid., 316.

"On the death of a man": Peary in ibid., 312.

"When a person is dying": Kroeber in ibid., 311.
"That night some of us gathered": *New York Evening Mail*, 21 April 1909.
"to appease the boy": *New York Evening Mail*, 24 April 1909.
"nothing particularly deserving": ibid.
"Oh, that was perfectly legitimate": ibid.
"Wallace made effort": AMNH, File 517; unsigned penciled notation on the first page of a typescript of a letter from William Wallace to Secretary Loeb, 14 January 1907.
"Dr. Boas requested me": AMNH, File 517; letter of William Wallace to Morris Jesup, 16 May 1898.
"We were only acting": *New York Evening Mail*, 21 April 1909.
"Now they talk of removing his flesh": *The New York Times*, 21 Feb 1898.
"There seems to be nobody": ibid.
"We have to fix up a grave": *The New York Sun* [supplement], 24 April 1898.

10. "In the Interest of Science"
"evidently possessed": Loring and Prokopec, 28.
"These six individuals": Hrdlička, 1910, 223.
"The brain in question": ibid.
Both the inspiration and the information for many of my comments on the early development of the science of anthropology come from Carl Sagan's brilliant essay, "Broca's Brain," in his book of the same name.
"gaunt and dedicated decapitator": Sagan, 13.
"it is a little unfair": ibid., 12.
The Inuit at the World's Columbian Exposition in Chicago in 1893 were from Labrador and had been brought to Chicago by a promoter who subsequently abandoned them. Dr. Frederick A. Cook, "out of the goodness of his heart, was taking care of them and seeing that they were returned to their home in Labrador." Cook planned to return the Inuit to Labrador in 1894 when he went north with the *Miranda* expedition, a popular excursion that he was organizing to the Arctic for fare-paying passengers; in the meantime he was exhibiting them and some "arctic paraphernalia" to raise interest in the trip. The quotations and the information are from Friis, 6. In 1894 these Inuit lived for a time in Cook's backyard in New York; see *The New York Times*, 10 September 1909.
"Many things heretofore unknown": *New-York Tribune* [illustrated supplement], 27 March 1898.
Regarding the boost to the careers of Boas, Kroeber, and Hrdlička by the publication of their research on the Polar Inuit, see relevant publications of Kroeber and Hrdlička in the bibliography. Boas did not publish directly on the Polar Inuit but oversaw the work of Kroeber.
"as a specimen of the race": *New-York Tribune*, 15 June 1899.
"It would be interesting": ibid., 14 June 1899.
"We think the body of the girl": ibid., 17 June 1899, 16.
"Little Eskimo girl died": AMNH, File 517; letter, Franz Boas to Dr. Bern Gallaudet, June 1899.
"Before Captain Bruce went away": *New-York Tribune*, 17 June 1899, 16.
"I am sorry to see": AMNH, File 517; letter, Franz Boas to Dr. Bern Gallaudet, June 1899.
"The newspapers had found out": *New York Evening Mail*, 21 April 1909.
"Unexpectedly one day": *San Francisco Examiner* [magazine supplement], 9 May 1909.

11. "The Very Pitiful Case of Minik"

"Esquimaux matter was fully settled": AMNH, File 517; letter of Wallace to Jesup, 10 January 1907.

"simply carrying out your unkindly feelings": ibid.

"a gentleman of your standing": ibid.

"I beg to call your attention": AMNH, File 517; statement of Chester Beecroft, 12 January 1907.

"a National guest," "his condition," and "the most abused": ibid.

"only interest in Minik": *The New York Sun*, 16 April 1909.

"particular and peculiar interest": ibid.

"meagerly clad" and "improperly cared for": AMNH, File 517; statement of Chester Beecroft, 12 January 1907.

"still forming" and "if he is allowed": ibid.

"an officer of the United States": ibid.

"gentle, kind and hospitable" and "received Peary warmly": ibid.

"It would be reasonable": ibid.

"What private griefs": ibid.

"right shall at last be done": ibid.

"I would thank you": AMNH, file 517; letter of Wallace to Loeb, 14 January 1907.

"No better": Roosevelt quoted in Eames, 69.

"afterward we learned": *New York Evening Mail*, 13 April 1909.

"urgent request": AMNH, File 517; notation in Bumpus's handwriting at end of typescript of article in *The Washington Post*, 12 January 1907.

"absolutely declined": ibid.

"do nothing whatever": ibid.

"insisting that I lay the matter": AMNH, File 517; letter of Wallace to Jesup, 21 January 1907.

"the President [Jesup] should be informed": AMNH, File 517; letter of Strong to Bumpus, 22 January 1907.

"You are not adapted": AMNH, File 561; letter of Bumpus to Jenness Richardson Jr., 15 February 1907.

12. "A Hopeless Condition of Exile"

"I am unwilling": *San Francisco Examiner* [magazine supplement], 9 May 1909.

"As far as Peary is concerned": ibid.

"ascertain how far": ibid.

"I can't be a burden": ibid. (The interview was not published until 9 May 1909, but must have been given in 1907, for in the article both Minik and Wallace refer to Jesup, who had died on 22 January 1908.)

"exceptional charm": *National Cyclopedia of American Biography*, vol. 32, 331.

"temperamentally unfit": NYHS, Osborn Papers, Box XX, File: Bumpus Affair, Item III—The Recent Administration of the Museum, Statement of Dr. Dean, page 50 of file.

"pleading for a Christian burial": *New York World* [magazine supplement], 6 January 1907.

"out of gratitude": ibid.

"If all these things happened": ibid.

"the skeleton of which": *New York World*, 13 April 1909.

"thoroughly mystified" and "As for his father's body": *The New York Sun*, 16 April 1909.

"Dr. Bumpus . . . has had some hesitancy": *New York Evening Mail*, 24 April 1909.

"he seemed inclined": ibid., 13 April 1909.

"I asked Dr. Bumpus": ibid., 26 May 1909.

"I attempted to do this": AMNH, File 517; "Notes on Mene . . ." memo by Bumpus, April 1909.

"Minik is very anxious": PFC, File 1908, Letter Received; letter of Wallace to Peary, 23 June 1908.

"I have your letter": PFC, File 1908, Letters Sent; letter of Peary to Wallace, 26 June 1908.

"If you expect": *The New York Sun*, 16 April 1909.

"The plight of this poor Esquimau": "Peary Dooms Esquimau Boy to Sorrowful Exile" (unidentified), 30 June 1908, copy in PFC.

"under one or another pretense": Rigsarkivet, no. 227, 10 September 1908.

"made room for the Eskimos": Rigsarkivet, no. 295, 9 November 1908.

"the boy would never have known": ibid.

"systematic campaign": ibid.

"He has heard so much": ibid.

"at least for the time being": ibid.

"down here, he will hardly become": ibid.

13. The Polar Plan

"Our . . . object": *New York Evening Mail*, 21 April 1909.

"The explorers who are trying": *The New York Sun*, 22 January 1909.

"They fit out nice comfortable ships": *The Evening Telegram*, 22 January 1909.

"The North Pole will never be discovered": *The New York Sun*, 22 January 1909.

"The record of recent Arctic exploration": *The New York Times*, 30 October 1876.

"I would like to return": *New-York Tribune*, 22 January 1909.

"I have known Minik" and "just let it rest": ibid.

14. Runaway

"I cannot bear": *San Francisco Examiner* [magazine supplement], 9 May 1909.

"more or less a freak": ibid.

Dr. Roswell O. Stebbins, chairman of the Arctic Club of America's committee on the relief of Cook, stated incorrectly in early June 1909 that Peary had never refused to take Minik back but "had simply made it a condition of giving him passage that the Eskimo should agree to remain in Greenland. The boy refused, desiring to be brought back here and permitted to join a circus." Dr. Stebbins added that "the Arctic Club of America would send the Eskimo north if he would agree to remain at Etah" (*New York American*, 10 June 1909).

"When this reaches you": *New York World*, 13 April 1909.

"If Minik is making for Newfoundland": *The New York Sun*, 16 April 1909.

"I want Minik to return": *New York Evening Mail*, 13 April 1909.

"The treatment which has been accorded": ibid., 21 April 1909.

"Everywhere Minik looked": *The New York Sun*, 16 April 1909.

"When I woke up": *New York Evening Mail*, 26 May 1909.

"This is probably": *New York World*, 23 May 1909.

"Think of the injustice [*sic*]": *San Francisco Examiner* [magazine supplement], 9 May 1909.

"I went to a boarding house": *New York Evening Mail*, 26 May 1909.

"I left New York": *New York World*, 26 May 1909.

"Yes, I had a hard time" and "I was not strong": *New York Evening Mail*, 26 May 1909.

15. "An Iron-Clad Agreement"

"I would shoot Mr. Peary," "I can never forgive Peary," and "And if he does meet Peary": *San Francisco Examiner* [magazine supplement], 9 May 1909.

"hopping mad": AMNH, File 517; quoted in letter from Bridgman to Bumpus, May 1909.

"our policy": AMNH, File 517; AMNH to Bridgman, 14 May 1909.

"Peary suspected": *New York World*, 27 May 1909.

"Minik is, you know": *The New York Times*, 14 April 1909.

"the conversation counted": PFC, letter of Bridgman to Mrs. Peary, 3 July 1909.

"we are under no obligation": ibid.

"an iron-clad agreement": PFC, letter of Bridgman to Mrs. Peary, 8 July 1909.

"Minik and his friends": PFC, agreement dated 9 July 1909.

"Thirteen years ago": ibid.

"Minik's feelings": PFC, letter of Bridgman to Mrs. Peary, 14 July 1909.

"to avail himself": ibid.

"I will endeavor": PFC, letter of Bridgman to Samuel Bartlett, 10 July 1909.

"Minik Wallace still has no contract": PFC, letter of Bridgman to Mrs. Peary, 13 July 1909.

"I hope you take Minik": PFC, letter of Josephine Peary to Robert Peary, 17 July 1909, as quoted in Bryce, 339.

"he had become my devoted slave": De Frece, 201.

"They say they are not": *New York Evening Mail*, 9 July 1909.

"You're a race of scientific criminals": ibid.

"bequeath his brain": *The New York Times*, 12 July 1909.

"To Minik, the polite request": ibid.

"I sail north tomorrow": *New York Evening Mail*, 9 July 1909.

"You Americans": ibid.

"To an Eskimo": *Daily Reflector*, 15 July 1909.

"It is this fact": *New York Evening Mail*, 10 July 1909.

"But even if he gets there": *San Francisco Examiner* [magazine supplement], 9 May 1909.

"They may balk": *Daily Reflector*, 15 July 1909.

"I bade Minik good-bye": PFC, letter of Bridgman to William Wallace, 10 July 1909.

16. Return to Greenland

"too many Eskimos" and "smoke cigarettes": *The New York Herald*, undated, 1909, clipping in PFC.

"Shortly after my arrival": Fleming, 38.

"My surprise and delight": ibid., 38–39.

"discontented and even bitter": ibid., 39.

"just waiting for him to die": ibid.

"My heart went out": ibid.

"a fine assortment": *The New York Herald*, undated, 1909, clipping in PFC.

"Minik was now a 'qallunaaq'": *The New York Herald*, 20 September 1909.

"Tell him to come up": *Galveston Daily News*, 25 October 1909.

"Climbing down into the small boat": ibid.

"he soon fraternized": *The New York Herald*, 20 September 1909.

"Commander Peary has given": ibid.

"made his peace": *The New York Times*, 13 September 1909.

"upon junction with Peary": PFC, agreement between *The New York Herald* and the owners of the *Jeanie*, as quoted in Bryce, 339.

"of special interest" and "Besides the obvious advantage": PFC, letter of Bridgman to Mrs.
    Peary, 15 July 1909.
"I hereby acknowledge": PFC, document, dated 23 August 1909.
"On this day": Gustav Olsen, 17.

17. An Inuk Again
"MINE . . .": Peary quoted in Eames, 92.
"The Pole at last": PFC, diary transcript, in Dick, 259.
"as subject to my will": ibid., 89.
"my little brown children": Peary, 1907, 190.
"although they were not qualified": Peary, 1917, 180.
"I had come to regard": Peary, 1910, 333.
"I have used the Eskimos": ibid.
"Can anyone think": Rasmussen, n.d., 7.
"The Eskimos here": Gustav Olsen quoted in Peary, 1917, 189.
Minik's mother, Mannik, had three older sisters, and two had children of their own. Man-
    nik's elder sister Siuleqatuk became the wife of Angutilluarsuk and bore him two sons,
    Ivik and Iggiannguaq. They were Minik's first cousins. A younger sister, Amaunnalik,
    married a man named Qujaukittoq. The couple and a daughter had died in the epidem-
    ic of 1895–96—it was their skeletons and crania (and one calvarium) that Peary had
    dug up from their fresh graves, taken to New York, and sold to the American Museum
    of Natural History in 1896 (see note to chapter 1). They had a daughter, Inugaarsuk,
    and a son, Inukittoq, who were both living when Minik returned. They were also
    Minik's cousins.
"The man who idles": Rasmussen, n.d., 1908, 55.
Majaq's mother was Arnaaluk. His father was an unidentified white man from the Hall
    expedition in the 1870s. Majaq was born in the summer of 1873. Majaq became a
    stepfather to Minik when Majaq and Qisuk swapped wives. Soqqaq married Arnaa-
    luk, thereby becoming Majaq's stepfather. Soqqaq was, therefore, a step-great-uncle to
    Minik.
"His tightly closed eyes": ibid., 38.
"An orphan who has a hard time": Freuchen, 1961, 60.
"The life I have led": Rosbach, *Avangnaamioq* 12, 98.
"I am still alive": Helgesen, 25 January 1916, 323–24.

18. The Thule Station
"like a native-born American" and "an extraordinarily": translation, Rasmussen to Nye-
    boe, August 1910, quoted in Gilberg, 1994, 469.
"I have gathered": letter to Rasmussen's mother, undated, provided by Knud Michelsen,
    now the property of Qaanaaq Museum.
"My father shall make": translation, Freuchen, undated manuscript, entry for 1 November
    1910, quoted in Gilberg, 1994, 477.
"Aja-ja-jah-ha": ibid.
"Great Peter": ibid.
On Minik's predictions that Ittukusuk and Iggiannguaq would die during the winter:
    There were two men of each name in the area. All four men survived the winter.
"he travelled about": ibid., 491.
"In a whisk": Freuchen, *Arctic Adventure*, 1935, 119–20.
"We must realize": ibid., 161.

"Up in our country": ibid., 263.

"spread the seed" Freuchen, 1953, 108.

"Don't you think": Freuchen, *Arctic Adventure*, 1935, 161.

"probably a good enough fellow": ibid., 162.

"I saw Minik": ibid.

"he did not want to make appointments": Freuchen, 1961, 104.

"To circumvent": Freuchen, *Arctic Adventure*, 1935, 163.

"none too enthusiastic": ibid., 168.

"Some of the women": Rosbach, *Avangnaamioq* 12, 98.

"an extraordinary fellow": Freuchen, 1953, 89.

"Minik was a great nuisance": Freuchen, *Arctic Adventure*, 1935, 142.

"the boy who had": ibid., 67.

"We had taken" and "even in Greenland": ibid., 67.

Inuit memories of Minik are from Harper interviews with Inuutersuaq, Qaaqqutsiaq, Qisuk, Amaunnalik, Imiina, and Navarana Qaavigaq, all in Qaanaaq, Greenland, at various times between 1977 and 1985. Gilberg, 1994, 447–51, uses interviews with Inuutersuaq, Iggiannguaq, Uutaaq, Imiina, and others; "another old hunter" is Porsimat; "one elderly woman" is Amaunnalik; "another" is Avoortungiaq.

"For a while": Freuchen, 1953, 89.

"It is not impossible": Freuchen, *Arctic Adventure*, 1935, 277.

"wholly Eskimo": Hunt and Thompson, 17. Hunt's full quotation is, "I went to examine the baby, and he was a tiny dark thing, about four pounds, but seemed healthy. He looked wholly Eskimo, and I think he was. The second child was Peter's."

Inuit beliefs that Minik had fathered Meqqusaaq were told to the author by Amaunnalik and Qaaqqutsiaq. Pipaluk Freuchen information is from Gilberg, 1994, 526.

Freuchen's novel *Ivalu* was published in Danish in 1930, and in English in 1935, with the expanded title *Ivalu: The Eskimo Wife*.

"brings her to the drama": from the dust jacket of Freuchen, *Ivalu*, 1935.

"Sad things" and "We must never speak": ibid., 309.

19. Uisaakassak: The Big Liar

"man-made mountains" and "The ships sailed in": Rasmussen in Gilberg, 1969–70, 85.

"the streetcars": ibid., 86.

"distance shrinker": ibid.

"Uisaakassak, go tell your big lies": ibid.

"can tell a lot": quotation from Mylius-Erichsen in ibid.

"a biting wind": PAC, File 1.2.11; report by Peary dated 28 August 1899.

Uisaakassak's wife was named Aleqasinnguaq. She was the daughter of the shaman Salloq and his wife Mikissuk. Uisaakassak was living with her in Inglefield Bay in 1903 when the Danish Literary Expedition arrived. She and Uisaakassak separated in or before 1905 when Uisaakassak moved to Tuttulissuaq, and she became the wife of Sigluk. Eventually Uisaakassak stole her back from Sigluk, but she became Sigluk's wife again after Uisaakassak's death. She was born about 1880 and died between 1910 and 1913. Similarity between her name and that of Piugaattoq's wife has given rise to confusion in some writings. Piugaattoq's wife, whom he sometimes exchanged with Uisaakassak and regularly shared with Peary, was named Aleqasina. To make the matter more confusing, Peary, in his written references to her, usually called her Aleqasinnguaq (although he spelled it in an irregular manner), the suffix -*nnguaq* being a suffix of endearment. He sometimes referred to her as Ally. She was born about 1881 and died in 1921. To

further muddy the matter, there was another woman at the time, somewhat older, born
    about 1869, with the name Aleqasina, whom the Inuit usually called Aleqaherruaq
    (Aleqasersuaq in standard Greenlandic); she was the wife of Soqqaq's son, Eri, and was
    Sigluk's sister.
"What shall one do": translation, Aleqasina quoted in Gilberg, 1994, 255.
"The following natives": PAC, File 1.2.10; instructions by Peary, written 31 March 1900.
"the belle of the tribe": PFC, Arctic Expeditions, 1896, journal, 74.
"who has a bad habit": quotation from Mylius-Erichsen in Gilberg, 1969–70, 86.
"not the kind of person": ibid., 88.
"Yes, Uisaakassak": Rasmussen in ibid., 89.

20. Wanted: Dead or Alive
Rosbach, who recorded an account of Minik's life, misunderstood Jesup's name and wrote
    it as "Josofi" and "Josoe" throughout the account. He also misdated the trip to America
    and the death of Qisuk by one year, as 1896 and 1897, respectively.
"There are many large ships": Rosbach, *Avangnaamioq* 11, 86.
"If I hadn't had": ibid.
"It was so hot": ibid.
"Unlike Jesup": ibid., 87.
"What are you doing here": ibid.
"I have never met": ibid.
The Wallaces were members of Park Presbyterian Church (now West Park Presbyterian
    Church) at 165 West 86th Street, New York, from 1886, the year of their marriage. Their
    son, William Jr., born in 1887, was baptized there the following year. The Register of
    Baptisms shows no baptism of Minik.
"There were many human skeletons": Rosbach, *Avangnaamioq* 12, 91.
"He lived in a large, fine house": ibid., 92.
"If Christian people": ibid., 95.
"I was the only one": ibid., 95.
"She was smiling": ibid., 96.
"In America": Freuchen, *Arctic Adventure*, 1935, 79.
"He believed that the world": ibid., 79–80.
"When you go" and "Poor woman!": ibid., 236.

21. The Crocker Land Expedition
"reach, map the coast-line": MacMillan, 1918, introduction.
"Our home was overcrowded": ibid., 33.
"Uutaaq was related": Freuchen, *Arctic Adventure*, 1935, 40.
"Have you forgotten": MacMillan quoted in Welky, 167.
"I guess not": Minik quoted in ibid.
"a fine fellow": Hunt in ibid., 168.
"Mac feels": AMNH, Rare Book and Manuscripts Collection, Fitzhugh Green, Journal on
    the Crocker Land Expedition, 1 December 1913.
"He is invaluable": Jerome Lee Allen, undated copy, typescript diary, private collection.
    Copy in author's possession.
"Minik Wallace, the English-speaking Eskimo": AMNH, Rare Book and Manuscripts Col-
    lection, Jerome Lee Allen, Journal on the Crocker Land Expedition, 1 December 1913.
"He seems to be": Hunt and Thompson, 39–40.

"Last month": AMNH, Crocker Land File, extract from letter of Dr. Harrison Hunt to Mrs. Hunt, 9 January 1914.

"Can't discover new land without tobacco": AMNH, Rare Book and Manuscripts Collection, Donald B. MacMillan, Field Note Book no. 22, Crocker Land Expedition, 13 February 1914.

"an almost vertical wall of ice": MacMillan, 1918, 56.

"who simply loved hard work": ibid., 57.

"our best man" and "the best Eskimo": MacMillan quoted in Welky, 234.

"loyal, capable, and energetic": Ekblaw quoted in Welky, 234.

"I feel that we are": MacMillan quoted in Welky, 212.

"when gossip and tobacco smoke": MacMillan, 1918, 56.

"Tautsiannguaq had": ibid.

"Young Eskimos": ibid., 54.

"greatest achievement": Welky, 365.

"I shot once": AMNH, Rare Book and Manuscripts Collection, Fitzhugh Green, Journal on the Crocker Land Expedition, 1 May 1914.

"a calm and extra-ordinarily": Rasmussen quoted in Welky, 236.

"not only a man": AMNH, File 1016; translation of letter from Rasmussen to Right Reverend Dean C. Schultz-Lorentzen, 6 January 1921.

22. On Thin Ice

"We cooked up some beans": AMNH, Rare Book and Manuscripts Collection, Jerome Lee Allen, Journal on the Crocker Land Expedition, 3 April 1914.

"Our supplies were gone": Ekblaw, "The Summer at North Star Bay," in MacMillan, 1918, 327.

"We untied our dogs" and "As Sechmann drew": Blossom, 86–92.

"very repentant": MacMillan, 1918, 143–44.

"At length": ibid., 151–52.

"The action began": ibid., 152.

"He wants the south" Fitzhugh Green quoted in Welky, 169.

"We hardly knew": MacMillan quoted in Welky, 220–21.

"absolutely unfit": ibid., 193.

"He asked me what crime": Freuchen, *Arctic Adventure*, 1935, 303.

"a mild little man": ibid., 300.

"a tactless, impolite person": ibid., 306.

"whined and expostulated": ibid., 304.

"called the Eskimos": Hunt and Thompson, 76.

"He showed me the gifts": Freuchen, *Arctic Adventure*, 1935, 301.

"Evidently he had believed": ibid., 301–02.

"I would have sat": Malaurie, 237.

"Not just a mannequin": ibid.

"We could all be rich": ibid.

"Now I am only waiting": Rosbach, *Avangnaamioq* 12, 99.

"I do not approve": Hovey quoted in Welky, 355.

"to the sorrow of no-one": translation, Freuchen quoted in Gilberg, 1994, 526.

"The captain made the mistake": Freuchen, *Arctic Adventure*, 1935, 274.

"our troubled soul": translation, Freuchen quoted in Gilberg, 1994, 526.

23. Back on Broadway

"various alleged Arctic explorations": Helgesen, 21 July 1916, 1626.

"Robert E. Peary's claims," and "for services": ibid.

"not a defender": Helgesen, 4 September 1916, 42.

"Is it possible": ibid., 70.

John Clark: Clark's reminiscences about Minik are from an interview with the author on July 21, 1994, when Clark was ninety-nine years old.

"I've got a big story": *New-York Tribune*, 22 September 1916.

"No, I don't know": ibid.

"All this information": *The Boston Post*, 22 September 1916.

"impart the information": *The New York Times*, 29 September 1916.

"I have no doubt": letter, secretary for Congressman Helgesen to Mene Wallace, 26 October 1916, in Private Archive of Minik (Mene Wallace), Registration NKA P.10.00.82, Greenland National Museum and Archives.

The United States effectively gave up any claim to Greenland with a treaty, "Cession of the Danish West Indies," signed at New York on 4 August 1916 and proclaimed into law on 25 January 1917.

"back on Broadway": *New-York Tribune*, 22 September 1916.

"took a bath": *The New York Times*, 22 September 1916.

"the igloos of Broadway": ibid.

"*Hip-Hip-Hooray*": *Logansport Daily Tribune*, 31 October 2016.

"B.F.B.": *The New York Times*, 29 December 1916.

"I had to learn": *New-York Tribune*, 22 September 1916.

"Was I satisfied": *The New York Times*, 22 September 1916.

"It would have been better": *New-York Tribune*, 22 September 1916.

"Of course, I made a hit": ibid.

"You can support": *The New York Times*, 22 September 1916.

"he did not get on with natives": Steele, 169.

"assisting the tribe": letter, Edwin S. Brooke Jr. to Mene Wallace, 24 September 1916, in Private Archive of Minik (Mene Wallace).

"Can we not find": AMNH, Department of Anthropology, File 1900-6; memo of Osborn to Sherwood, 13 January 1917.

Minik Qisuk: newspapers spelled it *Mene Keeso*. *Des Moines Daily News*, 30 March 1917.

"I don't know whether": *Ferdinand News*, 30 March 1917.

"neither fish nor fowl": Bunnell, 60.

24. The North Country

"nice fellow to have around": Bunnell, 61.

"It's hard for them": Ellsworth Bunnell, personal communication.

"I am asking a favor": *Evening Telegram*, undated (December 1918).

"he was a nice guy": Bunnell, 27.

25. "They Have Come Home"

"I asked about Qisuk": Aqqaluk Lynge in Cernetig, *The Globe and Mail*, 10 April 1992.

The 1992 newspaper articles that spurred new interest in Minik and in the bones held in the American Museum of Natural History were "Bones of History Buried in a Bureaucratic Limbo," by Miro Cernetig in *The Globe and Mail* (Toronto), 10 April 1992, and "The Skeleton in the Museum's Closet," by William Claiborne in *The Washington Post*, 5 April 1992.

These two newspapers were also the first to break the news of the impending return of the Skeletons to Qaanaaq for burial, three weeks before the event happened. Those stories were "Minik's Saga Will Finally Be Laid to Rest," by Miro Cernetig in *The Globe and Mail* (Toronto), 6 July 1993, and "The Eskimos Finally Go Home," by Charles Truehart in *The Washington Post*, 6 July 1993.

"In recent years": press release, Division of Anthropology Archives, American Museum of Natural History, filed as "Burial Service, Qaanaaq, Greenland. 8/1/93. Edmund Carpenter and Adelaide de Menil."

"the long-sought": address by Mayor August Eipe at the cemetery, 1 August 1993, in ibid.

"life was not kind": sermon delivered at the burial of skeletons, 1 August 1993, in ibid.

"Museums of natural history": remarks of Edmund Carpenter, 1 August, 1993, Qaanaaq, Greenland in ibid.

"ethnographic and linguistic": Carpenter, 27.

Epilogue

"in bad shape" and "comingled the funds": notes in a file on the estate of Willis Sharpe Kilmer, in the office of Colin T. Naylor III (lawyer), Binghamton, NY, page 12.

"stories hidden": and "How do you think": Tanya Linn Albrigtsen-Frable in Harper, *Nunatsiaq News*, 14 June 2013.

"[The play] is about": Susanne Andreasen quoted in Ducharme, *Nunatsiaq Online*, 6 July 2016.

BIBLIOGRAPHY

Archives and Libraries

American Museum of Natural History (New York, NY): Administrative Archives, Department of Anthropology Archives, and Rare Book and Manuscript Collection.
American Philosophical Society (Philadelphia, PA): Franz Boas Papers.
Cobleskill Town Library (Cobleskill, NY).
Explorers Club Archives (New York, NY): Peary Arctic Club records.
National Archives (Washington, DC): Record Group 401 (1), Peary Family Collection.
New-York Historical Society (New York, NY): Osborn Papers.
Manhattan College (Riverdale, NY): Newspaper clippings in a scrapbook.
Rigsarkivet (Royal Archives, Copenhagen, Denmark): Records of the Danish Ministry of Foreign Affairs, File A.S.95/08 of the Royal Danish Consulate, New York.

Newspapers

The New York Times
"The Arctic Mystery," 30 October 1876: 4.
"Mrs. Peary and Her Furs," 14 March 1897.
"Peary's Vessel Returns," 21 September 1897: 7.
"Peary Goes to Washington," 24 September 1897: 5.
"Peary to Stake His Life," 25 September 1897: 5.
"Returned from the Arctic," 27 September 1897: 8.
"Back from the Far North," 1 October 1897: 12.
"The Big Meteorite Landed," 3 October 1897: 24.
"Too Warm for Eskimos," 11 October 1897: 12.
"Topics of the Times," 28 November 1897.
"Kushan the Eskimo Dead," 19 February 1898.
"Topics of the Times," 21 February 1898.
"Deaths Reported March 16," 17 March 1898.
"Off for the North Pole," 3 July 1898: 11.
"The Art of Taxidermy," 25 June 1899.
"Young Eskimo Learns Fast," 27 June 1899.
"Judgments," 20 November 1900: 15.
"Peary's Athletic Protégé," 2 February 1902.
"Eskimo Skater Third," 19 February 1905.
"Mene to Be an Usher," 28 October 1907: 9.
"Eskimo Mene in College," 2 February 1909: 2.
"Mene Gone to Balk Peary?" 14 April 1909: 5.
"Latest Bulletin from Mene. New Letter Says Eskimo Boy Is Thinking of Suicide," 23 May 1909: 4.
"Equipping for Arctic Trip," 4 July 1909: 5.
"Mene Wallace Going Home," 9 July 1909: 10.

"Eskimo Mene Off for Home," 11 July 1909: 2.
"Mene's Opinion of Us" [editorial], 12 July 1909: 6.
"Mene's Opinion," 17 July 1909.
"Cook Gave a Show in a Dime Museum," 10 September 1909: 4.
"Cook Did Not Claim the Pole to Whitney," 13 September 1909: 2.
"Calls Peary a Falsifier," 14 September 1909: 2.
"Prof. Dean Reinstated," 11 February 1911: 4
"Peary Denies Mene Letter Charges," 14 February 1911: 3.
"Relief Ship Held in Crocker Land Ice," 25 June 1916.
"Says He Has Secret of Pole's Discovery," 22 September 1916: 7.
"Eskimo Going to Capital," 29 September 1916: 8.
"Eskimo Boy Will Appear at Benefit," 29 December 1916: 6.
"Mene Wallace to Become a Citizen," 28 January 1917.
"Peary's Eskimo Dead," 13 December 1918: 6.
"Obituary" [Chester Beecroft], 8 January 1959.

New York World
"Mene, the American, Late of Smith's Sound," 27 January 1899: 9.
"Eskimo Invalids Singing of the Snow," 31 January 1898: 12.
"Give Me My Father's Body" [magazine supplement], 6 January 1907: 3.
"Land of Snow Beckons Meenie, Esquimau Boy," 30 June 1908: 1, 3.
"Missing Esquimau Boy Mene Writes He's Going North," 13 April 1909: 1.
"Esquimau Boy Mene Threatens to End His Life," 23 May 1909: 2.
"Goes North to Save Eskimo from Suicide," 24 May 1909: 16.
"Esquimau Boy Mene Back in New York," 26 May 1909: 2.
"Peary Fears Him, Says Mene, the Esquimau," 27 May 1909: 6.
"Plans for Relief of Dr. Cook Are Complete," 10 June 1909: 4.

New York Evening Mail
"Angry Over Skeleton of Eskimo," 13 April 1909: 3.
"Why Mene, Young Eskimo Boy, Ran Away from His Home," 21 April 1909: 1, 4.
"Mene Reaches Ottawa on Way Home," 22 April 1909: 8.
"Prof. Boas Defends the Fake Funeral," 24 April 1909: 4.
"Eskimo Boy Tells of His Wrongs," 26 May 1909: 1, 13.
"Eskimo Boy to Go Home at Last," 8 July 1909.
"Mene Calls Us Race of Cannibals," 9 July 1909.
"Mene Goes, Agrees Not to Return Here," 10 July 1909: 1.
"Morris K. Jesup Left $12,814,894," 22 July 1909.

New-York Tribune
"Going Home to Greenland" [illustrated supplement], 27 March 1898: 7.
"An Attractive Esquimau" [illustrated supplement], 10 July 1898: 5.
"Mene in His New Home" [illustrated supplement], 8 January 1899: 1, 2.
"A Question Under the Burial Law," 14 June 1899.
"Esquimau Girl Dead," 15 June 1899: 10.
"It Has Not Been Dissected," 17 June 1899: 16.
"Esquimau Children" [illustrated supplement], 18 November 1900: 1.
"Work Halted for Inquiry," 20 March 1901: 1.

"Esquimau Hunts Pole," 22 January 1909.
"Mene Wallace, Eskimo, Back with North Pole 'Secret,'" 22 September 1916: 9.

New-York Daily Tribune
"Trouble Over the Dead Esquimo," 19 February 1898: 10.
"The Windward Sets Sail," 3 July 1898: 12.
"William Wallace Resigns," 14 January 1901: 4.
"Last of Peary's Esquimaus, Ill," 9 May 1903: 16.

The New York Herald
"Mene Wallace Catches Pneumonia," 18 November 1908: 4.
"Ready for Rescue of Dr. F. A. Cook," 4 June 1909.
"Mission of the Relief Ship Jeanie Ends," 20 September 1909.
"'My Word!' Says Briton of Mene Wallace," undated clipping, 1909.
"Holds Data at 'Million,'" 16 September 1916: 4.

The Brooklyn Daily Eagle
"The Esquimau's Body," 18 February 1898: 3.
Untitled, 7 April 1899: 13.

The New York Sun
"Eskimos at Highbridge" [supplement], 12 December 1897: 4.
"Three Unhappy Eskimos," 24 April 1898: 2.
"Eskimo to Hunt the Pole," 22 January 1909.
"Wallace to Seek Dr. Cook," 23 January 1909.
"Queer Case of the Lost Eskimo," 16 April 1909.
"Last Peary Eskimo Dies of Pneumonia," undated clipping, 1918.

The Cobleskill Index
4 November 1897: 8.
18 November 1897: 6.
28 April 1898: 5.
28 April 1898: 8.
19 May 1898: 1.
"The Esquimaux," 19 May 1898: 8.
16 June 1898: 5.
23 June 1898: 5.
30 June 1898: 8.
"The Esquimaux," 7 July 1898: 1.
7 July 1898: 4.
1 September 1898.
22 September 1898: 1.
20 October 1898.
2 February 1899.
"Wallace Prize," 8 June 1899: 1.
"The Wallace Prize," 22 June 1899: 1.
"Mene, the Esquimaux," 29 June 1899: 1.

6 July 1899: 2.
20 July 1899: 1.
27 July 1899: 2.
3 August 1899: 5.
19 July 1900: 5.
31 July 1902: 5.
21 August 1902: 5.
"Obituary" [Rhetta Wallace], 31 March 1904.
"Mrs. William Wallace," 18 March 1937: 8.
25 March 1937: 5.

Dansk-Amerikaneren
"Den forladte Eskimodreng!" 8 July 1908.
"Den Danske Regering Retter Forespørgsel om en Eskimodreng in New York," 23 September 1908.
"Eskimodrengen Meenie," 21 October 1908.
"Eskimoen Meenie funden i syg og hjælpløs Tilstand," 25 November 1908.
"Eskimodrengen Meenie, vil være Civilingeniør," 27 January 1909.
"Eskimodrengen Meenie," 3 February 1909.
"Eskimodrengen Meenie," 7 April 1908.
"Menee," 28 April 1909.
"Mene er gaaet hjem!" 14 July 1909.
"Mene Wallace," 4 August 1909.

Other
"Living a Fairy Tale," *Newark Daily Advocate*, 18 January 1899.
"Operation on Eskimo Boy," *Racine Daily Journal*, 9 May 1903: 3.
"Esquimau Mimi Now Selling Lots," unidentified clipping, 9 October 1904.
"To Train Young Eskimo," *The Washington Post*, 12 January 1907: 11.
"Peary Dooms Esquimau Boy to Sorrowful Exile," unidentified clipping, 1908.
"Dr. Cook's Wife Plans Arctic Relief Trip," *New York Evening Journal*, 8 January 1909.
"Eskimau Boy, First to Take College Course, Will Seek North Pole," *The Evening Telegram*, 22 January 1909.
"Why Arctic Explorer Peary's Neglected Eskimo Boy Wants to Shoot Him," *San Francisco Examiner* [magazine supplement], 9 May 1909.
"Peary Relief Ship Will Seek Dr. Cook," *New York American*, 10 June 1909.
"Off to Etah to Relieve Peary," *Bangor (ME) Daily Commercial*, 4 August 1909.
"Peary Relief Ship," *Lockport (NY) Union-Sun*, 17 August 1909.
"Eskimo Boy Who Declares He Will Lead His People to the North Pole," *The Fort Wayne Sentinel*, 14 July 1909: 3.
"Will Seek North Pole," *The Daily Reflector* (Jeffersonville, IN), 15 July 1909: 1.
"A Good Eskimo," *The Galveston Daily News*, 28 October 1909: 4.
"Peary Accused of Reading Mail Sent Out by Cook," unidentified clipping, 1909.
Untitled, *Clubfellow* (undated clipping), 1909.
"Intend to Search for Records of Cook," *Nevada State Journal* (Reno), 29 May 1910.
"Trip to Vindicate Cook," *Gulfport (MS) Daily Herald*, 7 June 1910: 6.
"Did Not Find Pole," *The Washington Post*, 10 January 1911: 6.
"A Boy Without a Country," *The Washington Post*, 20 January 1911.

"Says He Knows Who Won Pole," *The Boston Post*, 22 September 1916: 15.

"Did Cook and Peary Find the Pole? He Will Tell for a Million," *Des Moines Daily News*, 30 September 1916: 3.

"Eskimo to Test Show's Ice," *Logansport (IN) Daily Tribune*, 31 October 1916: 2.

"Eskimo Deserts Dane King," *Ferdinand (IN) News*, 30 March 1917: 2.

"The Tender Eskimo," *Chicago Journal*, 17 December 1918.

"Eskimo Guide Who Helped Peary Find North Pole Dies in New Hampshire," *The Evening Telegram* (New York), undated clipping, December 1918: 2.

"Peary and the Eskimos," *The Christian Science Monitor*, undated clipping, 1918.

"Confederate Money Held by East Orange Resident," unidentified clipping, 1938.

Olsen, Norman, "Eskimo Introduced at 1898 Cobleskill Fair," *Cobleskill (NY) Times-Journal*, 30 June 1976.

"Minik fra Thule—gangster i USA," *Jyllands-Posten* (Denmark), 9 October 1983: 5.

Cernetig, Miro, "Bones of History Buried in a Bureaucratic Limbo," *The Globe and Mail*, 10 April 1992: A1 and A5.

Claiborne, William, "The Skeleton in the Museum's Closet," *The Washington Post*, 5 April 1992: F1 and F6.

Cernetig, Miro, "Minik's Saga Will Finally Be Laid to Rest," *The (Toronto) Globe and Mail*, 6 July 1993: A1 and A2.

Truehart, Charles, "The Eskimos Finally Go Home," *The Washington Post*, 6 July 1993: C1 and C3.

"Ukiut 95-t qaanngiuttut inughuit iliverneqartut," *Atuagagdliutit/Grønlandsposten*, 7 August 1997: 32.

"Fire inughuit begravet 95 år efter deres død," *Atuagagliutit/Grønlandsposten*, 7 August 1997: 32.

Harper, Kenn, "The Minik Mural in Brooklyn," in "Taissumani," *Nunatsiaq News*, 14 June 2013.

Books, Manuscripts, Magazines, Journals, and Online Sites

Allen, Everett S. *Arctic Odyssey: The Life of Rear Admiral Donald B. MacMillan*. New York: Dodd, Mead & Company, 1963.

Andreassen, Janni. *Altid Frimodig: Biografi om Polarforskeren, Forfatteren og Eventyreren Peter Freuchen*. Copenhagen: Gyldendal, 2013.

Astrup, Eivind. *With Peary Near the Pole*. London: C. Arthur Pearson, 1898.

Aylmer, Kevin, and Roger Bowen. "The Lost Republic." *Yankee*, March 1968: 60–67 and 101–03.

Blossom, Frederick A. (ed.). *Told at the Explorers Club: True Tales of Modern Exploration*. New York: Albert and Charles Boni, 1936.

Borup, George. *A Tenderfoot with Peary*. New York: Frederick A. Stokes Company, 1911.

Brown, William Adams. *Morris Ketchum Jesup: A Character Sketch*. New York: Charles Scribner's Sons, 1910.

Bryce, Robert M. *Cook & Peary: The Polar Controversy, Resolved*. Mechanicsburg, PA: Stackpole Books, 1997.

Bunnell, Ellsworth H. "Mene." *New Hampshire Profiles*, January 1969: 26–61.

Burnes, J. Caldwell. "The Cape York Esquimaux." *Nickell Magazine* 8, no. 6 (January 1897): 323–26.

Carpenter, Edmund. "Dead Truth, Live Myth." *European Review of Native American Studies* 11, no. 2 (1997): 27–29.

De Frece, (Lady) Matilda Alice Powles. *Recollections of Vesta Tilley*. London: Hutchinson and Co., 1934.

Dick, Lyle. *Muskox Land: Ellesmere Island in the Age of Contact*. Calgary: University of Calgary Press, 2001.

Ducharme, Steve. "Nunavut Audience Moved by Retelling of Minik Tragedy." *Nunatsiaq Online*, 6 July 2016.

Eames, Hugh. *Winner Lose All*. Boston: Little, Brown, 1973.

Ekblaw, Elmer. *Along Unknown Shores: Narratives of Exploration in the Far North*. New York, London: Harper & Brothers, n.d.

_____. *The Polar Eskimo: Their Land and Life*. PhD thesis, Clark University, 1926 (unpublished).

Epps, Bernard. "The Republic of Indian Stream." *Canadian Frontier*, 1978: 72–74.

Fleischer, Jørgen. *Udsteder*. Copenhagen: Gyldendal, 1983.

Fleming, Archibald Lang. *Archibald the Arctic*. New York: Appleton-Century-Crofts, 1956.

Fogg, Katherine A. "Pittsburg, New Hampshire—The Last Frontier." *Outlook*, Winter 1977: 12–15.

Frandsen, Pertti, and Flemming Petersen. "The 100th Anniversary of the Mission Station 'The North Star' at Thule." *Greenland Collector* 14, no. 3 (September 2009): 9.

Freeman, Andrew. *The Case for Doctor Cook*. New York: Coward-McCann, 1961.

Freuchen, Peter. *Arctic Adventure*. New York: Farrar and Rinehart, 1935.

_____. *Ivalu, the Eskimo Wife*. New York: Lee Furman, 1935.

_____. *Vagrant Viking*. New York: Julian Messner, 1953.

_____. *Book of the Eskimos*. New York: World Publishing Company, 1961.

Freuchen, Pipaluk, Ib Freuchen, and Helge Larsen. *Bogen om Peter Freuchen*. Copenhagen: Forlaget Fremad, 1958.

Friis, Herman, ed. *The Arctic Diary of Russell Williams Porter*. Charlottesville: University Press of Virginia, 1976.

Gilberg. Rolf. "Uisaakavasak, 'The Big Liar.'" *Folk* 11–12 (1969–70): 83–95.

_____. "Changes in the Life of the Polar Eskimos Resulting from a Canadian Immigration into the Thule District, North Greenland, in the 1860s." *Folk* 16–17 (1974–75): 159–70.

_____. "En arktisk handelstation i 'ingenmandsland,' Thule." *Tidsskriftet Grønland* 9–10 (1977): 247–54.

_____. "Missionen iblandt Inuhuit." *Den Grønlandske Kirkesag* 120 (January 1984): 18–27.

_____. *Mennesket Minik*. Ilbe: Espergade, 1994.

Green, Fitzhugh. *Peary: The Man Who Refused to Fail*. New York: G. P. Putnam's Sons, 1926.

Hastrup, Kirsten. *Vinterens Hjerte: Knud Rasmussen og hans tid*. Copenhagen: Gads Forlag, 2010.

Helgeson, Henry T. "Analysis of Evidence Presented by Robert E. Peary to Committee on Naval Affairs, 1910–11." Extension of Remarks of Hon. Henry T. Helgesen . . . in the House of Representatives, 25 January 1916. *Appendix to the Congressional Record*. Washington: Government Printing Office, 1915: 268–327.

_____. "Peary and the North Pole." Extension of Remarks of Hon. Henry T. Helgesen . . . in the House of Representatives, 21 July 1916. *Appendix to the Congressional Record*. Washington: Government Printing Office, 1916: 1626–46.

_____. "Dr. Cook and the North Pole." Extension of Remarks of Hon. Henry T. Helgesen . . . in the House of Representatives, 4 September 1916. *Appendix to the Congressional Record*. Washington: Government Printing Office, 1916: 42–70.

Hendrik, Hans. *Memoirs of Hans Hendrik, the Arctic Traveller* (ed. Dr. Henry Rink). London: Trubner and Co., 1878.

Herbert, Wally. *The Noose of Laurels: The Discovery of the North Pole*. London: Hodder & Stoughton, 1989.

Hobbs, William Herbert. *Peary*. New York: Macmillan, 1936.

Holtved, Erik. "Contributions to Polar Eskimo Ethnography." *Meddelelser om Grønland* 182, no. 2. Copenhagen: C. A. Reitzels Forlag, 1967.

Hrdlička, Aleš. "An Eskimo Brain." *American Anthropologist*, 3, (1901): 454–500.

_____. "Contribution to the Anthropology of Central and Smith Sound Eskimo." *Anthropological Papers of the American Museum of Natural History* 5 (1910): 175–280.

Hunt, Harrison J., and Ruth Hunt Thompson. *North to the Horizon*. Camden, ME: Down East Books, 1980.

Kane, Elisha Kent. *Arctic Explorations: The Second Grinnell Expedition in Search of Sir John Franklin, 1853, '54, '55*. 2 vols. Philadelphia: Childs & Peterson, 1957.

Kaplan, Susan A., and Robert McCracken Peck, eds. *North by Degree: New Perspectives on Arctic Exploration*. Philadelphia: American Philosophical Society, 2013.

Kroeber, A. L. "Animal Tales of the Eskimo." *Journal of American Folk-Lore* 12, no. 44 (January–March 1899): 17–23.

_____. "Tales of the Smith Sound Eskimo." *Journal of American Folk-Lore* 12, no. 46, (July–September 1899): 166–182.

_____. "The Eskimo of Smith Sound." *Bulletin of the American Museum of Natural History* 12 (1899): 265–327.

Lee, Florence Leonard. "An Arctic Honeymoon." In Rudolf Kersting (ed.), *The White World: Life and Adventures Within the Arctic Circle Portrayed by Famous Living Explorers*. New York: Lewis, Scribner & Co., 1902: 161–74.

Lennert, Ulrik. *Angalatoorsuaq Oodaag*. Nuuk:Atuakkiorfik, 1997.

Loring, Stephen, and Miroslav Prokopec. "A Most Peculiar Man: The Life and Times of Aleš Hrdlička." In Tamara L. Bray and Thomas W. Killion (eds.), *Reckoning with the Dead*. Washington, DC: Smithsonian Institution Press, 1994: 26–40.

MacMillan, Donald B. *Four Years in the White North*. New York: Harper, 1918.

_____. *Etah and Beyond*. Boston, New York: Houghton Mifflin Company, 1927.

Malaurie, Jean. *The Last Kings of Thule*. New York: E. P. Dutton, 1982.

Meier, Allison C. "Minik and the Meteor." In *Narrative-ly*, published on the Internet in narrative.ly/minik-and-the-meteor, 19 March 2013.

Møller, Nuka. *Kalaallit aqqi / Grønlandske personnavne / Greenlandic personal names*. Nuuk, Greenland: Oqaasileriffik / Sprogsekretariat i Grønland / Greenland Language Secretariat, 2015.

Murphy, Robert Cushman. "Skeleton in the Museum Closet." *Peruvian Times*, 20 November 1959: 13.

National Cyclopedia of American Biography, vol. 32. New York: James T. White and Company, 1945.

Olsen, Gustav. *Palasip Ajoqersuiartortitap Gustav Olsen Ivnaanganermiititdlune Uvdlorsiutaisa Ilait*. Nuuk, Greenland, 1923.

Olsen, Knud. *Avanerssuarmiune Ajoqersuiartortitaq*. Nuuk, Greenland: Det Grønlandske Forlag, 1980.

Osbon, (Captain) B. S. "Cook and Peary." *Tourist* 6, no. 3 (September 1911): 208–16; and 6, no. 4 (October 1911): 309–18; and 6, no. 5 (November 1911): 443–50.

Oswalt, Wendell H. *Eskimos and Explorers*. Novato, CA: Chandler and Sharp, 1979.

Peary, Josephine Diebitsch. *My Arctic Journal*. New York: Contemporary Publishing Company, 1893.

Peary, Marie and Josephine ("The Snow Baby and her Mother"). *Children of the Arctic*. New York: Frederick A. Stokes, 1903.

Peary, Robert. *Northward Over the Great Ice*. 2 vols. New York: Frederick A. Stokes Company, 1898.

_____. *Snowland Folk*. New York: Frederick A. Stokes Company, 1904.

_____. *Nearest the Pole*. New York: Doubleday, Page and Co., 1907.

_____. *The People of the Polar North*. Philadelphia: J. B. Lippincott Company, 1908.

Rosbach, Sechmann. "Inuup Kalaatdlip Minik-mik Atigdlup Inuunera." *Avangnaamioq* 11 (1934): 84–88; and 12 (1934): 91–99 (manuscript translation by Kenn and Navarana Harper).

_____. *The North Pole*. New York: Frederick A. Stokes Company, 1910.

_____. *Secrets of Polar Travel*. New York: Century Co., 1917.

Rasky, Frank. *The North Pole or Bust*. Toronto: McGraw-Hill Ryerson Limited, 1977.

Rasmussen, Knud. *Greenland by the Polar Sea*. New York: Frederick A Stokes Company, n.d.

Sagan, Carl. *Broca's Brain*. London: Hodder and Stoughton, 1980.

Sand, Rudolf. *Knud Rasmussens Virke i og for Thule-Distriktet*. Copenhagen: Knud Rasmussens Mindeudgave, 1935.

"Search for Lost Arctic Film Footage Yields Orphaned Gem." *Bowdoin News* (Bowdoin College, Brunswick, ME). http://www.bowdoin.edu/news/archives/1academic-news/004171.shtml. Story posted 8 June 2007. Accessed 22 November 2016.

Sheldon, Mary B. "The Only Eskimo in the United States." *St. Nicholas* 28 (April 1901): 525–27.

Smith, Gordon W. *The Historical and Legal Background of Canada's Arctic Claims*. PhD thesis, Columbia University, 1952 (unpublished).

Steele, Harwood. *Policing the Arctic*. Toronto: Ryerson, 1935.

Sturm, Ruth. *When the Eskimos Came to Lawyersville*. 1950 (unpublished high school essay).

Tarrant, Isabel. *Dam It All*. Privately published, 1973.

Von Linden, Hal. "Cold Enough for an Eskimo. Old Schoharie Winters Weren't." *Schoharie County Historical Review*, Fall–Winter 1977: 20–21 (reprinted from *Knickerbocker News*, February 1961).

Weems, John Edward. *Race for the North Pole*. London: Heinemann, 1961.

_____. *Peary, the Explorer and the Man*. London: Eyre and Spottiswood, 1967.

Welky, David. *A Wretched and Precarious Situation: In Search of the Last Arctic Frontier*. New York: W. W. Norton, 2016.

Who Was Who in the Theatre: 1912–1976. Detroit: Gale Research Company, n.d.

ACKNOWLEDGMENTS

Since the original publication of *Give Me My Father's Body: The Life of Minik, the New York Eskimo*, I have acquired more information and gained new insights into the life of Minik. I want to acknowledge the assistance of the following who have helped to make this a different book:

Navarana Freuchen, for information on the Freuchen family;

Pia and David Goddard (Randall), for information on Jerome Allen of the Crocker Land Expedition;

Genny LeMoine, curator, Peary-MacMillan Arctic Museum, Bowdoin College, for information on Donald MacMillan and the Crocker Land Expedition;

Nuka Møller, of Oqaasileriffik, Nuuk, Greenland, for information on Minik's place in Greenlandic popular culture, and for his friendship over the years;

Lisathe Møller Kruse, Oqaasileriffik, Nuuk, Greenland, for information on Greenlandic place-names;

Inge Høst Seiding, archivist, Greenland National Archives;

Knud Michelsen, Danish author, for a copy of a letter written in Thule and bearing Minik's signature;

Rolf Gilberg, Danish researcher and author and retired museum inspector, for his publication of *Mennesket Minik*;

Aviaq Harper, my daughter, for translating some Danish and Greenlandic sources;

Niels Frandsen, former archivist, Greenland National Museum and Archives, Nuuk, Greenland;

Tanya Linn Albrigtsen-Frable, artist, for information on Minik's depiction in a mural in Brooklyn;

Jeremy Ward, curator, Canadian Canoe Museum, Peterborough, Ontario;

and the following writers, scholars, and friends for their encouragement, criticism, and friendship over the years:

Robert Petersen, retired professor, University of Copenhagen;

Peter Dawes, geologist and author, Denmark;

Pujo Olsen, linguist and scholar, Greenland;

Dr. Jonathan King, formerly of the British Museum, for many
    discussions on living ethnographic exhibitions;

Dr. Lyle Dick, for his insight into the character of Robert Peary;

Dr. Russell Potter, scholar and friend;

John and Carolyn MacDonald, for their generous friendship
    over forty years;

Jack Hicks, a tireless supporter;

Larry Millman, author and raconteur, for being Larry;

Kevin Spacey, for his friendship and interest in the story;

Claude Brunet, my lawyer, who, in the absence of an agent, has
    always provided good advice.

I would be remiss if I did not thank my editor, Dirk Van Susteren, for his patience in helping to shape this new edition of the life of Minik. Thanks are due also to my publisher, Chip Fleischer at Steerforth Press, for his unwavering belief in Minik.

Finally, my profound thanks and enduring love to my wife, Kathleen Lippa, for enduring my frustrations and idiosyncracies during the creation of this book. Without you, nothing is possible.

In the original publication of *Give Me My Father's Body: The Life of Minik, the New York Eskimo*, I acknowledged the assistance of the following, and have updated those acknowledgments ever so slightly:

Polar Inuit

Inuutersuaq Ulloriaq, historian of the Polar Inuit;

Qaaqqutsiaq, grandson of the shaman Soqqaq;

Qisuk, who bore the name of Minik's father;

Imiina, a hunter and friend;

Avoortungiaq, an elderly woman who knew Minik;

Amaunnalik, my former mother-in-law, named for Minik's
    mother's sister;

Navarana Qaavigaq, my former wife.

Greenlanders

Ulrik Lennert, chief of the Royal Greenland Trade Department in Qaanaaq, during the years I lived there. He had a deep and compassionate interest in the life of Minik;

H. C. Petersen, scholar, for directing me to Sechmann Rosbach's account of Minik's life in an old copy of *Avangnaamioq*.

In Schoharie County, New York

Jared Van Wagenen III, Lawyersville, who provided me with an excellent photograph of Minik, and whose father knew the Inuit boy;

Norman Olsen, town historian, Cobleskill, for running an article of mine soliciting information on the Wallace family;

Tom Johnson, Lawyersville, who lived at William Wallace's former Cold Stream Farm;

Ruth Sturm Graulich, Sharon Springs, who sent me a copy of a high school social studies essay she had written on the Inuit in Lawyersville thirty years earlier;

Reverend Jeffrey van der Wiel, of the Reformed Church of Lawyersville, who accompanied me on a visit to many of the eldest members of his church;

Bill McGovern, Mereness Funeral Home, Cobleskill;

Timothy Holmes, librarian, Cobleskill;

Mrs. Wanda Van Tassel, town clerk, Cobleskill;

Loraine Foster, Afton;

Edith Osterhout, Cobleskill;

Luanna Strouse, Cobleskill;

Frank Andrew, Cobleskill;

Margaret N. Bliss, Middleburgh.

In New Hampshire

Alice Young, niece of Afton Hall, Pittsburg;

Howard Young, nephew of Afton Hall, Littleton;

Fay Chappell, Pittsburg, who lived at the old Hall farm;

Joanne Carlson, town clerk, Pittsburg;
Ruth Dwinell, Pittsburg;
Ellsworth Bunnell, Colebrook;
Isabel Tarrant, Manchester.

Institutions

Lee Houchins, Smithsonian Institution, Washington, DC;
Alison Wilson of the Scientific, Economic and Natural Resources Branch, US National Archives, Washington, DC;
Beth Carroll, assistant manuscript librarian, American Philosophical Society in Philadelphia;
George Michanowsky, chairman of the Archives Committee, and Janet Baldwin, librarian, of the Explorers Club in New York;
Mary Genett, assistant librarian for reference services, the American Museum of Natural History in New York;
J. R. Starkey of East Orange Public Library, East Orange, New Jersey;
the staff of the New York Public Library, Newspaper Division;
Frank J. Carroll, head, Newspaper Section, Library of Congress;
James H. Hutson, chief, Manuscript Division, Library of Congress;
Edward P. Cambio, reference specialist (international political scientist), Library of Congress;
Lee Birch, executive director, National Taxidermists Association, Cleveland, Ohio;
Annegret Ogden, reference librarian, University of California, Berkeley;
William Asadorian, Long Island Division, Queen's Borough Public Library;
Brother Philip Braniff, Admissions Office, Manhattan College, New York;
the late Dr. Junius Bird, Department of Anthropology, American Museum of Natural History;
Paul Woehrmann, Milwaukee Public Library;

Hans Sode-Madsen, archivist, Second Department, Rigsarkivet,
  Copenhagen, Denmark;
Harriet Culver, Culver Pictures Inc., New York;
William Finley Dailey, curator of the Theodore Roosevelt Col-
  lection, Harvard College Library, Cambridge, Massachusetts;
Richard A. Baker, historian, US Senate, Washington, DC;
Stuart W. Campbell, archivist, Robert Hutchings Goddard
  Library, Clark University, Worcester, Massachusetts;
Jeanette McBride, West Park Presbyterian Church, New York
  City.

Others

Hans Engelund Kristensen, editor, *Hainang*, the local newspa-
  per of Qaanaaq, Greenland;
Janet Vetter, Tequesta, Florida, granddaughter of Dr. Frederick
  Cook;
Lars Toft Rasmussen, Copenhagen, Denmark, journalist,
  former information officer, Inuit Circumpolar Conference,
  Nuuk, Greenland;
Ruth Hunt Thompson, Hancock, Maine;
Dangler Funeral Home, Morristown, New Jersey;
Greystone Park Psychiatric Hospital, Parsippany, New Jersey;
Gloria Ann McCausland, Great Neck, New York;
Mrs. Lauraine Horbak, Fallsburg, New York;
Mrs. Stanley Smith, Cooks Falls, New York;
R. A. Mickler, Montgomery, Alabama;
Kathleen Minckler Dolan, Spring Lake Heights, New Jersey;
Willis Kling, Lima, New York;
Mrs. Tricia Becknell, Franklin Lakes, New Jersey;
Mrs. Joyce Clark, Staten Island, New York;
Mrs. Louis Zeh, Binghamton, New York;
Colin T. Naylor III, Binghamton, New York;
Prof. Iain Prattis, Carleton University, Ottawa, Ontario, for
  encouragement and insight;
Dr. Trevor Lloyd, Ottawa, Ontario, for critical comment and
  inspiration;

Hon. Dennis Patterson, former minister of education, Northwest Territories, and presently a member of the Senate of Canada, for support and encouragement.

The author acknowledges permission to quote from archival material from the following institutions: New-York Historical Society; American Philosophical Society; Explorers Club Archives; National Archives, Washington, DC (and Mr. Edward Stafford for the Peary Family Collection); the Royal Archives, Copenhagen, Denmark; and the American Museum of Natural History.

The author acknowledges the following permissions to quote from published material: (1) E. P. Dutton, Inc., for selections from Jean Malaurie, *The Last Kings of Thule*; (2) Elsevier-Dutton Publishing Co., Inc., for selections from Archibald Lang Fleming, *Archibald the Arctic*; (3) Harold Matson Company, Inc., for selections from Peter Freuchen, *Arctic Adventure* and *Book of the Eskimos*.

PHOTO CREDITS

1 Explorers Club.
2 Harper Collection.
3 in Kroeber. "The Eskimo of Smith Sound." *Bulletin of the American Museum of Natural History*, vol. xii (1899), following p. 326.
4 Ibid.
5 Courtesy Peabody Museum of Archaeology and Ethnology, Harvard University.
6 in Hrdlicka. "Contributions to the Anthropology of Central and Smith Sound Eskimo." *Anthropological Papers of the American Museum of Natural History*, vol. 5 (1910), following p. 233.
7 Ibid.
8 Ibid.
9 Harper Collection.
10 Photo: Kenn Harper. Harper Collection.
11 Ibid.
12 Ibid.
13 Ibid.
14 Harper Collection.
15 Ibid..
16 in Hrdlicka, op. cit.
17 Harper Collection.
18 in Green. *Peary, The Man Who Refused to Fail.* New York: G. Putnam's Sons, 1926, facing title page.
19 Library of Congress: 12244 US262 8234.
20 Library of Congress: 12244 USZ62 30426.
21 Harper Collection.
22 Library of Congress: 12244 USZ62 42993.
23 Dartmouth College, Rauner Special Collections Library, Stefansson Collection, Manuscript Collection 198, item 5:84.
24 in "The Snow Baby and Her Mother" (Marie and Josephine Peary). *Children of the Arctic.* New York: Frederick A. Stokes Company, 1903, p. 73.
25 Peabody Museum, Harvard, N31253H2974.
26 *New York Tribune* (illustrated supplement), 8 January 1899.
27 Photo: Kenn Harper. Harper Collection.
28 Ibid.
29 *New York Tribune* (illustrated supplement), 18 November 1900.
30 *The Evening Mail* (night edition), 21 April 1909, p. 1.

31 Photo: Kenn Harper. Harper Collection.
32 Neg. no. 220545, Courtesy Department Library Services, American Museum of Natural History.
33 Courtesy: Jared van Wagenen III.
34 Courtesy: Cobleskill Public Library, Cobleskill, New York.
35 Neg. no. 46326. Courtesy Department of Library Services, American Museum of Natural History.
36 Neg. no. 2A 5161. Courtesy Department of Library Services, American Museum of Natural History.
37 Library of Congress: 12244 USZ62 16216.
38 Neg. no. 319950. Courtesy Department of Library Services, American Museum of Natural History.
39 in *The White World*. New York: Lewis, Scribner and Co., 1902, p. 192.
40 Ibid, p. 360.
41 *The World* (magazine supplement), 6 January 1907.
42 San Francisco Examiner (Magazine Supplement), 9 May 1909.
43 in De Frece. *Recollections of Vesta Tilley*. London: Hutchinson and Co. Ltd., 1934, facing p. 198.
44 Harper Collection.
45 Library of Congress: 12243 B2–881-7.
46 Harper Collection.
47 Photo: Thomas N. Krabbe. Neg. L 199. Danish National Museum, Ethnographic Department.
48 Photo: Thomas N. Krabbe. Neg. L 214. Danish National Museum, Ethnographic Department.
49 Photo: Thomas N. Krabbe. Neg. L 202. Danish National Museum, Ethnographic Department.
50 Photo: Thomas N. Krabbe. Neg. L 205. Danish National Museum, Ethnographic Department.
51 Photo: Thomas N. Krabbe. Neg. L 209. Danish National Museum, Ethnographic Department.
52 Neg. No. 234232. Courtesy Department of Library Services, American Museum of Natural History.
53 Photo: Thomas N. Krabbe. Neg. L 210. Danish National Museum, Ethnographic Department.
54 in Peary, *Northward Over the Great Ice*, vol. 1, New York: Frederick A. Stokes Complany, 1898, p. 478.
55 Photo: Thomas N. Krabbe. Neg. L 212. Danish National Museum, Ethnographic Department.
56 Photo: Thomas N. Krabbe. Neg. L 207. Danish National Museum, Ethnographic Department.

57 Photo: Thomas N. Krabbe. Neg. L 211. Danish National Museum, Ethnographic Department.
58 Harper Collection.
59 Photo: Erik Holtved. Arktisk Institut, #42.594.
60 Neg. L 186a. Danish National Museum, Ethnographic Department.
61 No. 161889. Royal Library, Copenhagen, Denmark.
62 Photo: probably Peter Freuchen. Neg. L 1066. Danish National Museum, Ethnographic Department.
63 Harper Collection.
64 Courtesy: Knud Michelsen.
65 Neg. no. 230128. Courtesy Department of Library Services, American Museum of Natural History.
66 Harper Collection.
67 Photo: Peter Freuchen. Danish National Museum, Ethnographic Department.
68 Photo: W. Elmer Ekblaw. Neg. no. 233668. Courtesy Department of Library Services, American Museum of Natural History.
69 Photo: W. Elmer Ekblaw. Neg. no. 233666. Courtesy Department of Library Services, American Museum of Natural History.
70 in MacMillan. Four Years in the White North. Harper, 1918, facing p. 33.
71 Photo: W. Elmer Ekblaw. Neg. no. 233667. Courtesy Department of Library Services, American Museum of Natural History.
72 Photo: E. O. Hovey. Neg. no. 234193. Courtesy Department of Library Services, American Museum of Natural History.
73 Neg. no. 36573. Courtesy Department of Library Services, American Museum of Natural History.
74 Photo: D. B. MacMillan. Neg. no. 231238. Courtesy Department of Library Services, American Museum of Natural History.
75 Harper Collection.
76 Courtesy: Alice Young.
77 Courtesy: Alice Young.
78 Courtesy: Alice Young.
79 Courtesy: Alice Young.
80 Photo by Kenn Harper, Harper Collection.
81 Harper Collection.
82 Photo: Kenn Harper, Harper Collection.
83 Photo: Kenn Harper, Harper Collection.
84 Photo: Kenn Harper, Harper Collection.
85 Photo: Kenn Harper, Harper Collection.
86 Photo: Kenn Harper, Harper Collection.

INDEX

The italicized numbers refer to the numbered photographic plates in the photo inserts and not to page numbers in the text.

and Polar Inuit in New York, 8, 37, 45, 46
and relationship with Minik, 47, 49, 50,
54, 74, 75, 95, 105–6, 136–37, 183
and relationship with Wallace, 71, 72, 74,
78, 95, 101, 105, 138
and revenge fantasy of Mink, 187–88
and remains of Qisuk, 186, 187
Wallace letters to, 45–46, 74, 95, 101, 103

Kane, Elisha Kent
Arctic explorations of, 29, 30, 118
and Polar Inuit, 17, 19–20
Kroeber, Alfred
as anthropologist, 90, 91, 235
study of Polar Inuit, 41, 81–82, 83, 88, 91
Krueger, Hans, 235
Kuuttiikittoq, 209–10

Lennert, Ulrik, xiii, xiv
Lizzie (nurse), 58, 219
Loeb, William, Jr., 96, 98, 99–100

MacMillan, Donald Baxter, 73
and Crocker Land expedition, 194–95,
196, 197, 198–99, 200, 201
expeditions of, 205–6, 207–8
film shot by, 240
and Minik, 195–96, 199, 205, 207
and North Pole controversy, 213–214
Majaq, 31, 32, 157, 169
Malaurie, Jean, xiii, 209, 210
Mannik, 31, 32
Margrethe, Queen of Denmark, 232
McKinley, William, 28, 45
Melgaard, Jørgen, 229, 230
Meqqusaaq (elder), 161, 173, 175
Meqqusaaq (younger). See Freuchen,
Meqqusaaq
Mequpaluk. See Freuchen, Navarana
Michanowsky, George, 239
Minik. See Wallace, Minik
Møller, Nuka, 242
Moore, Charles A., 28
Murphy, Robert Cushman, 238–39
Mylius-Erichsen, Ludvig, 164, 179

Naalagapaluk, 195
Nansen, Fridtjof, 5

Nares, George Strong, 117, 118
Navarana. See Freuchen, Navarana; Harper, Navarana
Nordenskiöld, Adolf Erik, 24
Nukappiannguaq, 207, 208
Nuktaq, 6, 14
bust of, 12
death and disposition of, 46, 48, 84, 86,
87, 228, 230, 232
and death of Atangana, 41–44, 87
and death of Qisuk, 82, 83
family of, 30, 31, 34, 41. See also Atangana; Aviaq; Eqariusaq; Qulutana
and Peary, 19–20, 27, 29, 30, 34, 35,
47–48

Olsen, Gustav "Guutak," 61
and Inuit language, 158, 160
relationship wtih Minik, 150–51, 160,
167, 169, 170
as priest at North Star Mission, 155, 165,
166
and Rasmusen, 166, 167
Operti, Albert, 1, 69
Orchard, William C., 240
Osbon, Bradley S., 40
Osborn, Henry Fairfield
and museum fund manipulation, 59,
63, 64
as museum president, 70, 106–7, 218

Peary, Josephine Diebitsch, 45
concerns over Minik, 137, 138–39, 140
in Greenland, 12–13, 21, 29
and marriage to Peary, 5, 29
as Peary advocate, 132–33, 134, 135,
148–49
and sale of meteorites, 70
Peary, Marie Ahnighito "Snow Baby," 3, 21,
23, 24, 33
Peary, Robert Edwin "Piuli," 3–6, 18, 19,
20, 21
and Aleqasina, 13, 179
and American Museum of Natural History, 6–7, 10
and American Route, 27, 142
arrival in New York City, 1–3
and attitude toward Inuit, 21–23, 153,
154, 164